Christmas
dear Tokkie
wishing you a very
Merry Christmas and a
Happy New Year.
with much love
Rex & Sarah

A glassy peeler rolls into Great Western Beach, Cornwall, with Chris Jones in the slot, August 1967. PHOTO: DOUG WILSON.

THE SURFING TRIBE

A HISTORY OF SURFING IN BRITAIN

BY ROGER MANSFIELD | EDITED BY SAM BLEAKLEY AND CHRIS POWER

ORCA PUBLICATIONS

St Agnes surfer Martin Wright lays down a bottom-turn at Porthleven, circa 1983. PHOTO ALEX WILLIAMS.

**THE SURFING TRIBE
A HISTORY OF SURFING IN BRITAIN**

BY ROGER MANSFIELD
EDITED BY SAM BLEAKLEY AND CHRIS POWER

COPYRIGHT © 2009 ORCA PUBLICATIONS LIMITED. ALL RIGHTS RESERVED. NO PART OF THIS BOOK MAY BE REPRODUCED IN ANY FORM WITHOUT WRITTEN PERMISSION FROM THE PUBLISHER.

ISBN 978-0-9523646-5-8

PUBLISHED BY ORCA PUBLICATIONS LIMITED,
BERRY ROAD STUDIOS, BERRY ROAD, NEWQUAY, TR7 1AT,
UNITED KINGDOM.
01637 878074
WWW.ORCASURF.CO.UK

PROJECT DIRECTORS CHRIS POWER, MIKE SEARLE
PUBLISHING EDITOR / PHOTO EDITOR CHRIS POWER
ASSOCIATE EDITOR SAM BLEAKLEY
DESIGN DAVID ALCOCK
SUB EDITOR / PROOFREADER KAT DAWES
EDITORIAL CONSULTANTS STEVE ENGLAND, LOUISE SEARLE

PRINTING GARNETT DICKINSON GLOBAL, PRINTED IN SHENZHEN, CHINA.

The Surfing Tribe is dedicated to all those people who have shared my life within surfing. Above all it is dedicated to the blue-eyed beauty who showed up for a surfing lesson – my wife Hilde. Without your emotional support and patient understanding, I could not have researched and written this tale about my own spiritual ocean tribe. Thank you.

– Roger Mansfield

FRONT COVER: Jersey Surfboard Club, 1959. PHOTO: JOHN D HOUIELLEBECQ/ROGER MANSFIELD COLLECTION.

BACK COVER: TOP Newquay pro Russell Winter, slotted in Scotland. PHOTO: ALEX WILLIAMS.
MIDDLE LEFT On the road, '70s style. PHOTO: PETE BOUNDS. MIDDLE RIGHT Sixties superstar Rod Sumpter. PHOTO: DOUG WILSON.

OPPOSITE: Dawn Patrol, Pembrokeshire, 1979. PHOTO: PETE BOUNDS.

CONTENTS

An international rendezvous at La Barre in Southwest France, August 1965. Britain's Rod Sumpter (far right) greets American and Aussie surfers including Greg Noll's brother Jim (far left), and Dennis White (third from left). PHOTO DOUG WILSON.

	FOREWORD	010	
	PREFACE	012	

PART ONE — THE SEEDS OF BRITISH SURFING

1 FIRST CONTACT 016 Captain Cook watches surfers in Hawaii • Bellyboarding: Britain's original wave-riding pastime • Duke and the prince go surfing • A present from Hawaii? • Papino 'Pip' Staffieri: Europe's first surfer • Surf lifesaving clubs and the first travelling surfers

PART TWO — LOCAL FLAVOURS – THE STORY OF BRITISH SURFING UNTIL 1990

2 THE CHANNEL ISLANDS DID IT FIRST 030 Jersey: where the British surf scene was born • Gordon Burgis: Britiain's first champion • Guernsey: Island style • Dave Grimshaw: the architect of British surfing

3 CORNISH GOLD RUSH 046 St Ives: surfing gets cool • Newquay: surf city UK • Bill Bailey: the father of British surfing • Rod Sumpter: the king of the malibu

4 KERNOW'S CORNERS 072 Sennen and the south coast: way out west • Mid and North Cornwall: the Badlands to the borderlands • Tiger Newling: counter cultural icon

5 DEVON TAKES OFF 088 England's oasis • South Devon: laid back locals • Tim 'Tiki' Heyland

6 WALES ON BOARD 096 The dragon stirs • Pete 'PJ' Jones: a passion to be the best • Carwyn Williams: surf hard, party hard

7 ENGLAND'S ENCLAVES 114 Brighton, Bournemouth and the Isle of Wight: South Coast surf fever • From Kent to Cromer: finding waves in every corner of the Isle • Riding the Severn Bore

8 NORTHERN LIGHTS 124 Edging into the cold: the North East • Nigel Veitch: North Sea wave warrior

9 SCOTLAND'S BEAUTIES 130 Searching for hidden treasure • Andy Bennetts: Scottish surf pioneer

PART THREE — EXPLORATION, EQUIPMENT, EQUALITY AND CULTURE

10 EXPLORATION 138 The quest for the perfect wave • Vive la France! • The magic of Ireland • Rob Ward: underground explorer

11 GIRLS IN THE CURL 154 Jumping the gender gap • Linda Sharp: Welsh wonderwoman

12 BOARDS FOR BRITS 160 The shaper: feeling the foam • Matters of size: the shortboard revolution • Stepping forward: the longboard renaissance

13 TOP GEAR 172 Surfwear: image is everything • Wetsuits and leashes: keeping warm and hanging on • Skateboarding: the street child of surfing

14 COMMUNICATION SKILLS 178 Celluloid sliding • Writing style

15 LIVING FOR SURFING AND SURFING FOR A LIVING 182 Getting paid to surf? You must be joking! • Brits on the global scene

16 SURFING THE NEW WAVE 194 Greening the green room • History is the future

CODA	202	
APPENDIX	204	
BIBLIOGRAPHY	204	
ABOUT THE AUTHOR	205	
INDEX	206	

foreword

Riding waves has always been my passion and I have lived my whole life as a surfer. I have also been fortunate to meet many other remarkable individuals, at home and on foreign shores, united through this single link of going surfing. Many of these great characters feature in this book.

Immersed in wave-riding since the early '60s, I watched British surfing evolve as I grew up. I was both participant and observer in a new and unique way of life. Surfing gripped my soul. At peak moments it was so intense that it bordered the spiritual. It was like a form of worship that upheld the wave, a spiralling pulse of natural energy, as its dominant focus, worthy of praise. The essence of membership of the surfing tribe was each individual's desire to ride waves in the spirit of fun. This was the magic glue that bound us all together as if a tribe. It was exhilarating, intoxicating and quite addictive. It still is.

For the committed surfer, the invariable cost of this activity was the thousands of hours spent sitting in the sea waiting for waves – often a significant percentage of one's life. This devotion becomes a communion with another element, the life of the worlds' oceans. To meet dolphins, whales and even sharks in their own territory are among the many gifts that such a life can offer.

On land, surfers adapted their unique identity to fit in with the simple reality of making a living. The artisan became the surfboard builder or wetsuit maker. Other surfers were channelled into competition, while others capitalised on the growing commercial niche in shops and surf fashion companies.

After more than 40 years in the waves it seems like quite a journey. I always thought someone would write it down and tell the story of the many adventures of this modern tribe along the way. Some tales were caught in magazine articles or films, but the big story was drifting away as significant members of the tribe started to pass on. We reached a critical moment in British surfing. A history of it had to be put together, so I marshalled my own memories, researched old magazines and films, listened to the testimonies of many of my lifelong friends, then started talking to other surfing acquaintances and their significant friends. The openness and willingness of all concerned to talk was obvious. They too had noticed the void in recording what we all had shared and loved.

So this is it – The Surfing Tribe. I can only say to the tribe for which I speak that if we have forgotten you, or an event you think was important, our apologies. It was not intentional and this is not a perfect work, in the same way that so many waves do not peel with perfect shape, yet they still get joyfully ridden.

Roger Mansfield

preface

below
When Pip Staffieri began surfing in 1941 he could never have imagined how popular the sport would become by the end of the century.
PHOTO: UNKNOWN/ROGER MANSFIELD COLLECTION.

Silhouetted against a setting sun, a 23-year-old lone surfer paddles into the third wave of a clean three-foot set, the faces brushed by a crisp offshore. He climbs to his feet, finds control, gains speed and a beautiful sound emerges as the wave unzips behind him. But he does not hit the lip or launch an air or even walk to the nose. He remains still and upright, with an elegant stance. No wonder, his board is 13'6". He has no language to describe what he is doing, no surfer-talk to capture his 'turn', his 'trim', or his evident 'stoke'. No wonder, it's 1941. This is Europe's first stand-up surfer, Papino 'Pip' Staffieri, an ice-cream seller, testing his newly designed four-inch fin on a hand-built hollow board at Great Western Beach, Newquay.

Pip could not have imagined that half a century later his beloved Newquay beaches would become 'Surf City UK', and the ocean would be dotted with surfers riding miniscule fibreglass boards. Today, the surfing lifestyle and industry embraces tens of thousands of people strung out along our extensive coastline. The British Surfing Association estimates that the island hosts as many as 300,000 surfers. But, until now, the history of British surfing was an untold story.

The Surfing Tribe is the first comprehensive history of British surfing. It can never be definitive, as history conceals as much as it reveals, but this snapshot of Pip Staffieri will at least alert surfers to the fact that surfing in Britain has deeper roots than most people imagine. From these roots has grown a sport that is perhaps better described as a lifestyle and a culture. Once it grips you, it never lets you go. Surfing will take you to places you would never otherwise visit. And once there you'll meet like-minded people with whom you can instantly trade stories about magic dawn sessions, encounters with dolphins, heart-stopping wipeouts and time-defying tube rides.

There are still plenty of surfers around who can remember having to round up friends so that they would not be surfing alone, when there were no such thing as crowds. This book is for them, the trailblazers. But, most importantly, this book is for the future of surfing, because we can only track where we are going by recounting the past.

British surfing has a rich yet largely untold past. There were few photographers around to document the early days, and very little media coverage. The original '60s scene was even lampooned in the American magazine Surfer in an infamous Stoner-Griffin article, 'Surfing in the United Kingdom'. As a consequence many Californian surfers probably imagined that everyone in Britain wore beefeaters or bowler hats, and that every building in Scotland was a castle. In fact, the article was written without a visit ever being made – it was pure fiction. Early '60s British surfers chuckled at this stereotype. We didn't surf in bowler hats. We had good waves and a vibrant surfing culture built along miles of coastline, some of it as stunning as anywhere in the world. Yet records and accounts of the early days were scattered, and just how surfing evolved across Britain remained a mystery to many. Thankfully there are still plenty of the '60s surfers around who can provide a reliable oral history, and many of them still surf. This book is their testimony.

The surfing cultures of Australia, South Africa and America deeply influenced our own surfing tribe as it grew from a minor cult into a national identity in just 50 years. But we have been reticent to fully articulate the rich and varied regional surf identities, the local flavours. Although united in the quest for 'the perfect wave,' Britain is a patchwork surfing nation, deeply influenced by each coastline's cultural and social history, whether Welsh, Cornish, Scottish or whatever. Geography has also shaped our waves, from frigid Scottish barrels to crystal Jersey peelers. Region by region this book looks at the developments in performance and equipment, and the iconic personalities who have pushed the art of wave-riding forward.

Britain's neighbours, France and Ireland, are interwoven into the story but they each have their own unique histories. Ireland is a treasure trove of surfing potential with a fascinating past, but we have not included Northern Ireland in the regions section of the book; instead we've considered Ireland as a whole (see Chapter 10) because, as surf legend Barry Britton explains, "Surfing in Ireland is a cross-border sport, in the same way that Irish rugby is." Hopefully the brief overview here might inspire a separate book examining the full history of Irish surfing.

The Surfing Tribe is a collection and distillation of a thousand different tales.
The story starts with Captain Cook's first encounter with Hawaiian surfers in 1778, then jumps forward to the birth of stand-up surfing in Britain in the 1940s, which was inspired by photographs of traditional Hawaiian wave-riders. The core of the book celebrates half a century of surfing from 1940 to 1990. It was during this period that surfing evolved from the pioneering days to become the 'cusp of cool' in Britain. We track how the rip 'n tear shortboarding of the contemporary era was established, how the thruster became the dominant species of board, and how the British surf industry was born and boomed. Along the way surfers rediscovered 'style' and longboarding returned from the grave to supply a breath of fresh air to an otherwise punk-infested aerial-infused youth driven surf market. The gender balance also changed as the decades passed; the average lineup tended to be 'men only' in the '60s and '70s, but by the '90s there were plenty of women surfers out there enjoying the waves.

Every book has to end somewhere, and we decided on a 1990 fade out, with two significant exceptions. The pair of chapters at the end of the book, which discuss professional surfing and contemporary British surfing, build a bridge from past to present and place surfing in the here and now. The post-1990 era saw surfing spin off in many new and varied directions that will hopefully be tracked in detail in later editions of this book. 'New School' surfers took their ultra-thin performance boards through lightening fast tailslides and aerials. While the power surfing generation that went before them wanted to carve heavy moves on the face, the new breed wanted ledging hollow tubes and wedging sections. In Britain, Russell Winter single-handedly redefined the achievements of European professional contest surfers, while a newer generation of Brits began to make a living from free-surfing and the associated media exposure. Finally, in the last five years, jetski assisted tow-in surfing has taken British big-wave riding to a new level.

While the last two chapters highlight important contemporary aspects of British surfing, this story is primarily about what made them possible, and the fun that was had along the way. It's a celebration of the people, the places and the events that made and defined British surfing.

Sam Bleakley

below
A triumphant Russell Winter wins the 2002 Rip Curl Boardmasters pro contest at his home break, Fistral Beach in Newquay.
PHOTO: AL NICOLL.

PART ONE
THE SEEDS OF BRITISH SURFING

Newquay's waves have been a source of fun for the best part of a century. Bellyboarders at Great Western in 1925. PHOTO: COPYRIGHT THE FRANCIS FRITH COLLECTION.

1 | first contact

CAPTAIN COOK WATCHES SURFING IN HAWAII

Between 1768 and 1779, British explorer Captain James Cook made three groundbreaking voyages to the Pacific Ocean. Cook and his expeditionary force aboard *HMS Discovery* and HM*S Resolution* were also the first Westerners to witness surfing, off the island of Kauai in Hawaii in 1778.

Cook's family gravestone in Yorkshire bears the inscription, 'James and Grace Cook were the parents of the celebrated circumnavigator Captain James Cook who was born at Marton, October 27th 1728…and killed at Owhyhee, December 14th 1779.' The latter date is actually incorrect. Cook died on 14 February, at Kealakekua Bay in Hawaii. Yet this simple gravestone speaks more eloquently of the distance Cook had travelled than any of the grand monuments erected in his name. 'Owhyhee', a tropical paradise unknown to the West before Cook arrived, was about as far as a man from Yorkshire could go. "Ambition leads me not only farther than any other man has been before me, but as far as I think it possible for man to go," Cook once observed, writing in his journal.

In 1768 he embarked on his first voyage aboard *HMS Endeavour*, having been commissioned by the Royal Society to observe and record the transit of Venus across the Sun from the mid Pacific. At the time, roughly a third of the world's surface remained 'nondum cognita' (not yet known) on maps. To the superstitious, this vast area was the domain of sea monsters, Patagonian giants and imaginary continents. But Cook sailed into this void in a small wooden ship, and returned three years later with charts so accurate that some of them stayed in use until the 1990s.

During his two later voyages, Cook explored a huge area of the Pacific: from the Arctic to the Antarctic, from Tasmania to Terra de Fuego, from North America to Siberia, and from Tahiti to Hawaii.

In total, he sailed more than 200,000 miles – roughly equivalent to circling the equator eight times.

During his third and final expedition Cook visited Tahiti, in December 1777. There he witnessed Polynesians riding waves in canoes at Matavai Point. Cook's diary entries were later published in *A Voyage to the Pacific Ocean*. "He went out from the shore until he was near the place where the swell begins to take its rise. Watching its first motion very attentively, (he) paddled before it with great quickness, until (it) had acquired sufficient force to carry his canoe before it without passing underneath. He sat motionless, and was carried along at the same swift rate as the wave, until it landed him upon the beach. Then he started out…and went in search of another swell. I could not help concluding that this man felt the most supreme pleasure while he was driven on so fast and smoothly by the sea."

From Tahiti, *Resolution* and *Discovery* sailed north, and in January 1778 Cook and his crew became the first Europeans to set foot on the Hawaiian Islands. While exploring and mapping the archipelago, the visitors witnessed an impromptu demonstration of stand-up surfing off the island of Kauai. "Twenty or thirty of the natives, taking each a long narrow board, rounded at the ends, set together from shore," wrote Cook in his journal, while the ship's artist sketched a (somewhat exaggerated) picture of naked natives surfing on carved koa and wili-wili planks. "As soon as they have gained – by repeated efforts – the smooth water beyond the surf, they lay themselves at length on their boards and prepare for return. As the surf consists of a number of waves, of which every third is remarked to be always larger than the others and to flow higher on the shore, their object is to place themselves on the summit of the largest surge, by which they are driven along with amazing rapidity towards the shore."

below
Captain James Cook was the first European to discover and map vast areas of the Pacific, including Hawaii, New Zealand and the east coast of Australia. PORTRAIT: NATHANIEL DANCE.

16 THE SURFING TRIBE

The ancient Hawaiian art of standing upright on a surfboard (to *he'e nalu* or slide a wave) must have been a revelation to a Britannia that supposedly 'ruled the waves'. Cook was impressed. "The boldness with which we saw them perform these difficult and dangerous manoeuvres was astonishing."

Cook named his discovery 'the Sandwich Islands', in honour of the Chief of the British Navy at the time, the Earl of Sandwich. This kind of imperialism was typical for the time; it was as if the natives did not have their own place names, history or culture. (Obviously they did, and surfing was actually an intrinsic part of that culture.)

Resolution and *Discovery* did not stay long in 'the Sandwich Islands', and sailed east to explore the west coast of North America. But the Bering Strait proved impassable, and Cook returned to Hawaii in 1779. The two ships sailed around the archipelago for eight weeks, mapping the islands. In mid February they anchored at Kealakekua Bay, on what is now called the Big Island. Cook had done much to establish friendly relations with the Polynesians. But on 14 February a group of Hawaiians stole a small boat belonging to the British. Cook, who was by this time ill after spending months at sea, went ashore with a party of marines to recover the boat. A large crowd gathered. The confrontation between Cook's men and the Hawaiians turned aggressive. In the frenzy, Cook and four of his men were clubbed to death.

It was left to Lieutenant James King to take over command of the expedition, and to complete Cook's journals before the ships returned to England. King subsequently devoted two full pages to a description of surfing, later published in *A Voyage to the Pacific Ocean*. He wrote: "They lay themselves flat upon an oval piece of plank. They wait (until) the time of the greatest swell…and push forward with their arms to keep on its top. It sends them with a most astonishing velocity, and the great art is to guide the plank so as always to keep it in a proper direction on top of the swell. If the swell drives him close to the rocks before he is overtaken by its break, he is much praised. Just before they reach the shore, if they are very near, they quit their plank, and dive until the surf is broke, when the piece of plank is sent many yards by the force of the surf from the beach. By such exercises, these men may be said to be the most amphibious."

Over the decades that followed, Western contact nearly killed the natives of the regal home of surfing. Diseases previously unknown to the Polynesians almost wiped out the local population. To add insult to injury, the Christian missionaries who subsequently arrived repressed surfing due to its nudity and perceived frivolity. Work, not play, was the stern Calvinist philosophy, and surfing was 'against the laws of God'.

In surfing terms, however, contact had been made, and surfboard riding would come to find an audience in Britain centuries later.

below
Surfers riding waves off the island of Kauai in 1778, as observed by the ship's artist aboard *HMS Discovery*.
ILLUSTRATION: BISHOP MUSEUM COLLECTION.

BELLYBOARDING: BRITAIN'S ORIGINAL WAVE-RIDING PASTIME

opposite
Bellyboarders at Perranporth, Cornwall, in the '20s, with boards made by the local coffin-makers.
PHOTO: UNKNOWN/ ROYAL CORNWALL MUSEUM COLLECTION.

below
Jersey bellyboarder Nigel Oxenden, who founded the Island Surf Club at St Ouen's Bay in 1923. PHOTO: UNKNOWN/JEREMY OXENDEN COLLECTION.

The seeds of surfing were already sown in the early part of the last century, through the long-established activity of bellyboarding. In the early 1900s seaside holidays soared in popularity in Britain, and by the 1920s bellyboard surfing had become a popular pastime at many beaches.

Jenny Rilstone, a life-long resident of Perranporth in Cornwall, recalls that bellyboarding began there soon after the end of the First World War, when young soldiers from the town returned from the Western Front. Two of theses young men, George Tamlyn and William Saunders, were among the first in Cornwall to ride broken whitewater waves lying on wooden boards. Their inspiration had come from contact with South African soldiers. Stories about their lives back home had been exchanged in lulls between the fighting, and the lads discovered that they had something in common – they all lived next to surf-pounded beaches. The difference was that the South Africans, from Durban and Cape Town, talked of their surf-riding antics on flat boards.

Jenny began bellyboarding at Perranporth in 1921, "as soon as I had two bob for a board," when she was just seven years old. Jenny's timber board was made by the local coffin-makers, TB Tremewan; it was totally flat and built from two pieces of tongue-and-groove screwed to three wooden cross cleats. Bellyboarding was a sporting pastime she was to pursue until she was 82 years old. Jenny explained that by the 1930s "many Perranporth beach people were going surf-riding. It wasn't just young men, but women, local families and an increasing number of weekend visitors."

This ocean pastime spread rapidly to other beach communities around Britain's shores. On Jersey, 150 miles to the southeast, a similar journey of discovery about the joys of riding waves had been unfolding. Long-time Jersey surfer Jeremy Oxenden recalls that his grandfather, Nigel Oxenden, travelled to South Africa, Australia and Hawaii after the First World War and along the way got hooked on bellyboarding.

"When he got back to Jersey he built a summerhouse down at the beach, and in 1923 he formed the Island Surf Club. He used to make his own boards, and he would tie a rope from the tail of his board to the back of his belt and swim or paddle out to sea to catch the green waves."

Nigel Oxenden was an accomplished waterman and a master of his art, possibly the best exponent of prone surfing in Britain during his time. His surfboards were carved out of solid wood, normally about 5'6" long, 18" wide and 1-1/2" thick. They weighed about 40 lbs and were decorated with various hand-painted heraldic crests on the nose. His personal passion was for 'deep water surfing' which required him to swim out beyond the surf, in order to take off on green waves as they were peaking. It was an incredible display of skill for the period. Once he'd ridden the green section of a wave, he'd bounce along in front of the whitewater into the area he called 'the nursery', where his less accomplished disciples enjoyed catching whitewater rides, closer to shore. So, the critical division between green water and whitewater surfing was established.

As Nigel Oxenden gained followers they formed a sporting identity based around his small beach house beside St Ouen's Bay. The Island Surf Club was the first of its kind in Europe, and the 'green hut' still stands.

By the '30s and '40s, bellyboarding was firmly established as a popular summertime pastime on Britain's beaches. The boards had become lighter, smaller and more sophisticated; they were made from marine plywood and had upturned tips to reduce 'pearling'. By this time the railways had dramatically improved access to coastal Britain. In the seaside tourist boom of the era, the Great Western Railway was able to transport large numbers of passengers to the coast for a cheap holiday or weekend away. It was a common sight to see whole families at the beach, sometimes spanning three generations, who would all go bellyboarding together. On a hot summer's day when there was a clean swell running, you could often see hundreds of people bellyboarding a single beach in Cornwall.

DUKE AND THE PRINCE GO SURFING

After being discouraged for over a century, surfing was revived in Hawaii in the 1900's as tourism became popular among affluent Americans. The ancient sport of the islands became a symbol for American tourists to consume as a mark of a healthy lifestyle. At the forefront of this revival was Duke Kahanamoku, who found international fame as a swimmer when he won gold medals at the 1912 and 1920 Olympic Games. ('Duke', incidentally, was his given name, not a title.) American surf pioneer Tom Blake gave Kahanamoku much of the credit for the sport's renaissance. "Surfing has been rescued from the lost arts and encouraged by Duke and his beach boys. It now promises to give health and pleasure to the youth of the world." Kahanamoku subsequently travelled to California and Australia, and became recognised internationally as the first emissary of surfing.

In 1920 Prince Edward became the first recorded Briton to surf when he had lessons from Duke at Waikiki. A very English press release from the royal entourage described how Edward enjoyed the experience. "He was especially delighted with surfing. He was frightfully keen about it."

The events of April 1920 are recorded in The Diaries of Lord Louis Mountbatten, 1920-22: Tours with the Prince of Wales. A month after leaving Portsmouth, HMS Renown and the royal party aboard were escorted into Honolulu Harbour by 12 US Destroyers. That same afternoon, Prince Edward and his party were lead down to the beach where they changed into bathing suits and were taken for a ride in a large surf canoe. "Duke Kahanamoku, the world's champion swimmer, was the coxswain," wrote Mountbatten. "When Duke saw a big wave approaching he ordered 'Paddle!', and everyone paddled for all they were worth. The stern of the canoe was lifted up by the wave as it caught up with her, and the canoe, with its great outrigger, appeared to be racing downhill into a non-existent valley in the water, which it never reached, and at a speed which must have been over 20 knots. HRH (Prince Edward), who was sitting right in the stern sheets, had the crest of the wave all round him, nearly as high as his head. The canoe was then turned, and this performance repeated three times."

Mountbatten continues: "After the third ride, HRH dived overboard and tried a surfboard. He had hardly mounted when he slipped off again. However, he was soon on and had one or two successful rides. The others then all dived overboard and swam about, most of them trying surfboards also." Does 'successful ride' imply he stood, or simply clung on, going prone? We do not know. But the lineup was crowded, as Mountbatten explained: "The great danger was that if one was just swimming alone, it was exceedingly difficult to keep out of the way of all the canoes and surfboards that came racing down on top of one." Surfing was happening in Hawaii again.

After the surf session Edward went to meet Hawaiian royalty for a late-night Luau with earth-baked pigs and Hula dancing girls.

Years later, in 1936, Edward became King Edward VIII. He lasted 325 days before abdicating the throne to marry twice-divorced American, Wallace Simpson. They lived in France until the outbreak of World War II, when they retreated to the Caribbean and Edward became Governor of the Bahamas, clearly bitten by the beach bug.

above right
Hawaiian surfer Duke Kahanamoku, who gave Prince Edward a wave-riding lesson at Waikiki in 1920. PHOTO: UNKNOWN/BISHOP MUSEUM COLLECTION.

below
Prince Edward prepares for his lesson in an outrigger canoe, which was followed by a brief session on a surfboard. PHOTO: UNKNOWN/BISHOP MUSEUM COLLECTION.

20 | THE SURFING TRIBE

A PRESENT FROM HAWAII?

Stand-up surfing could have started in Europe in 1938 when Jimmy Dix, a young dentist from Nuneaton in Warwickshire, experimented with a 14-foot Tom Blake board in Cornwall. It's possible, even probable, that he stood up and rode a few Cornish waves at this time, but we have no definite proof.

Jimmy had been a keen swimmer and water polo player while at university, and during the '30s he and his future wife often spent their summer holidays in Newquay where they enjoyed bellyboarding.

Around this time Jimmy became interested in surfing, possibly after seeing an iconic photo of Hawaiian surfers at Waikiki in the 1929 edition of the Encyclopedia Britannica, or some other publication. He was fascinated by the idea of surfing and became determined to try it for himself. Jimmy was a keen craftsman in his spare time and shared a workshop with his neighbour. Since he would have known nothing about surfboard construction, we assume that sometime in the mid '30s he obtained the address of a wave-riding club in Hawaii and wrote them a letter asking for information.

We don't know who Jimmy addressed his letter to, but the Outrigger Canoe Club in Waikiki is the most likely recipient. This was one of two wave-riding clubs in Hawaii at the time, founded in 1908, "For the purpose of reviving and preserving the ancient Hawaiian sport of surfing on boards." The members of the club must have been astonished to receive a letter from England, of all places, enquiring about surfboard specifications. The image of a pale Englishman wanting to surf the cold waters of the North Atlantic must have been quite amusing to these tropical island dwellers. Yet Britain was still a superpower in the '30s with a sprawling global empire, and its citizens were universally respected. On top of this, Hawaii had historic links with Britain going right back to its discovery by Captain Cook in the 18th Century. The Outrigger Club enjoyed the patronage of some wealthy men, which certainly would have enabled it to consider a grand gesture of goodwill.

above
Jimmy Dix getting the feel of his Tom Blake board, river paddling in 1938. PHOTO: UNKNOWN/ CHRIS DIX COLLECTION.

Two of Hawaii's best surfers at the time were Duke Kahanamoku and Californian-raised Tom Blake. Blake was an expert surfer who had recently begun building hollow wooden surfboards; these were considered 'state-of-the-art' by the surfers of Waikiki.

Back in England, many months after sending his letter, Jimmy Dix eventually received a reply. Not a letter, but a huge 14-foot Tom Blake surfboard. It weighed 66lbs and was signed by Blake himself.

Did Jimmy buy the board? Or was it a present from the magnaminous Hawaiians? We don't know. Either way he was evidently delighted to receive it because he promptly built a smaller replica for his wife. And that summer, the couple drove down to Newquay to try surfing.

We don't know whether Jimmy Dix learnt to stand up and ride his board that year. He died in 1989 leaving no records about his attempts at surfing, and presumably unaware of the significant part he'd played in the history of the sport.

However, the presence of the Dixs' boards in Newquay unquestionably had an inspirational effect on a young man who would become Europe's first documented stand-up surfer. That man was Pip Staffieri, and his story follows next...

PAPINO 'PIP' STAFFIERI: EUROPE'S FIRST SURFER

opposite
Pip with the hollow wooden board he built, 1940. PHOTO: UNKNOWN/ROGER MANSFIELD COLLECTION.

below
A photo of Hawaiian surfers in the 1929 edition of the Encyclopedia Britannica inspired Pip Staffieri to try stand-up surfing. PHOTO: JAMES SANDERCOCK / SANPIX.

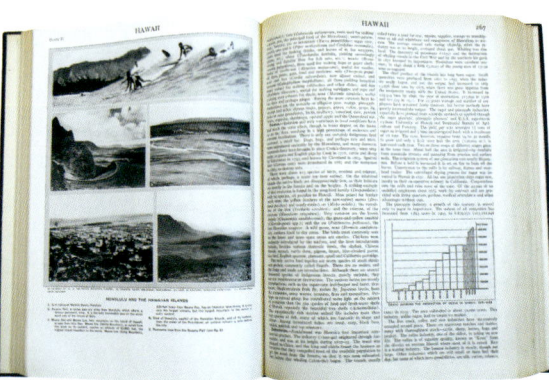

At the same time as Jimmy Dix's adventure, another Brit was developing an interest in surfing, inspired by an image in the 1929 Encyclopedia Britannica showing Hawaiians riding waves at Waikiki. Since he lived in Newquay, Papino 'Pip' Staffieri was better placed to get to grips with surfing and he became Europe's first stand-up wonder.

Pip was born on 5 August 1918. His Italian parents had moved to Newquay at the turn of the century to set up an ice cream business as seaside holidays in the Southwest became popular. Pip contracted polio when he was two years old; yet, despite some muscle loss in his left leg, he grew up to become a keen swimmer with a strong love of the ocean. In his teens he regularly swam off Towan Beach, and some summer evenings he'd be spotted powering the mile-long circuit out to Dane Rock and back to Towan.

By the 1930s Newquay was a genteel summertime bathing resort which attracted wealthy holidaymakers, like the Dix family, for a healthy escape from the city. Pip worked for the family business selling ice creams, and he also serviced the bathing machines that stored beachgoers' clothing. Pip had to work hard to support his family, as his father had been killed in the First World War while fighting with the British forces.

In the evenings, Pip and his friends would often go along to the Pavilion Cinema above Towan Beach to watch the thrilling Pathe newsreels. Occasionally these included footage of surfboat races from Australia. The 22-foot boats, each with four oarsmen, launched from the shore and raced one another boats around a buoy beyond the surf zone, before paddling back to the beach, catching waves (and sometimes colliding) on the way in. The chaos was a real crowd pleaser. Pip loved it, and was aware that similarly impressive waves also rolled into the beaches in Newquay.

After trying flat wooden bellyboards, Pip began to think about other, more exhilarating ways to ride the waves. His first opportunity came when he joined a group of Newquay lads who had taken to building canoes. Local man George Old had perfected their construction using canvas stretched over a wooden frame, and was the most skilful canoeist in the area. But Pip dreamed of emulating the surfers of Waikiki, and he was unfulfilled catching waves in canoes.

Then, one day in 1938, when he took his pony and trap to the beach to sell ice cream at the harbour, he saw two surfboards. "I was amazed," said Pip. "They lay side by side, alone on the sand. I stopped and examined them closely. The smaller one was quite crude, but the other was beautiful. It was 14-foot long and exhibited real craftsmanship, with a map of the Hawaiian Islands hand-painted on its deck."

Work commitments compelled Pip to continue down the beach, but whenever he looked back he saw no-one claiming the boards. He didn't meet Jimmy Dix or his wife that day, but the sight of their surfboards was sufficient to stir him into action. He left the beach with a working design for a board in his head.

Pip was skilful and innovative, and pursued the construction of his own hollow wooden board with some variations on the Tom Blake design. In the 1930s the working-class were confined to an existence of working, eating and sleeping, just to make ends meet. As Pip working more than 12 hours a day, seven days a week during the season, it took him almost two years to save up, acquire the materials and build his board.

Pip finished his hollow wooden board in 1940. He was 22. The board was 13'6" long and slightly wider than the Tom Blake board, constructed from 3/8 inch wood strips attached to oak frames by brass screws. The whole shell was sealed with varnish, and it had a nose plug to drain any water that might seep in. Dry, it weighed 112 lbs; wet, it was 165 lbs. "It was too heavy to be carried," said Pip, "so I built a little trolley with a

above
Pip's ice cream van.
PHOTO: UNKNOWN/
NEWQUAY HISTORICAL
SOCIETY COLLECTION.

below
The earliest known photo of a stand-up surfer in Europe. Pip Staffieri rides into the shallows at Great Western. PHOTO: UNKNOWN/ROGER MANSFIELD COLLECTION.

set of bicycle wheels to transport it to and from the (Newquay Bay) beaches, half a mile from our house."

The mantle of 'the true beginner' would fall squarely on Pip's shoulders as he learned to surf himself, with no example to follow, in the summer of 1940. "The family ice cream business was a seven-days-a-week work commitment in the summer, so I surfed in the evenings off Tolcarne," said Pip. "If the tide was high I would go in at Great Western. There were never many people on the beach in the evening. I would stay in for two hours sometimes." On cold, windy evenings Pip would wear a sleeveless woollen pullover on top of his swimming costume to break the chill. Pip was hooked. If he had been a Californian, he would have been 'stoked'. His inner fires were certainly burning...and he needed them to survive the Atlantic's evening chill.

"I'd push the board out to neck-deep water," said Pip, "and when there was a lull I'd paddle hard to get out. If some bigger waves caught me, I'd jump off and hold the nose of the board to push it under the wave. That's the way I got out back. I'd always go right outside. I had plenty of confidence. I never thought of the danger of the rocks or currents when I was young. Sometimes the big waves looked like a row of houses coming at you. It was great! I could catch green faces very early because the board was so long and it paddled fast. When I started I'd just lie down. Then I learned to kneel, and with more practice I could stand. What a thrill, especially if you made it right to the sand."

As Pip's surfing progressed he realised that a slight modification to his board would give it more control. "Soon I learned to get some angle on the wave. That's when I got the idea to put a four inch tail-keel on the bottom to give it better directional stability." Pip's fin design was an isolated inventive refinement of global significance. Unbeknown to Pip, American Tom Blake had placed the first fin on a surfboard just five years earlier.

In 1941, 23-year-old Pip was photographed riding a wave standing at Great Western. It's the first shot of its kind in Europe. Jimmy Dix, on holiday in Newquay again, also watched Pip surfing, and he was so impressed that he visited Pip at his house. It was unusual for the different classes to mix socially in this era, but Jimmy was a friendly, unpretentious man and he invited the young ice-cream seller out for a ride in his Alvis. They went to a pub for a drink and talked about riding surfboards. Pip recalls how Jimmy explained his inspiration to try surfing: "Jimmy Dix told me that he'd seen photographs of Hawaiians surfing, and he had to give it a try. But he needed a real surfing board, so he wrote to the Hawaiian Islands for information. Jimmy suggested that the Tom Blake surfboard he received in 1937 had been a gift, but he never revealed who it was from."

Jimmy also told Pip that trying to ride the board was a lot harder than he'd expected. "He said building the replica had been the easiest part, and learning to ride the board was the real challenge. He told me that surfing was a lot more difficult than he'd anticipated. I saw some box-camera photographs of Jimmy and his wife attempting to stand, riding whitewater near the beach." Whether Mr and Mrs Dix actually stood up is not known. Jimmy and Pip never surfed together. August was a busy time and Pip spent all day selling ice cream before taking to the water in the evenings, just as Jimmy, the professional man, would retreat to the hotel for dinner with his family.

Where Jimmy was trying to surf as a holiday activity, for Pip it had become a lifestyle. Pip's favourite spot was off the point between Great Western and Tolcarne beaches. "I don't want you to think I was a great surfer," said Pip many years later, "nothing like all the acrobatic stuff young people do on waves today. Some waves I'd ride lying down or on my knees part of the way, in between standing. But every ride was always exciting."

In the early 1940's, as the Second World War raged, Pip's

involvement with surfing waned. However, in 1943 a group of Australian Air Force officers (on a reprieve from service) stayed at the Great Western Hotel and borrowed Pip's board for paddling and wave-riding sessions.

After the war, the story of surfing in Britain entered a lull. Times were hard, and Pip did not have the money or social opportunities to pursue surfing, until 1960.

above
A typically busy summer's day at Towan Beach, Newquay, in 1933. PHOTO: COPYRIGHT THE FRANCIS FRITH COLLECTION.

But finally, when he was 42, Pip embarked on a long-awaited world tour, which took him to several islands in the Pacific, including Oahu. At Waikiki, he hired a 10-foot fibreglass board and went surfing; this made him the first Briton to ride a fibreglass surfboard. Europe's first surfer had finally succeeded in living his dream – the one embodied in that inspirational photograph from the Encyclopedia Britannica.

Pip's return from his Polynesian trip marked the end of his surfing endeavours. He continued to sell ice creams in Newquay, but away from work he turned his attention to sailing. He had always been a skilful woodworker and his next project was to build a beautiful wooden yacht. He named it *Symmetria* and spent many happy years sailing it around the coast of the Southwest.

Just as Pip devoted himself to another watersport, a new wave of surfing hit the continent. The early 1960s ushered in a cult of surfing in Europe, initially inspired by visiting South African, Australian and American lifeguard surfers. Images from magazines, surf films and surf music inspired the first serious core of wave-riders. The influence radiated outwards from Jersey, St Ives, Newquay and Biarritz simultaneously as individuals in Britain and France got their hands on the new foam-and-fibreglass 'malibu' surfboards, named after their testing ground in California.

As the decades passed and surfing boomed, Pip often spent time watching the surfers riding the waves in the bay. He was amazed and enthralled how popular the sport had become. "I never in my wildest dreams thought that what I was doing could ever grow and become so big in Newquay, let alone the rest of the country," he smiled, in an interview in 2004. "It gives me such pleasure to see all the fantastic things surfers do on waves these days."

SURF LIFESAVING CLUBS AND THE FIRST TRAVELLING SURFERS

Although surfing is an individual sport, the larger social structures of clubs have been instrumental in its development. In the early 1950s the strongest influence on British beach culture came from the Southern Hemisphere, when a representative of the Surf Life Saving Association of Australia, Alan Kennedy, toured southern Britain. With evangelical fervour, Kennedy promoted the creation of lifesaving clubs based on the Australian model. This was a timely cultural input – with the rise of post-war tourism, the number of fatalities from drowning had risen alarmingly, particularly in Devon and Cornwall.

Kennedy started his crusade in Brighton, which historically had a high profile as a holiday resort for the London masses. It was here in 1954 that Britain's first surf lifesaving club was formed, initially using volunteers until paid lifeguards were employed in 1956.

In Cornwall, the response to Kennedy's call was also good, since a large proportion of the local population already used the beaches as a playground. It was these same folk who normally had to risk their lives in rescues when tourists got into danger.

Bude already had a small lifesaving club at this time, which was affiliated to the Australian SLSA. In 1955 it expanded and became an official surf lifesaving club, soon followed by St Agnes and Porthtowan further along the Cornish coast. Each club was made up of local volunteers who patrolled the water's edge and were trained in resuscitation and rescue techniques. As a result, many lives were saved.

Later in 1955 the Surf Life Saving Association of Great Britain was formed to co-ordinate the development of the movement across the nation. The Association's motto was 'Vigilance and Service', and their mission statement was "To provide a safe and enjoyable environment on our beaches". In subsequent years many other communities with surf beaches formed surf lifesaving clubs. But it was Brighton, Bude, St Agnes and Porthtowan that led the way. Bude hosted the first Surf Life Saving Association of Great Britain Gala in 1955, and the following year Porthtowan was the venue for the inaugural SLSA National Championships.

During the late '50s nearly all the people who developed an interest in wave-riding were members of the newly-formed surf lifesaving clubs. By 1963, one of the highlights of the annual SLSA Championships (and most SLSA carnivals) was the surfing competition on the last day of the event. So before surfing became a sport in its own right, the 'surfers' were hidden inside the ranks of these new and enthusiastic surf lifesavers. Paradoxically then, the 'alternative' subculture of surfing grew from a conventional beach culture of safe practice.

Through their direct links and personal contacts with either Australian or South African clubs, British clubs fostered visits, in both directions. Information and ideas started to flow. The tradition of using 'surf-skis' as rescue vehicles in the water had been widely adopted, and dozens of the broad hollow wooden boards were built from Southern Hemisphere designs by North Atlantic lifesavers. The same happened with the 14-foot racing paddleboards.

For some individuals the temptation to abandon the paddling squat, or the paddle, was too much to resist. The chance to shrug off the traditional disciplines and ride towards the beach standing up was ever present. Surfing was poised to steal the attention of many hundreds of young beach users.

Over time it was inevitable that the surfers would seek to detach themselves from the constrictive structure of the surf lifesaving clubs. In Australia this had already happened; a group of Sydney surfers split from the SLSA and formed the Australian Surf Board Association in 1945. The next seismic shift occurred in California in 1956 when a lifeguard team led by Malibu's Tommy Zahn and Greg Noll put on a surfing display riding their

below
Many of the surf lifesavers of the early '60s enjoyed riding their hollow wooden boards standing up. Trouble was, the boards only went straight! PHOTO: DOUG WILSON.

26 | THE SURFING TRIBE

above
A group shot of the Australian lifeguards employed to patrol the beaches of Newquay in 1964. (Back row, left to right) Ian Tiley, John 'Bull' Campbell, John 'General' Greaves, Bob 'The Bear' Head, Mick 'The Phantom' Irwin, (middle) Wayne Mitchell, Don 'Bombhead' Mitchell and (seated) Mick 'Pump' Jackman.
PHOTO: UNKNOWN/DOUG WILSON COLLECTION.

new 'malibu' boards. These round-nosed boards were smaller, lighter and easier to turn. Suddenly surfing had its own unique equipment. The new boards allowed far more expression on the wave face, compared to the surf lifesaving boards which only went straight. In California, Australia and South Africa, surfing quickly took on its own identity and style.

In '60s Britain the social climate was ripe for the emergence of surfing. Many beaches saw the arrival of Australian and South African lifeguards, employed by local councils to work the summer season. They brought surfing with them, and paraded a carefree lifestyle totally at odds to the austerity of the post-war years. Amid the social revolution of the era, colourful subcultures quickly flourished. Everything was directed toward a freethinking, open-minded lifestyle...and this eventually materialised into the hippy movement of the mid '60s.

Around the world, surfing became something of a cult with its own language, fashion and lifestyle. The sport developed its own heroes, its own rules and rituals.

In Britain this tribal ethos developed in numerous separate areas around the country, with important regional variations. The earliest surf community in Europe originated in Jersey, our first regional port of call...

PART TWO
LOCAL FLAVOURS – THE STORY OF BRITISH SURFING UNTIL 1990

A South Coast gem. PHOTO: AL NICOLL

2 | the Channel Islands did it first

JERSEY: WHERE THE BRITISH SURF SCENE WAS BORN

Tucked in close to the French coast, the vibrant island of Jersey has played a huge part in the history of European wave-riding. It is home to Britain's oldest surfing community, and has produced some of the country's biggest stars. The sweeping five-mile expanse of sand at St Ouen's Bay dominates the western coast. The Watersplash complex, midway along the bay, has been the epicentre of the Jersey scene since two South African lifeguards introduced stand-up surfing here in the late '50s. At the north end of the bay is Secrets, identified by visiting Australian and Surfer magazine photographer John 'Wheels' Williams in 1967 as "a prime place to surf alone either side of high tide". Not today: surfing is now one of the Channel Islands' most popular sports, with deep roots and champions to match.

'Surf planing' was introduced to Jersey in 1922 by well-travelled Jerseyman Nigel Oxenden. He was an adept waterman who rode the outside peaks on his wooden bellyboard, and he even made himself a leash some 50 years before surfboard leashes were popularised. Nigel and his followers formed the Island Surf Club, based in a small wooden house near St Ouen's, and slowly the summer pastime grew in popularity.

By the '50s, bellyboarding on five-foot plywood boards had become an accepted and common beach activity. But St Ouen's Bay could be a dangerous place when a swell was running, with extreme tides and strong rips. "There were no States (local authority) lifeguards in the '50s," remembers Dr Peter Lea, a radiologist at the General Hospital and a keen bellyboarder, "but the sea at St Ouen's was quite dangerous and bathers drowned there every year. So Harry Swanson, who owned the Watersplash Inn, hired three South African beach guards for the summer season in 1958. It was a shrewd move on Harry's part."

The three South Africans were Bobby Burden, Shorty Bronkhorst and Cliff Honeysett. They were used to swimming and surfing in the powerful waves of Durban, where they had worked as lifeguards. Stand-up surfing had been introduced to South Africa several decades earlier, when Australian surf lifesaver Charles 'Snowy' McAlister toured the country in 1928. Soon after their arrival in Jersey, Bobby, Shorty and Cliff became tempted by the consistent, although cooler, beachbreak conditions and made themselves hollow 14-foot boards out of plywood.

Charles Harewood, a friend of Dr Lea and chief pharmacist at the same hospital, remembers the day they first saw the South Africans riding the waves at St Ouen's. "I was with Peter that day. We couldn't believe what we saw – surfers sweeping in on their boards, standing up all the way to the shallows. Peter ran up the beach to speak to the South Africans when they came out of the water, and then came sprinting back all excited to tell me about their plywood boards."

Slicing across the waves at St Ouen's in 1958, the Durban surfers fired up the local watermen. Peter bought one of the huge boards when the South Africans left at the end of the summer season. "They were incredibly heavy," he recalls. "You had to carry them down the beach on your shoulder. I could hardly pick one up now!" The craze quickly gathered momentum as other local lads started building their own plywood boards. But soon there were complaints coming from the already established group of bellyboarders. "There were no leashes back then, so when you fell off, these heavy things would come in sideways and they could hit people really hard," explains Peter. "The States (Jersey's government)

below
Durban lifeguard Cliff Honeysett (left), one of the three South Africans who visited in Jersey in 1958.
PHOTO DEREK JARDINE

30 | THE SURFING TRIBE

above
The founding members of Jersey Surfboard Club line up for a photo in June 1959. (Left to right) Unknown surfer, 'Willy' Williams, Robin Stevens, Gordon Wilkinson, Graham Sutton, Mike Wilkinson, Jeff Alker, Tom Williams, South African lifeguard Denis Everett (with surf ski and paddle), South African lifeguard 'Shorty' Bronkhorst, Brian Rolland, 'Scrubber' Amy, John Rumball, Peter Lea, Charlie Maine and Albie Coxall.
PHOTO: JOHN D HOUIELLEBECQ.

below
Jersey was the venue for the 1964 Great Britain National & International Surfing Championships. Aussie lifeguard Bob Head and several other surfers from the mainland travelled over to take part. PHOTO DOUG WILSON.

began to take an interest, and considered dividing the bay into separate areas. Obviously us 'big-boarders' were going to have to organise ourselves into a group. So we did, and I found myself appointed President of the Jersey Surfboard Club."

When the Jersey Surfboard Club was formed in August 1959 it sported more than 20 members and 14 boards. Only Biarritz could rival that, but there were only had a handful of stand-up riders and seven boards

in the Waikiki Club, formed at Cote des Basques in September 1959. In Jersey, Charles Harewood became the club's first Secretary, and by the following summer the membership had grown to 40. The club went on to become the main vehicle for the development of organised surfing in Jersey and Britain.

When surfing first appeared as a collective group activity, the public viewed it as a cult. The surfers themselves were caught up in a fraternal enthusiasm for this stand-up wave riding they had recently discovered, following no plan other than to have fun

at the beach and in the waves. Practitioners began to define themselves quite simply as 'surfers' and used esoteric language such as 'dropping-in', 'walking the board', 'big sets', 'malibus', 'baggies' and 'woodies', language which created an identity for the surfers. It took on a uniquely British style, a paradoxical mixture of adventurousness and reticence.

In the summer of 1961, Cliff Honeysett and Bobby Burden returned to Jersey to work the season with fellow lifeguards Denis Everett, 'Bull' Laverick and 'Chookie' Saltzman. This time they brought state-of-the-art 12-foot resin-bonded wooden boards with a more rounded shape. Several Jersey surfers began experimenting with similar laminated balsa boards, while others ordered the latest models from Australia. Gradually fibreglass became established as the key component of surfboard production, and in 1963 Silva Yates, a local company that produced fibreglass tanks and boats, started building surfboards.

The rising star on the Jersey scene was an energetic naturalfoot called Gordon Burgis. He started surfing in 1959, sharing a wooden board with friends Peter Gould and Mike Forest. Others followed their example when better boards became more accessible in 1961. Dave Grimshaw, Dave Beaugard, John Bisson, Graham Sutton, Barry Jenkins, Alan Guy, Steven Aston, Ian Harewood and Mick Emms were some of the core surfing clan.

In September 1962, eight Jersey surfers

set off for Biarritz in southwest France, their boards piled high on the roof of a green Ford Thames van. Peter Gould takes up the story: "Mike Forest had been down to France the year before. He noticed there were good waves in the Biarritz area, so we knew we should head straight there. After surfing at Chambre d'Amour, where we were the only ones in the water, we drove towards Biarritz town. We drove around a corner, with all the boards on top of the van, and saw a French car with boards on it coming the other way. What a moment! We all stopped in the middle of the road and got out to meet each other like spacemen meeting another lifeform on Mars. The French guys turned out to be Joel de Rosnay, Jo Moraiz, and the Lartigau brothers. They were as surprised as we were. Over the next few days they showed us their surf world on the Basque Coast."

Gordon Burgis also has fond memories of the trip. "I remember one merry evening when we all got thrown into the clink for testing the durability of French cars' roofs! Thankfully Jo Moraiz bailed us out of jail.

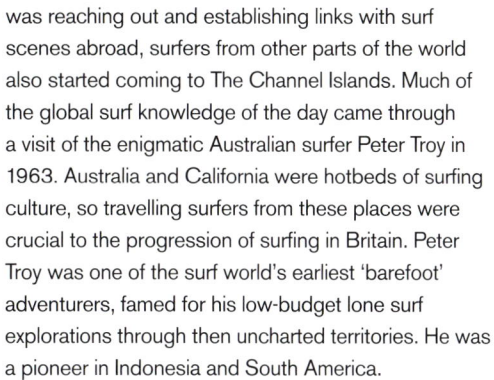

The French surfers treated us like royalty. And the surf was pretty magic too."

The first contact with surfing in France had been made. It proved a vital link in the future chain of European surfing, and the Jersey crew returned again the following year to cement the relationship.

While Jersey Surfboard Club

was reaching out and establishing links with surf scenes abroad, surfers from other parts of the world also started coming to The Channel Islands. Much of the global surf knowledge of the day came through a visit of the enigmatic Australian surfer Peter Troy in 1963. Australia and California were hotbeds of surfing culture, so travelling surfers from these places were crucial to the progression of surfing in Britain. Peter Troy was one of the surf world's earliest 'barefoot' adventurers, famed for his low-budget lone surf explorations through then uncharted territories. He was a pioneer in Indonesia and South America.

In autumn 1963, fresh off the boat from Sydney, Peter arrived in Jersey. He was en route to the Makaha International surf contest in Hawaii, but that was not until December so he planned to check out Europe first. The blonde 25-year-old fell in with the Watersplash gang, which accorded him cult hero status. He was dubbed 'The Messiah', thanks his superior surfing ability. "I took up residence in a shed at The 'Splash which was used to store inflatable rubber surf mats, and I stayed for the next six weeks," recalls Peter. "This loose and friendly group of surfers kept asking me about life in Australia, the design of Australian boards and how to perform hotdog manoeuvres. The young kid Gordon Burgis was always by my side, like a shadow. He appeared totally committed to copying my every move, particularly in the water."

Gordon Burgis showed the benefits of his apprenticeship to Troy by winning the inaugural Channel Islands Championships later that year. The event was well funded, well organised and was Britain's first surf contest.

As a consequence, the following year Jersey was invited to send a representative to the inaugural World Surfing Championships in Australia. Gordon,

above
September 1962: eight Jersey surfers prepare to set off to France on their first ever surf trip. Among the group are Peter Gould, Mike Forest, Gordon Burgis, Ian Harewood and Mick Emms.
PHOTO: PETER GOULD. COLLECTION

above
Low-tide Watersplash, lined up and pumping.
PHOTO: DAVE FERGUSON

below
Dave Grimshaw was a standout in the '60s and went on to become the first president of the BSA.
PHOTO: JERSEY EVENING POST ARCHIVE.

the clear choice, now had a chance to ride with the best — Americans Joey Cabell and Mike Doyle, and the eventual World Champion, Midget Farrelly from Australia. Gordon duly attended the event at Manly Beach, Sydney, and put in a good performance in the clean two to four-foot waves. A British surfer had joined the inner circle of Australian, American, Hawaiian, New Zealand, South African and French surfers at the first ever world contest.

Back on the island, the Jersey Surfboard Club, with

Dave Grimshaw and Dave Beaugard in the driving seat, was becoming ever more resourceful. After getting Peak Lager to sponsor the Channel Islands Championships, they gained financial backing for the 1964 Great Britain National & International Surfing Championships from the island's tobacco distributors. Hundreds of spectators attended the contest at St Ouen's, many just curious to see what all the fuss was about. Gordon Burgis, fit and focused from his overseas experiences, won again. He beat the first group of contest surfers to visit from the British mainland, among them masterful naturalfoot Bob Head and free-flowing St Ives surfer Charles Williams. Gordon Burgis was the first 'Great Britain' Surfing Champion.

The following year Gold Leaf stepped up to sponsor the Great Britain & International Surfing Championships. As it was the only international surfing event in Europe at the time, several top foreign surfers were tempted over to British shores. The skilful and hyper-competitive Rod Sumpter had just won the US Open Junior title at Huntington Beach in California, against many of the best in the States, and he was hungry for more. Although he was raised in Australia, Rod was a born in Britain, and thus able to compete in the Great Britain division. The final was held in choppy waves at St Ouen's, and Rod threw in every trick in the book, from skeg-first takeoffs to nose rides. He could even hang ten, then the ultimate objective in surfing. The versatile Charles Williams powered his way to second, ahead of local naturalfoot Steve Harewood (son of Jersey surf pioneer Charles Harewood). Rod's win gained him entry to the international event.

In the August heat, thousands of people watched the 30-minute International final. Enterprising French surfer Jean-Marie Lartigau had an excellent start, showing a smooth style and smart wave selection. Californian Geoff Roberts put in solid bottom-turns and big dropknee cutbacks, constantly threatening for the title. But the swell was dropping in size and an onshore wind began to ruffle the faces. Rod did not falter and adapted to make the best of the conditions, milking the waves with finesse. He pushed Geoff into second and Australian John 'Wheels' Williams into third. Rod had the audience in awe, displaying a new level of surfing. Clutching his two huge trophies, he instantly became the hero of British surfing. He promised to return the following year (and did so, winning the British & International title again in '66), and talked about possibly coming to live in Jersey, but ended up making his home in Cornwall.

Jersey was the first European port of call for many colourful travelling surf messengers in the mid '60s, like the effervescent American Bob Cooper and the iconic Australian Keith Paull. An result of this international contact was the Jersey Surfboard Club's recognition that Britain needed some form of national identity in the global surfing world. Spearheaded by Dave Grimshaw and Dave Beaugeard, the club reached out to a wider surfing audience on the mainland with the message that British surfers should get themselves organised into a national governing body, and this culminated in the formation of the British Surfing Association in 1966. This new era of organisation led to the Great Britain Championships being run as an annual event, held at Fistral Beach in Cornwall in 1967, before returning to St Ouen's in 1968. Once again Jersey put on an impressive event. Gordon Burgis, finely tuned from another extended period of surf travel, regained the title, renewing Jersey's faith in its competitive surfing supremacy.

That same year, the nation's four-man team for the World Championships in Puerto Rico contained three Jersey surfers. Out in the Caribbean, Steve Harewood, Gordon Burgis, Barry Jenkins and Cornishman

below
Steve Harewood's progressive designs made Freedom Surfboards one of the top brands in Europe.
PHOTO: GERRY GEORGE.

Charles Williams were riding egg-shaped, vee-bottomed rounded pintails, around 7'10" in length. The shortboard revolution had hit and the innovative Steve Harewood was fast becoming a top shaper, as well as being a top surfer. Steve was awestruck when he saw Reno Abellira from Hawaii racing along on a 6'7" 'pocket-rocket' shaped by Dick Brewer. "It was such a futuristic board," remembers Steve, "but the design was far too extreme to bring back to Jersey." Steve turned his attention to the board being ridden by rising international star David Nuuhiwa, also from Hawaii. "Nuuhiwa was my hero, a radical guy with long hair and a rockstar image. He was tearing it up on a 7'3" single-fin mini-gun. It was far more manoeuvrable than our thick chunky Bilbo's."

After the contest in Puerto Rico, Steve Harewood travelled on to California where he worked with Dewey Weber for six months, helping to produce a model known as The Ski. This was 7'3" long, 13" in the nose and 14" in the tail, with a foil that reflected a scaled-up version of Reno Abellira's board. The Golden State sojourn was life-changing for Steve: "I went out there as a clean-shaven schoolboy, and came back with beads, bells and hair down to my shoulders!" While he was over there, Steve had direct access to all the latest ideas and developments in shortboard surfing and production. The whole trip was a huge inspiration. When he returned home in 1969, Steve set up Freedom Surfboards with business partner and flamboyant surfer Barry Jenkins. A cool-looking, radical surfer with an expressive modern style, Steve would go on to shape cutting-edge surfboards for decades to come and inspire a new generation of young surfers.

Jersey's biggest contribution to early British surf culture, however, was its surf club and their pioneering surf contests. The Jersey Surf Club showed the rest of Europe how to put a commercial and promotional face on surfing. In 1969 they threw their decade of expertise into presenting the first officially sanctioned European Surfing Championships. Players No.6 sponsored the event, but it was almost the end of an era for this type of sporting support. The health consciousness of surfers and parents was rising and they could recognise the irony of awarding a champion surfer with a trophy, 400 cigarettes and an embossed table lighter! Players No.6 had the cash, however, to arrange to have the reigning Miss World, Penny Plummer, on hand to award the prizes. The gorgeous Australian made men melt when she blew a kiss. A record-breaking crowd of 5,000 cheering spectators watched the hotly contested final, and Gordon Burgis beat Rod Sumpter to claim the first European title for Jersey. It was testament to Gordon's competitive zeal that a homegrown hero could beat the internationally acclaimed Sumpter. Gordon knew the importance of such events. "Contests are good," he commented in a 1972 interview in Surf Insight magazine. "They bring people together and at the same time build interest. People formulate ideas and communicate from contact with each other, raising standards and helping to improve equipment."

The next surfer to take centre stage in Jersey was the dynamic Bobby Male.

Lean and lanky with incandescent white hair, Bobby won the Channel Islands title numerous times and the British title twice, in 1974 and 1977. It's an impressive competitive record, but contests weren't really his calling, as Dave Grimshaw explains: "Bobby was the original laid-back soul surfer. I had great problems getting him to enter contests. I actually had to plead with him to enter the Europeans one year. He finally consented, and ended up winning the thing and becoming European Champion!"

As well as being a brilliant surfer, Bobby was also a talented and innovative shaper who worked for Steve Harewood at Freedom Surfboards. He loved to travel, visiting France, Spain, Portugal and Morocco over the years. During a trip to northern Spain in 1971, he pushed his fluid smooth style to the limits. "Tigger Newling, Roger Mansfield and I did this incredible trip to Mundaka," recalls Bobby. "We went to Biarritz, then toured the north coast Spain with no idea about this perfect rivermouth wave. We just stumbled across it. What a find!" The trio were among the best surfers in the country at the time. "To be able to push one another on a perfect canvas at Mundaka just took our surfing to totally new and exciting levels."

"Bobby's tube riding was legendary," says Gordon Burgis. "His loose style was totally effective. It was all natural ability. He always had good timing as well. It meant he could put himself back in the pocket and get enviably deep inside the tube whenever the waves offered the chance."

The twin temptations of warm water and hollow waves eventually got the better of Bobby, and he emigrated to Australia in 1988 to shape boards and

below
Jersey's quality waves provided the training ground for the island's surfers throughout the '70s, '80s and beyond.
PHOTO: DAVE FERGUSON.

ride the barrels of Queensland's fabled Gold Coast.

Despite Bobby Male's lead, by the mid '70s the primacy of Jersey had given way to the rapidly expanding surfing culture of mainland Britain, centred in Cornwall and South Wales. However, individual surfing talent kept emerging from the Islands. Determined and competitive goofyfoot Dave Ward came to prominence when he won four Channel Islands Championships between 1979 and 1983.

The next Jersey star was Arlene Maltman, who won the British Women's title in 1984. Arlene was blonde and attractive, with sun-kissed curly hair and a radiant style. Thanks to sponsorship from British Airways, she was able to compete internationally and became the Channel Island's most successful female surfer.

Second generation surfer Renny Gould, the middle son of Jersey pioneer Peter Gould, rose through the ranks to become the island's top performer in the late '80s. Alongside Mark Durbano, Jon Carden and younger brother Piers, Renny helped raise British performance levels to unimaginable new highs. Lightfooted and spontaneous, Renny was British Champion in 1987 and came close to winning a second British title in '88 as well as a European title in '89. "Renny deserved more in contests," says Dave Grimshaw. "If he'd become more of a dedicated heat surfer he really would have made it big in European professional surfing. He was a free spirit and a real class act, able to perform in everything from slop to treacherous Thurso barrels."

But Renny, like Jersey champions Bob Male and Gordon Burgis before him, was more interested in travelling to find quality waves than being a contest machine. That trait seems to be common to Jersey surfers over the generations – surely the lure of The Continent, just 14 miles away, must have had something to do with it.

above
Bobby Male won a cupboard full of trophies in the '70s, including the British, European and Channel Islands titles.
PHOTO: GERRY GEORGE.

Second generation surfer Renny Gould was one of the island's top competitors in the late '80s and '90s, and remains a standout in any lineup.
PHOTO: DAVE FERGUSON

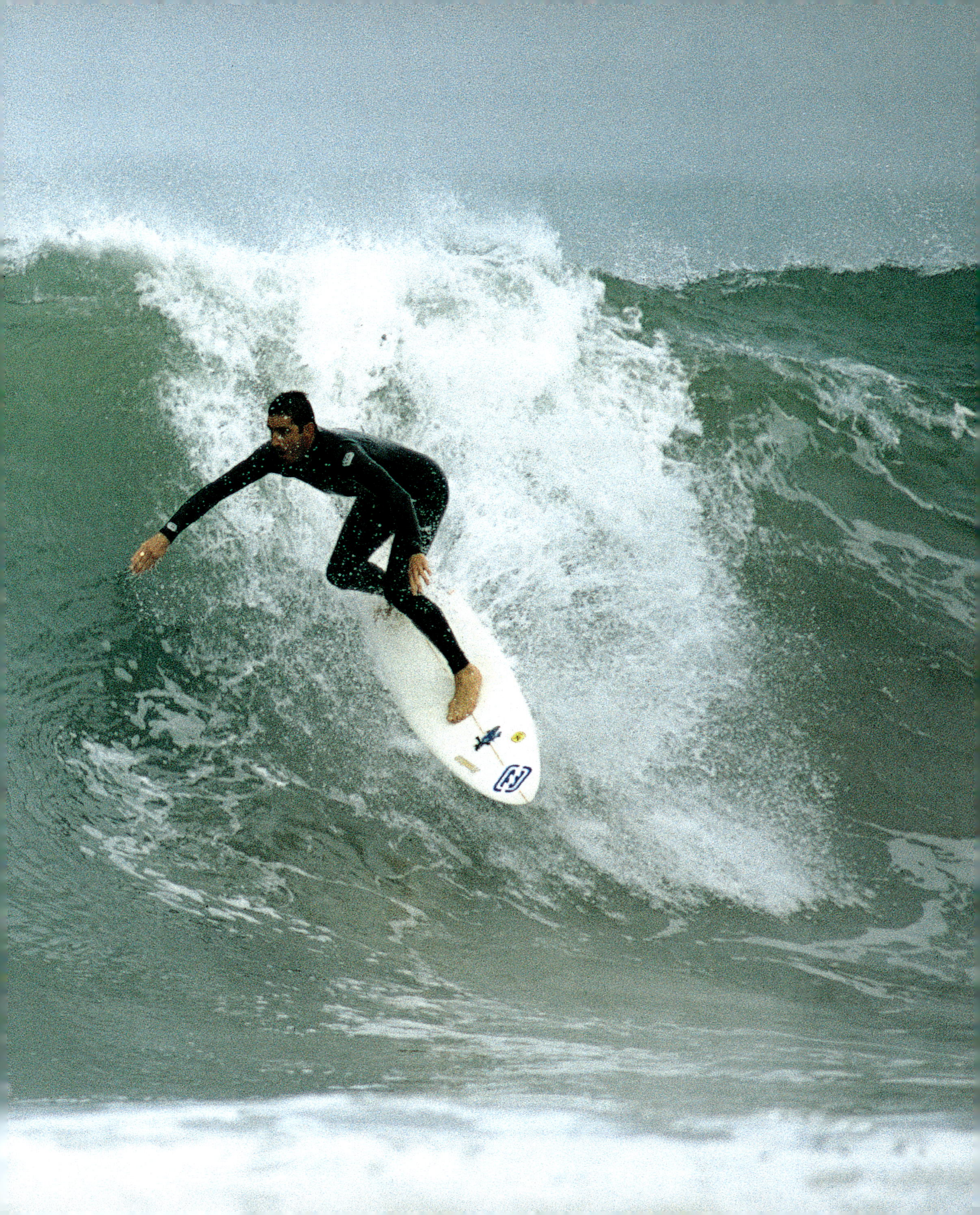

GORDON BURGIS: BRITAIN'S FIRST CHAMPION

Gordon Burgis is more than just a legend in British surfing.

He was our first British-raised national and European Champion, and the only local surfer to push Australian-trained Rod Sumpter in '60s competitions. After becoming the country's first representative at the World Championships in 1964, he set the travel mould for countless surfers to follow. He was the original and archetypal surf explorer, and went on trips to dozens of the most famous waves of the '60s and '70s. More importantly he helped put British surfing on the international stage. Later Gordon switched his attention to skiing and sailing, but never lost his competitive flair and ability to inspire new generations.

Gordon started surfing in 1959, already a keen bodysurfer. "My first board was a 14-foot plywood log which I shared with two friends, Mike Forest and Peter Gould," he recalls. "It weighed 40 pounds, so it took three of us to carry it down to the water's edge. We called it 'big board' riding back then."

By 1962, Gordon and the rapidly expanding posse of local surfers had gained access to fibreglass-covered balsa boards copied locally from from South African imports. These boards were lighter and far more manoeuvrable than the plywood boards, which opened up all sorts of possibilities for turning and walking the board. However, it wasn't until Gordon got his hands on an even lighter foam-and-fibreglass surfboard from Australia that his surfing really took off. Over the next two years, the agile naturalfooter honed his hotdog style and became the best surfer on the island.

In 1964 the Australian Surfriders' Association invited Jersey to send a representative to compete at the World Championships at Manly Beach, Sydney. There was no doubt that Gordon was the man to go. He flew to Oz and put in a respectable performance in the contest which was held in clean two- to four-foot waves. More importantly, he watched and met some of the world's best surfers. It was a great inspiration.

Gordon was flying home via California, and on the Pacific leg of the journey he had a chance meeting with a surfing superstar. "Out of the blue, Phil Edwards wandered down the aisle and took the seat beside me." At the time, the Californian was the most famous surfer in the world, and he'd long been treated as the unofficial world champion. His smooth moves adorned countless pages of Surfer magazine, and he won their first ever 'best surfer' poll. Gordon could hardly believe that he was getting the chance to meet his boyhood hero. "We talked about surfing for hours. By the time we landed in Los Angeles, Phil had given me the whole history of the growth of surfing in California!" The pair got on so well that Phil invited Gordon to stay with him and his wife at their home in Oceanside, although the Brit had to decline as he had a connecting flight to catch. But the invitation was open.

Buzzing from his trip, Gordon won the 1964 Great Britain National & International Surfboard Championships. First prize in those days equalled a big trophy, respect and maybe a free surfboard, but unfortunately none of the sponsorship deals common in the modern world of competitive surfing. Nevertheless, Gordon was determined to travel abroad and ride some of the waves he'd seen in Surfer magazine. So he worked and saved, and that winter he and fellow freethinking Jersey surfer Barry Jenkins set off on a two-year round-the-world trip.

In November 1964, Gordon and Barry arrived in Sydney.

Gordon recalls how quickly they got into the swing of things. "We got off the plane and that very first evening we went to the Australian premiere of *The Endless Summer*. We'd never been in the company of so many surfers all hooting and hollering at the action on the big screen. The atmosphere was intoxicating. And the next morning Manly was three- to four-feet and kissed by a light offshore. What an arrival to Australia!"

After spending a while in Sydney, Gordon and Barry headed north up the New South Wales coast in an old VW camper, with an Aussie friend they'd met called Bernie Huddle. The highpoint of the trip was driving down a dirt road to the fishing village of Yamba to check the righthand point at Angourie. Today it's a world renowned break, but back then it was just an isolated spot with little notoriety. "We scored it perfect, with just three of us out. And over the next few days the swell picked up to a good six- to eight-feet, with occasional 10-footers. Perfect peeling righthanders...and no one else turned up." A cracking photo of Gordon on a big clean face was printed in Bob Evans' Australian Surfing World magazine the following year.

After scoring more great waves at Kirra and Bells, Gordon and Barry travelled to New Zealand. The charismatic pair were a hit wherever they went. Both surfed expertly, but Gordon was a standout every session with his near-perfect pocket riding and canny wave judgement. He was filmed at Whangamata Bar, a lefthand rivermouth on the Coromandel Peninsula, surfing with total control in prime conditions. The footage appeared in Andrew McAlpine's 1968 film *Children of the Sun*.

By now an accomplished international surfer,

Gordon returned to an expanded British competition scene in 1968. A new British Champion, Rod Sumpter, had dominated since Gordon's departure. But 28-year-old Gordon had nine years of surfing experience under his belt, the last few in some of the best-known peelers on the planet. Keen to re-establish his place in the surfing pecking order, he won the Great Britain Surfing Championships at St Ouen's and the inaugural European Surfing Championships the year after.

Burgis seemed unbeatable on home turf. The art of riding the nose had become defunct now longer boards were old hat, but Gordon had adapted to the shorter board designs with ease. Climbing and dropping along the waves, he was able to put the early single-fin shortboards on the rail with speed and style. He continued to surf competitively into his thirties. He represented Britain again at the World Championships in Australia in 1970 and California in 1972.

Gordon also discovered other adrenaline kicks. He was one of the first British surfers to cross over into skiing, and spent two winters working as a ski instructor in the Austrian Alps in the early '70s. This inspired him to set up a groundbreaking business back home, the Jersey Surf School, where he taught surfing to eager novices until the late '70s.

In the '80s Gordon changed tack again and began racing Hobie 16's, a type of high-performance catamaran. His competitive instinct remained strong and he subsequently won seven Channel Islands Championships, and took part in several European and World Championships.

These days Gordon devotes a lot of his spare time to coaching Jersey's junior sailing squad, although he still surfs when conditions are good.

Gordon Burgis, the archetypal champion, made Jersey tops in surfing and inspired three generations of British surfers. He remembers the '60s as a special time. "I don't think we'll ever be able to recapture the unique spirit of those early days. It was the dawn of an era. A golden era."

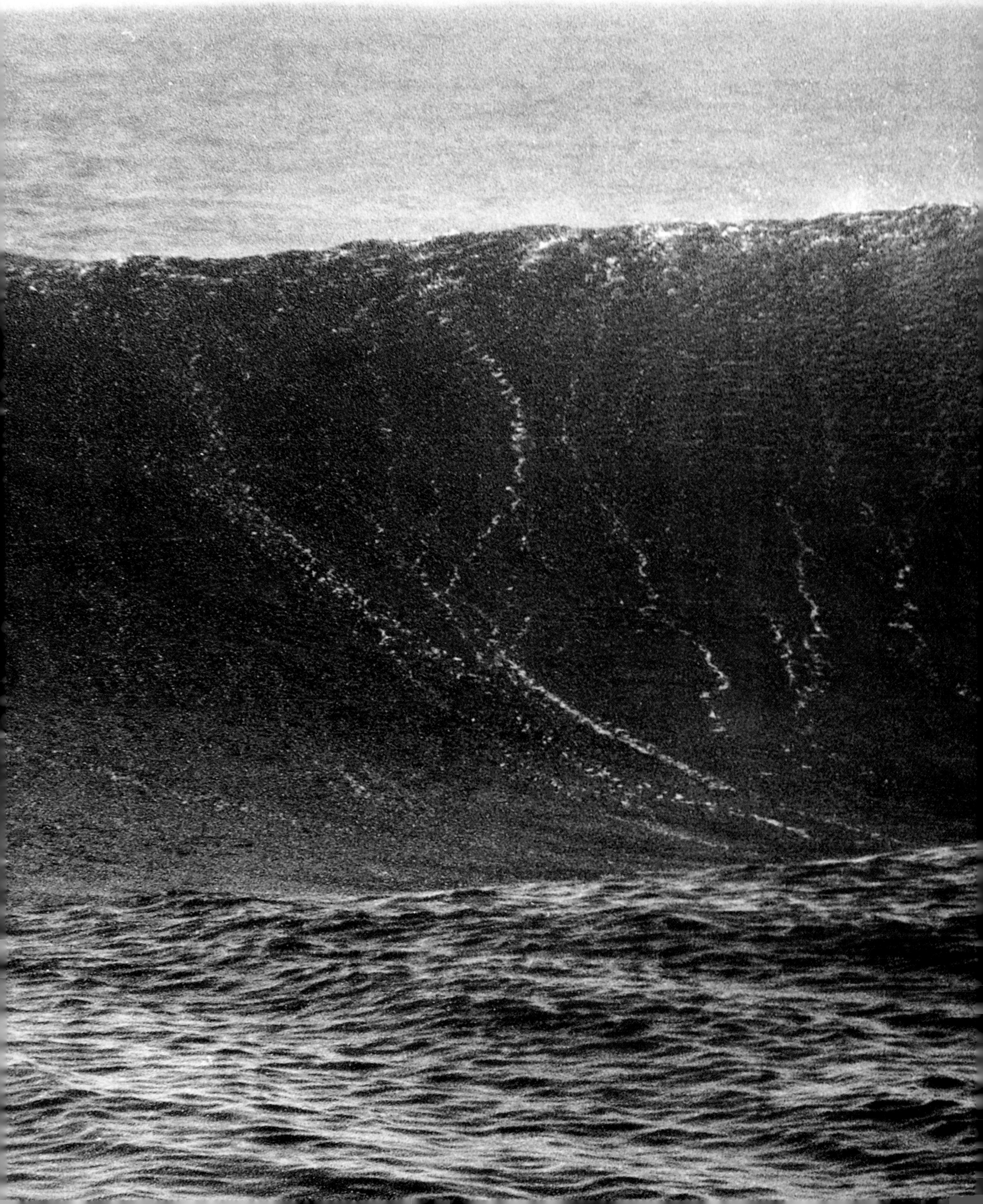

A classic shot of Gordon Burgis at Angourie in New South Wales from 1965. PHOTO: BOB WEEKS.

GUERNSEY: ISLAND STYLE

below
Guernsey surfer Terry le Pelley enjoys a crisp offshore day at Vazon Bay in the mid '60s. PHOTO: UNKNOWN/ROGER MANSFIELD COLLECTION.

bottom
Portinfer took over as the island's favoured beachbreak in the '80s. PHOTO: MATT BAIN.

Guernsey, 20 miles northwest of Jersey, has a range of beaches and rocky reefs on its west coast for surfers to enjoy. Roger Berry and his father Kenneth are credited with making and riding the first surfboards in Guernsey in the late '50s; they experimented with them at Vazon Bay, the island's most consistent spot. Vazon later became the water park for the island's first group of regular surfers in the early '60s, by which time Roger had moved away to work in England. Dave Fletcher, Tom Woodford, George Head, Roger Blanchford and Paul Birtwhistle were the core group of these Guernsey pioneers, learning to ride on a 12-foot hollow wooden board and a 15-footer that only Paul could carry to the water. "They were dinosaurs of the surfboard world," says Dave Fletcher, "but they got us started."

Fletcher, who ran an eponymous sports shop on the island, founded Guernsey Surf Club in 1961. For a few years the club members used a hut at Vazon to store their boards; but when that was demolished they moved their hangout to a nearby farmer's cottage. They would surf Vazon on the pushing tide until the backwash kicked in, then walk back to the cottage and warm up next to the paraffin heater.

In the mid '60s Peter Bachmann started importing foam-and-fibreglass boards for his shop under the Focus Gallery in St Peter Port, supplied by French company Barland-Rott. The availability of modern surfboards here and at Fletcher Sports lit the fuse of enthusiasm for surfing on the island. Other surfers who joined the scene at this time included Vince Chapple, John Halliwell, and Barry Hughes. Dave le Tissier helped the local crew make rudimentary wetsuits, extending the surfing season beyond the warm summer months. Before long, commercial interests on the island began to pick up on the buzz being generated. Coca Cola were the first big brand to get involved, sponsoring an inter-island competition between Guernsey and Jersey in 1966. The locals – among them Richard Browning, Bob Warry, Keith Ogier and Brian Corbet – showed just what they could do, beating some of the best surfers from the Big Island. Later, cigarette company Gold Leaf sponsored the Guernsey & Open Surfing Championships.

In 1968 Guernsey Surf Club leased Fort Richmond from The States (the island's government), a larger and more prestigious clubhouse with a view of Vazon Bay. By this time membership numbers had risen to more than 150, and fundraising efforts were proving highly fruitful. This explains why American writer Peter Dixon commented in his book *Where The Surfers Are*: "The surfers of Guernsey are perhaps the best organised in the world." Indeed there were three pages devoted to The Channel Islands in the book, which claimed to be the definitive guide to the top surf spots of the world. In the early days these islands were more than just dots on the map – they were epicentres of European surfing culture.

The outstanding Guernsey contest surfer throughout the late '60s and early '70s was the energetic Dave Wilson. He dominated the Junior division as the era of shortboards began, and went on to win the European Junior title in 1970, thanks to his distinctive hard turns and aggressive style.

In the mid '70s, clubs and contests became somewhat 'uncool', and the Guernsey Championships were not held between '75 and '85. Many of Guernsey's best surfers chose to spend time travelling abroad in search of perfect waves. Notable surfers from the wilderness years were Chris Ashwell, Kev Warr, Tim May, Steve Mollet, 'Pedro' le Poidevin, Kev Hinshaw, Richard Gillingham, Allan Bichard and Dave Taylor. It was during this time that many of Guernsey reef's were surfed for the first time, aided of course by the introduction of the surf leash.

In 1985 Guernsey Surf Club swung back in action and soon re-established its reputation as a well-organised club thanks to the efforts of Chris Ashwell, Matt Brouard and Kev Hinshaw. Top performers of the time included Mike de Garis, Matt Hoare and Indo pioneer Steve Johns. In the subsequent decade Robin Ozanne, Jon Baird, Paul Bishop, Nathan and Jeremy Browning rose to the fore.

In January 1990 the club produced a souvenir publication celebrating 'The first 25 years of Guernsey Surfing', packed with photos and stories. It was an impressive testament to Guernsey surfers' long-time devotion to the Atlantic, island style.

44 | THE SURFING TRIBE

DAVE GRIMSHAW: THE ARCHITECT OF BRITISH SURFING

The man who must take most credit for the formation of the British Surfing Association in 1966 is Jersey's Dave Grimshaw.

Grimshaw began surfing at St Ouen's in the early '60s, along with his mates Dave Beaugeard and Gordon Burgis. They were quick to appreciate the performance benefits of the new foam-and-fibreglass boards, and within a couple of years young entrepreneur Grimo was importing boards from France and Australia.

Beaugeard and Grimshaw became leading figures in the Jersey Surfboard Club in the mid '60s and it built a reputation as a supremely well-organised outfit. The club forged links with surf associations abroad, and these efforts were rewarded in 1964 when Jersey was invited to send a representative to the inaugural World Championships in Australia. Gordon Burgis accepted the honour, and Britain had its first born-and-bred competitor on the international stage.

As a surfer and club administrator, Grimo became aware of the growing rift between surfers and lifesavers. In the early '60s the only surfing competitions were those held at the Surf Lifesaving Association of Great Britain's National Championships (and various SLSA carnivals); but these were merely a side-show, and they were always criticised for poor judging.

Many of the surfers within the lifesaving movement wanted surfing to develop along its own path, but the SLSA leadership wasn't buying it; they felt that surfing and surf lifesaving were inextricably linked, both culturally and historically. At their Annual General Meeting in 1964, Secretary Keith Slocombe and Chairman Jack Simmons ruled that the SLSA should continue to represent surfing.

In Jersey, however, the surf club went ahead and organised its own contests. Their '64 and '65 events boosted surfing's national credibility; these and subsequent surfer-organised events at St Ives and Porthtowan encouraged surfers to break away from the SLSA and do their own thing.

Grimshaw recognised the need for the sport to be organised under its own governing body, so he started writing to clubs and key individuals in Cornwall and Wales about the idea of forming a Great Britain Surfing Association. He didn't expect everyone to agree with his vision. "I had a lot of correspondence with Keith Slocombe. But he was adamant that the surf contests organised through the SLSA had to be restricted to surf lifesaving club members. 'Sorry, not acceptable,' was my response."

Grimo got a much more positive reaction from Penzance surfers Mike Carr and Tony Hole, so he travelled to Cornwall to meet them. The three surfers realised they shared a common aim and drew up a plan of action. In April 1966 the British Surfing Association was formed. It was initially run from Tony Hole's menswear shop, Modern Man, in Penzance. In recognition of Jersey's prominent role in its creation, Dave Grimshaw was made President. Pete Griffin, who ran the Porthmeor Surfing Association in St Ives, was voted in as Chairman, and Mike Carr and Tony Hole became Secretaries. Other key members included Newquay surfers Dave Friar, Bill Bailey and Doug Wilson, and Bob Groves from Bournemouth. British surfers finally had an organisational and political voice.

The BSA's first objective was to create an annual British Surfing Championships, which would have more credibility than the surfing competition at the SLSA National Championships. Thankfully, the Gold Leaf Great Britain Surfboard Championships at Fistral Beach in 1967 lived up to expectations, and British-born surf star Rod Sumpter took the Open title.

By the '70s Dave Grimshaw was Britain's most experienced surfing official. His diplomatic duties took him around the world for meetings, events and social occasions. In 1975 he was appointed Vice-President of the European Surfing Federation, and in 1983 he was made Secretary General of the International Surfing Federation. For 10 years he served on the Executive Committee of the ISA, and he played a leading role in bringing the World Championships to Britain in 1986. But for all the prestigious posts he held, Grimo's proudest moment came in 1983 when he was made the Honorary Life President of Jersey Surfboard Club.

below
President of Jersey Surf Club in the '70s and '80s, Dave Grimshaw was also a key figure in the formation of the BSA.
PHOTO: JERSEY EVENING POST ARCHIVE.

3 | Cornish gold rush

ST IVES: SURFING GETS COOL

above
St Ives Bay, with the town of St Ives in the background, as seen from Godrevy. PHOTO: MIKE SEARLE.

Squeezed between four beaches, a granite harbour and a maze of cobbled streets, there is something indefinable, even magical, about St Ives. Set at the edge of a rugged landscape of wild moorland, prehistoric remains and the haunting ruins of the once great tin mining industry, St Ives has a distinctive feel and a cultural sophistication that sets it aside from its surroundings. This has made it one of Britain's most popular and stylish seaside towns.

Porthmeor beach is the backbone of St Ives and a natural amphitheatre for surfing. Although sheltered from the prevailing southwesterly winds, it still picks up plenty of swell, and this enabled the sport to flower over the decades.

It was at Porthmeor that two sets of brothers, the Williams and Griffin brothers, got hooked on surfing and led its growth in West Cornwall. Twins Charles and James Williams were 11 when their parents moved to St Ives from Zimbabwe to run a hotel in the late '50s. The twins and younger brother Peter-George were all strong swimmers, used to playing in the waves at Durban in South Africa, where they went on family holidays. Naturally, as soon as they arrived in St Ives they began swimming at Porthmeor. At their new school, St Ives Grammar, they became friends with Pete and Dave Griffin, who were members of St Ives Surf Lifesaving Club. The Griffins encouraged the new boys to join the club, so they did and the gang spent most of the following summers at the beach.

The club was run by volunteer lifeguards Keith Slocombe and Dave Lobb, who trained the youngsters and bought (or made) all the equipment. "It was a big scene for both the girls and the boys at the school," remembers Charles Williams. "We learnt to do all kinds of stuff – dragging reels around, swimming tow lines out to sea, and pulling 'torpedoes'. Eventually we got to use the surf skis and rescue boards." The rescue boards were 12-foot hollow wooden boards made from marine ply. The club had several of them, all imported from South Africa or Australia. It took two people to carry them down the beach, so they were kept at the water's edge in case there was an emergency. "Standing up on them was just an extension of learning how to control them when you rode a wave in. For me, my brothers and the Griffin boys, standing on the rescue boards was the most fun we could have with the lifesaving equipment."

The surf lifesavers were having fun trying to ride the rescue boards standing up as early as summer 1959. But the boards had their limitations, to say the least. "You could only ride them straight in," recalls Charles, "if you tried to angle off in any direction, they immediately started to broach and you were flipped off!"

In 1961 Keith Slocombe and Dave Lobb ordered a balsa malibu board from Australia for the club. The new board duly arrived, and the young surfers were thrilled to discover how manoeuvrable and responsive it was.

The Williams and Griffin brothers were buzzing on surfing. Several of their schoolmates also caught the bug, among them Mike Lake, Geoff O'Neill, Dave and Pete Dearnley and Jimmy Walcock. The boys got hold of a few copies of the American magazine Surfer, and became captivated by articles about the scene in California. Being schoolkids, they didn't have the money to buy expensive boards from the States, so they began thinking about making their own. "In woodwork we started making fins," says Charles, "and some of us were studying science so we began to think how we could shape surfboards from foam, and glass them with fibreglass."

The boys gleaned some information about making boards from Surfer, but they wanted to know more so Pete Griffin wrote to the magazine to ask about board dimensions and shaping tools. Thankfully, they didn't have to look so far for information about materials; as well as running the surf lifesaving club, Keith Slocombe already knew a fair bit about board building as he'd made several fibreglass-coated paddleboards for the club. Keith helped the boys obtain the materials they needed including, eventually, the foam. "We ended up getting the foam from a refrigeration company in Liverpool," remembers Dave Griffin. "It was brown and came in two-foot by three-foot blocks, which we glued together [to make a blank]. Keith helped us get the fibreglass resin and cloth, and we got some advice about how to use them from the ICI office in London."

By spring 1962 the boys had made six surfboards. Although crude, these were the first batch of homemade foam-and-fibreglass surfboards built in Britain. (The homemade boards built Freddie Blight in Plymouth a year earlier were balsa and fibreglass.) The lads were keen to check out their new craft, so they braved the cold water for as long as they could, wearing woollen jumpers to protect them from the chill.

One weekend the whole St Ives crew gathered to watch a demonstration by 'The Springboks', a touring team of lifeguards from the South African SLSA. Dave Griffin remembers being particularly impressed by their brilliant bodysurfing. Their surfing might have had more of an impact if team member Cleo Maranges hadn't sold his balsa-and-fibreglass board during their previous stopover in Jersey. Max Wetteland and Cleo did however surf on the paddleboards. Their surfing skills had quite an effect on the St Ives youngsters. "They really inspired us to be more committed and progressive with our surfing," says Charles Williams.

The St Ives Surf Lifesaving Club was thriving, but the growing number of surfing enthusiasts among its ranks were becoming aware that the Shangri-La of surf culture was California, where surfers had totally detached themselves from the lifeguard movement.

The St Ives boys had only read about these 'real' surfers in Surfer magazine; but bizarrely, thanks to the innocuous letter Pete Griffin had written to the magazine, they were about to meet one...

The passion for surfing in St Ives

was truly set alight with the unexpected arrival of flashy American surfer Dave Rochlen in the spring of 1962. Rochlen was one the most famous surfers in the US at the time, and often hung out at California's famous pointbreak, Malibu. As well as being a top surfer he also enjoyed skiing, and after winning a surf contest at Malibu he decided to celebrate with a ski trip to Zermatt, Switzerland. He'd heard rumours that there were waves in Britain and France, so he brought his surfboard with him on the trip. His only contact address in Cornwall was that of the Griffin brothers in St Ives, which he'd been given by one of the staff at Surfer magazine.

"He arrived at our house carrying a 9'6" Dewey Weber board and introduced himself," remembers Dave Griffin. "He ended up staying at our house for three weeks. His surfing just blew our minds. He did things in the water nobody could believe – bottom-turns, cutbacks, rollercoasters..." Every time Rochlen hit the water at Porthmeor he put on an awesome display of the latest hot-dogging style.

The St Ives boys could hardly believe it. The US was the prominent force in global surf culture at the time, and its top man was living in their own town. Besides his amazing surfing skills, Rochlen was the living embodiment of the Californian surfer lifestyle, a genuine alternative role model. He wore red floral-patterned surf trunks. He could walk the board and ride the nose. And when he pulled off after a good wave he'd declare the experience, "Bitchin'!" The guy simply lived for surfing, an attitude epitomised in a subsequent interview in Surfer magazine when he was asked about the appeal of surfing. "It's simple," said Rochlen, "the ocean is the most wondrous thing on the planet, and a breaking wave is the single most exciting thing happening in the ocean. Riding a wave allows you to reach out and touch the face of God."

Dave Rochlen's presence was to profoundly influence the lives of several of the young locals, especially surf-stoked teenager Charles Williams. "Rochlen showed us how to perceive ourselves as surfers," says Charles. "We realised that surfing was more than just a sport – it incorporated your clothes,

below
St Ives' schoolboy surf lifesavers, with a home-made surfboard and a couple of trophies they 'liberated' from the SLSA National Championships in 1961. Among the faces are Dave Dearnley, Pete Griffin, Dave Lobb and Charles Williams.
PHOTO: DAVE LOBB COLLECTION.

your shoes, your car, even how you moved on the dance-floor. From then on all I wanted was to be at one with the wave, have a rapport with the ocean, and surf as well as I could." Charles became the undisputed St Ives silver surfer and a new star of the burgeoning scene in Cornwall.

With Keith Slocombe as its head honcho, the beach community in St Ives embraced a new surf-orientated lifestyle. Keith understood the beach life perfectly because of his passion for surf lifesaving. He also could act as a promotional force for surfing due to his position as Honorary Secretary of the Surf Lifesaving Association of Great Britain. Early in 1963 Slocombe set up a small board-building factory in Lelant, and later that year he opened a shop called The Surfer's Store in a cobbled side street in St Ives. It was the first specialist surf shop in Britain, proof that in 1963 St Ives had the largest surf scene in Cornwall.

Slocombe was the spark for the surf industry in St Ives. While Charles Williams was away studying at college, brothers James and Peter-George started their own board brand, Williams Surfboards, at Keith's Lelant factory.

Two years later, Charles quit his studies and returned home to set up his own brand, Atlantic Surfboards, with local wheeler-dealer Colin Prior. The pair found a derelict two-up two-down cottage at the top of the town and converted it into a surfboard factory. Colin made rough blanks from refrigeration foam, Charles did the shaping, and Dave Griffin helped to glass and sand the boards.

In 1965 Pete Griffin formed the Porthmeor Surfing Association

and staged the earliest and best-organised surfing contest in mainland Britain. Previously, surf on the mainland were merely a side-show to the SLSA National Championships or one of their carnivals.

above
Top Californian surfer Dave Rochlen in action at Porthmeor in 1962. Rochlen's unexpected visit had a profound effect on the young surfers of St Ives. PHOTO: DAVE LOBB.

below
Dave Rochlen (left) with Pete Griffin. PHOTO: DAVE LOBB.

The Porthmeor contest attracted surfers from across Cornwall and enabled them to do their own thing, away from the SLSA. "That competition was great," remembers Charles Williams, "it got everyone who called themselves surfers together to show off their abilities. There was a really good festive atmosphere, and it was home turf for us as well."

The surfers who gathered for the contest were fascinated to see what boards the other guys were riding, what they were wearing, and what they were thinking. A clan identity was in the making, inspired by the surf lifestyles of California, South Africa, Australia and Hawaii, but with a unique British edge. "We even had our own Surfers' Dance after the contest, an idea we picked up from Dave Rochlen," continues Charles. "It was a stomping night of loud music and everyone totally let loose."

By the second half of the decade word had spread that there was a cool surf scene in St Ives. Tourists could hire boards from the Man Friday cafe, and the beach became a magnet for flamboyant travelling surfers working the summer lifeguard season. This was a time when the Vietnam War gave many young American and Australian men good reason to pursue a life on the road. Californian Richard Neff and Australians Chris 'The Animal' Cannings, Neil 'The Gnome' Redding, John Brown and Johnny Ryland all came to Cornwall as so-called 'draft dodgers'. These talented surfers worked as lifeguards in St Ives, and entertained the locals with their antics. They installed a live-for-the-moment party attitude common to Australians that was different to Dave Rochlen's laid-back Californian approach. They surfed hard and played hard. More importantly, Chris Cannings and Neil Redding also worked part-time at Atlantic Surfboards where they had a massive influence. "They brought fresh ideas and cutting edge shaping and finishing skills to our board business," says Charles Williams.

The late, great Chris Cannings also gravitated to Newquay, where his reputation as a surfer and party animal grew. After several nights of drunken debauchery he was banned from the Cellar Bar in Newquay's Great Western Hotel. One evening he sneaked back in with a couple of mates. The bar manager spotted him and asked him to leave. Chris stood his ground, until there was a big flare up. Chris dashed behind the bar and ran along it turning on all the beer taps, with the bar manger chasing him turning them off again. Chris did a few more laps, the beer taps going on and off, on and off. "If I stop, will you lift my ban?" laughed Chris. The bar manager agreed.

By the late '60s, however, St Ives was no longer thought of as Cornwall's leading surf town as the focus had shifted to Newquay. Atlantic Surfboards also suffered a major setback. In the summer of 1968 a fire destroyed the small board factory. Fortune smiled on Charles and Colin, however, when they secured a Government grant to set up a purpose-built factory at Penbeagle. "It was state of the art," says Charles. "We had a shaping bay, a glassing bay with extractor fans, and a sanding room with water jets running down the walls to keep the dust down." Atlantic Surfboards developed to become a leading brand in the expanding British market over the next seven years. Its success was promoted by Charles Williams' own well-travelled competition appearances. He rapidly evolved into one of Britain's most stylish performers and represented Britain at international events throughout the '60s. His good looks also earned him a brief career as a model for London tailors Austin Reed. His picture appeared in high street shop windows and newspaper advertisements. He also had a starring role in a 1973 BBC television documentary The Surfers, which attempted to depict the philosophy and lifestyle of the band of devoted wave-riders inhabiting the beaches of Cornwall.

By the mid '70s Charles found himself doing more and more foreign surf trips. "I'd been able to use my shaping income to live at home, and my modelling money to fund contest trips abroad, often with the British team. But after being runner-up three times in the British Championships I got disillusioned with the contest scene. It wasn't a very important part of

below left
Charles Williams graduated from nine-footers to six-footers at the end of the '60s, and remained one of Britain's biggest talents right through the '70s. PHOTO: TONY HOLE.

below right
The beachfront at Porthmeor made a perfect base for summer surf contests in the '60s. PHOTO: DOUG WILSON.

the surfing lifestyle to me. I wanted to improve my own personal ability. I started to realise that there were only a few reefs in Cornwall, and I knew I couldn't reach my full potential as a surfer by staying at home. So I travelled, and I got hooked on spending months and months abroad. Everything else in life became peripheral. I just wanted to be immersed in good waves."

In the '70s a new generation

of surfers came to the fore, including Tim Symons who won the British Junior title in 1974. Tim was an outstanding talent who attacked Porthmeor's fast sections with his radical, yet fluid style. He and his family went on to run several successful businesses throughout the town.

As the neon-fuelled '80s took grip, surfing entered a radical period of board design and experimentation. "It went a bit crazy on fluoro colours, but the boards were changing so much it was great," says local Duncan Hall. "I think I had a different board every six months! We had single fins, twins, thrusters then quads. Porthmeor has always been a great wave to feel out different boards. I remember having a twin-fin with two wings and a swallowtail. I chopped off the end of the tail so there was only one wing, put two extra fins on and turned it into a 5'4" quad. It went really well! It was typical of the experimentation of the time."

Porthmeor remains a superb wintertime surfing beach; at four-foot-plus it can be heavy and hollow. Peeling best on the dropping tide, there are zippy rights on north swells and reeling lefts on southwest swells. It's no surprise the place has created generation after generation of outstanding surfers. Few have been as talented as James and Charles Williams, however. They became two of Cornwall's best surfers and earliest proponents of the cool surfer lifestyle, founded a couple of classic British board labels, and travelled the world. It must seem a long, long time ago that they began daydreaming of becoming surfers in those science classes at school.

above
Stefan Harkon attacks a Porthmoer wall in 1988. PHOTO: ALEX WILLIAMS.

NEWQUAY: SURF CITY UK

The Great Western Railway ushered in a new era of tourism in Cornwall during the early 20th century. Many of the visitors came to the then small fishing town of Newquay on the north coast. With nine golden sand beaches open to ocean swell, Newquay was naturally equipped to become a centre for surfing. Bellyboarding was the post-war summer buzz and a local culture emerged that was all about playing in the waves. This evocative image was used to promote Newquay as the tourist capital of the new 'Cornish Riviera', easily accessed by train (and increasingly by car) in the '50s and '60s.

Local surfing pioneer Pip Staffieri had aroused mild curiosity by riding waves in Newquay during the '40s, but the austerity of the post-war years prevented the emergence of surfing for another 20 years. By the '50s, Pip was better known for making ice creams than surfing, but he still liked to park his van in a good spot and quietly watch the waves while he was working.

Newquay became a magnet for alternative subcultures that changed the cultural landscape of the post-war years, such as the 'beat generation' beatniks who came to town on the back of the folk music scene in the late '50s. Early pioneers such as Pete Stanley and Wiz Jones played impromptu concerts at the Fly Cellars on Pentire Headland

and fired up their young audience with social protest songs, to herald a freethinking new generation.

A rudimentary lifeguard service

operated on Newquay's beaches throughout the '50s. Two local families – the Williams and Simpson families – spearheaded this early movement, recognising the dangers of the unpredictable Atlantic to the growing number of bathers and bellyboarders. Inspired by the arrival of expert South African lifeguard Kams Veeran, this group of concerned beach users formed the Newquay Surf Lifesaving Club in 1958. The following year Newquay Council (and private beach-owners in the town) took on full-time lifeguards who were paid to work at Watergate, Towan, Great Western, Tolcarne, Porth, Crantock and Fistral throughout the summer season. It was from this diverse group of watermen that surfing and surf culture would emerge in Newquay. At its core was the unlikely pair of Doug Wilson and Bill Bailey.

Doug Wilson had been a musician in the army and he moved from Sussex to work as a lifeguard at Fistral in 1959. Two years later Bill Bailey, an ex-engineer in the RAF, came down from Somerset to work as a lifeguard at Porth. The pair became central to the social and sporting activities of the Newquay SLSC, alongside Doug Turner and Newquay-raised Richard Trewella. Bill was a keen craftsman and in 1961 he built

above
Fun waves at Fistral, September 1966.
PHOTO: DOUG WILSON.

opposite, top
Roger Mansfield enjoys a clean summer wave at Great Western in 1966. PHOTO DOUG WILSON

opposite, bottom left
1964. A group of young Newquay surfers hang out on 'the Slope' at Great Western, with lifeguard Bill Bailey. Among the faces are Alan McBride, Rod Sumpter, Dave 'Moby' Patience, John Conway and Robin Wilson. PHOTO DOUG WILSON

opposite, middle
Newquay gremmies Chris Jones (far left), Roger Mansfield (far right) and friends wait for the tide to turn at Great Western in 1963.

opposite, bottom right
Newquay's first surf shop, The Surf Centre, which opened on Fore Street in 1965. PHOTO DOUG WILSON

a wooden surf ski for Doug Turner. He also made two 14-foot hollow wooden 'okanui' boards for himself and Richard Trewella. He copied these from an Australian design in the manual of the Australian Surf Lifesaving Association.

When a visiting team of surf lifesavers from South Africa put on a demo at Tolcarne Beach in early spring 1962, the Newquay crew were hugely impressed. The standout was three-times South African paddling champion Max Wetteland. The Springbok team had already visited Jersey and St Ives, but it was in Newquay that Max had the biggest impact. "His speed and his paddling power were incredible," remembers Richard Trewella. "Max could also surf the paddleboards with style and control. It was an inspiring sight and it spurred me, Bill and Doug to start experimenting with stand-up rides on the buoyant two-man wave-skis."

Later that spring, a sequence of chance events unfolded which would form a core group of surfboard riders in the town. One morning, Bill Bailey received a telephone call from Peter Cox, a friend who lived on the island at Towan Beach. "Bill, get over here!" said Peter excitedly. "Someone's surfing right out front!" Bill rushed down to Towan, where he saw a distant figure riding the waves on a revolutionary-looking board. The mystery man turned out to be a visiting American called Doug McDonald, and the board he was riding was a state-of-the-art 9'6" Bragg fibreglass malibu board.

On the very same day, four Australian lifeguards who had just arrived in town, took their first look at Newquay Bay. In the chilly April air a clean swell was rolling in, the wave faces held up by a stiff offshore wind. "Check this, mate, they've got some decent surf here!" was the surprised observation of Bob Head, who had come to Cornwall with fellow Avalon SLSC members John Campbell, Warren Mitchell and Ian Tiley.

All four lifeguards were top watermen, fresh from the 'surfer' versus 'clubbie' culture-rift that was manifesting itself on Australia's east coast. Bob and John had brought their surfboards with them in the hope of finding waves. These boards were foam-and-fibreglass malibu boards made by Barry Bennetts in Sydney; boards with polyurethane foam cores (instead of balsa wood) were the latest innovation to sweep the surfing world.

The next day, the Aussie lifeguards were back at Great Western, this time with their boards. Doug Wilson and Bill Bailey chased after them to meet them and find out about their equipment.

Later that eventful day Bill learned that Doug McDonald, the American surfer he'd watched at Towan, was returning home to California and was keen to sell some equipment. Bill tracked him down and bought his 9'6" board on the spot. To top off the deal, he bought McDonald's bright yellow Ford van as well.

The international cast for the launch of surfing in Newquay grew further when American lifeguard and surfer John Lydgate arrived a few weeks later. 'Mahogany Jack' (as he became known) was a tall, tanned, well-educated post-grad student; he'd attended Yale University and was now studying for a PhD in London. He had swum for Yale since the late '50s and had worked as a lifeguard at Nantucket on the east coast of America for several summer seasons. Before college he went to high school in Hawaii, where he learned to ride big waves on the North Shore.

Bill Bailey and Doug Wilson welcomed and befriended all the new arrivals. Bob Head and Jack Lydgate were now the best surfers in town, and both became instant heroes to the local beach-going youngsters who watched them cruise effortlessly along the waves. Goofyfoot Jack was not a 'performer', but an elegant straight-ahead stylist in the smooth Hawaiian and Californian tradition. Naturalfoot Bob was burly and heavy set, but beautiful in the water; he had a powerful style and liked to carve turns along the wave, typical of the hottest Aussies.

Amid the excitement of the sudden influx of surfers into Newquay, Doug Wilson noticed a red balsa-and-fibreglass surfboard for sale in the window of a shop at the bottom of Marcus Hill in Newquay. The price tag was £11, more than a week's wages, but Doug snapped it up. It turned out that the board had been built by Freddie Blight, a cabinet maker from Plymouth. Inspired by a Life magazine covershot of Greg Noll standing on a beach in Hawaii, Freddie had built three balsa-and-fibreglass boards in 1961, the earliest of their type in Britain. His two sons, Richard and Ajax, learnt to surf on two of these (in the Padstow area), but the third board went unused and Freddie sold it to the shop. This then was the first commercially-built balsa-and-fibreglass board in Britain. Doug later made contact with Freddie and introduced him to the Newquay surfing crew.

By the spring of 1963 a small but
dedicated surfing clan had formed in Newquay, with all the action going down in the bay. Great Western deck chair attendants Dave Friar, Trevor Roberts and

RETURN TRAYS HERE
Wall's
ICE CREAM
SURFING PROMOTIONS
NEWQUAY

The Surf Centre
HOLLOW DAYS
FOLLOW THE SUN

above
Fistral Beach was rarely surfed in the early '60s. But on offshore days surfers began to sit up and take notice.
PHOTO DOUG WILSON

Alan 'Mac' McBride were drawn in and became the town's first beach boys. They were soon joined by other locals such as Richard Trewella, Brian and Dave Daniels, and peroxide blonde brothers Viv and Robin Wilson. The Wilson's family home became a popular social hangout for many of the young surfers.

Bill Bailey noticed there was a growing demand for surfboards, so he tried his hand at building some in a town garage. One of his first tasks was reshaping and re-glassing parts of Doug Wilson's crude Freddie Blight board. Further up the coast at Mawgan Porth, Bob Head also began building malibu boards, in a disused chicken shed. He called his label Friendly Bear Surfboards. Bob had never built a board back in Australia, but he saw the opportunities emerging in Britain. His surfing skills and intimate knowledge of the Australian surf scene served him well. The seeds of an industry were being sown.

As the town's sons saw the fun that was being had in the waves, younger kids found their way into the lineups. Chris Jones was an enthusiastic 14-year-old bellyboarder at the time. His parents managed St Brannock's Hotel above Tolcarne Beach. "I was given the chance to try stand-up surfing by Jack Lydgate, the lifeguard there," says Chris. "I was hooked straightaway. It was the best thing ever. So I worked all summer long, cleaning beach huts and hustling deck chairs to earn the £25 to buy my own board." At Great Western, 11-year-old Roger Mansfield was similarly encouraged to learn to surf by lifeguard and part-time shaper Bill Bailey. It wasn't long before CJ and Roger became the keenest 'gremmies' in town.

At the end of the 1963 season, the visiting Aussie lifeguards and Bill Bailey headed off on a trip to Biarritz to discover the delights of France and find out if the rumours of incredible waves were true. There Bill learned to ride bigger more powerful waves, and he laid the foundations for a future business partnership with Bob Head. Unfortunately Bill's travel money ran out sooner than expected, and he was forced to sell his beloved Bragg surfboard to fund the journey home.

Once back in Newquay, Bill and Bob continued to build boards independently for another two years, supplying hot gremmies Chris Jones and Roger Mansfield as well as a second wave of youngsters who caught the surfing bug later in '63 and '64. These included Alan 'Fuz' Bleakley, Colin Christian, Ian 'Porky' Morcom, John Conway, Neil Mason and Paul Holmes. Some of these newcomers came from the surf lifesaving club, others simply used to hang out at the beach. Whatever their background, Bill Bailey and the Newquay lifeguards encouraged and inspired them all.

Fuz Bleakley recalls the board his dad gave him for his 15th birthday in January 1964. "It was a green-and-white striped 9'8". It originally belonged to Bob Head, then he passed it on to one of the other lifeguards, a guy they called 'Phantom' [Mick Irwin]. Phantom and the other guys used to drink and play poker late into the night at my parents' hotel, The White House on Headland Road. One night, Phantom was losing heavily to my dad, but he didn't have the money to pay the debt. Instead, he gave Dad his surfboard...and he passed it on to me as a birthday present. My friend Porky [Morcom] had just scored a beavertail wetsuit top so we pooled resources, taking turns to use the board and wetsuit at Towan."

By 1964 surf fever was building in Newquay, and at the end of that long hot summer it was obvious that there was not only a new sport emerging, but also a new lifestyle. All the action was focused on Tolcarne, Towan and Great Western. Sometimes crowds would line the clifftops to watch the spectacle put on by of the small band of regulars, which included Dave 'Moby' Patience, Dave Friar, and Trevor Roberts on his trademark red-and-black board. Virtually every holidaymaker who visited the town must have stopped to watch this new breed of wave-riders. Soon, even the national press started printing stories about the new 'cult of surfing'.

The emerging surf culture was further stimulated by the arrival of surf music from California. First came the guitar bands such as The Ventures and The Chantays, then the vocal harmony groups like The Beach Boys and Jan & Dean. As primarily a boys' sport in those early days, who could resist lyrics such as "...two girls for every boy"? Following Jan & Dean's song 'Surf City', Newquay imagined itself to be 'Surf City UK'.

The hub of the Newquay scene at this time was 'the Slope', the area at the bottom of the road to Great Western, next to the lifeguard hut. In the film *Big Wednesday*, a fictional crew of Californians hang out at a flight of broken steps leading down to a Malibu-style pointbreak. The Slope was Newquay's equivalent, a genuine hotbed of Newquay surf culture. Travellers and locals alike would congregate on the Slope, then paddle out for a session. Here, lifeguard and board maker Bill Bailey commanded a masterful aura. If you were an aspiring surfer wanting a locally-built board, you had to prove to Bill that you were a good swimmer and had the right to own a surfboard.

The scene extended into the Cellar Bar below the Great Western Hotel. Here Trevor Roberts (now a lifeguard at Tolcarne) would fill the bar with his big personality and social charm. Tall and bearded, Trevor seemed to be in charge of every situation he entered. His hilarious jokes and all-around ability to entertain became legendary. He was a big-hearted lover of life, forever positive, always describing things as "magic". In fact, it was under Trevor's wing that many young surfers sneakily sipped their first pint. "Trevor was the life and soul of the party," remembers Chris Jones. "He was everybody's mate and a surrogate dad to the young guys hanging down the beach."

Another gang hung out at the Blue Lagoon, a popular dancehall which teetered precariously on the clifftop above Great Western. Here was a happening 'mod' scene where lads arrived on Lambretta scooters, wore mohair suits and skinny ties, and danced to Tamla Motown and ska music. Both the Cellar Bar and the Blue Lagoon reflected the wider cultural influences that made Newquay such an exciting town in the early '60s.

Out in the water, surfing was clearly an athletic pursuit, but it was mainly about having fun. "We used to do some pretty stupid things like ride into the cave at Great Western at high tide, just for the hell of it!" remembers Chris Jones. "If there was a good swell running, we'd call the biggest wave of a set 'the widowmaker'. And if there were quite a few guys out, we'd get everybody to catch the same wave and shout 'GLITTERY GLIDE-DOWN!'. Occasionally we'd all paddle out and do a glittery glide-down on a widowmaker!"

These antics in the ocean and on land caused confusion and mild consternation among the general public. "What is this surfing craze?" they wondered, bemused by the strange-looking boards, the lingo, and the apparently frivolous beach lifestyle. A whole new social group was emerging in coastal Britain.

The tourist industry was quick to pick up on the hedonistic new 'surfie' lifestyle. The cover of the Newquay Town Guide in 1964 showed a picture of two girls riding the whitewater (prone) on a malibu board. Inside there was a colour spread of two surfers riding 'Hawaiian style' across a green wave in Newquay Bay.

Paul Holmes reckons that it was an amazing time to be a teenage surfer. "The early '60s was a period of total transformation for us young surfers. I was caught up in some kind of dream state, partly inspired by Californian surf magazines and movies, and partly by the 'live for the moment' attitude of early British surfers like Bill Bailey and Trevor Roberts. It felt like we were at some kind of new frontier. That was so radical for a kid brought up in a small seaside town…it was literally blowing my mind. Remember, there were few opportunities in Cornwall back then. I was at school with kids who were mostly sons and daughters of farmers and fisherman, or small-minded lower middle class professionals."

By 1964 Newquay's fledgling surf industry was beginning

to take shape. Surfers could purchase boards from one of three shapers in the town: Bill Bailey, Bob Head or Freddy Bickers.

Freddy was a skilful craftsman who had run a successful cabinet making business in Plymouth. Resolute, attentive and slightly built, he was a classic artisan of the era. Freddy was in his fifties when surfing caught his attention; typical of the social conformity of that particular generation he wore tweed trousers, a cardigan and delicate oval spectacles. In the summer of '64 he stepped up his production to three boards a week, employing young local surfer John Conway as an apprentice carpenter and shaper.

Bill Bailey and Bob Head had become good friends on their trip to France the previous year. In the autumn of '64 they felt the time was right to join forces and set up a proper business, uniting their talents as well as those of Doug Wilson (by now a keen surf photographer) and Freddie Blight. The four of them sat down and agreed a business plan. They called their new business the European Surfing Company, and named their board label Bilbo Surfboards (combining the names of their shapers, Bill and Bob). In February 1965 they set up a small surfboard factory on Pargolla Road, on land leased from the council. In the spring they opened a shop on Fore Street called The Surf Centre. Bill and Bob ran the factory, Doug managed the shop, and Freddie worked behind the scenes as the company's financial director.

Business thrived and within a year the company opened a second outlet, Bilbo Surf Shop, on Cliff

above
Crowds gather on Towan Head to watch Australian and American lifeguards tackle huge waves at The Cribbar in September 1966.
PHOTO DOUG WILSON

Road at the north end of town. Across the road was another new venture, Maui Surf Shop, just opened by Australian Mick Jackman. Easy going Mick had come to Newquay to work as a lifeguard a couple of years earlier. He'd supplemented his income by working as a piano player in a hotel jazz band, but he soon realised there was more money to be made from the expanding British surf market.

It was the perfect time for new styles and brands of clothing to take off. In the swinging '60s, Britain was in the grip of a whole new fashion movement, and fresh new ideas were lapped up by the nation's youth. In order to expand the product range in the European Surf Company's shops, Doug Wilson set up a new brand called Force Nine Surfwear. Shorts and jackets were manufactured by a local clothing company to Doug's specifications...although these weren't always entirely original. One jacket design was literally ripped off the back of a visiting Aussie traveller called John Brown; Doug liked John's Hang Ten jacket so much that he bought it off him and 'borrowed' the style and design!

Mick at Maui also started making good money from surf clothing, selling floral shorts obtained from Bob Westlake, who later started the British surf company Alder. More surf shops subsequently opened in Newquay, allowing British surfers to get the look they wanted as well as the hardware.

Although the surfwear industry was flourishing, the development of the wetsuit was still in its infancy. In the earliest days, surfers survived the cold months by wearing multiple layers of clothing, which was not very effective. Around 1964 Cornish surfers starting making their own neoprene wetsuits, using patterns for diving wetsuits. These early suits were warm, but stiff and uncomfortable. Newcomer Dennis Cross from London made a few suits for himself and his friends, then realised he could make a bit of money using his know-how. He came up with a design for a one-piece long john wetsuit, specifically for surfers, and sold a couple of dozen of them that season. The new wetsuits were highly popular, and Dennis was soon asked to supply wetsuits for the Bilbo shops. Demand was high because surfers realised they could continue surfing right through the year in the comfortable new cuts.

Three years later Dennis set up Gul Wetsuits, and began producing ever better suits using the latest neoprene and new methods of stitching. The Bodmin-based company grew dramatically over the next decade, fuelled by the absolute necessity for every British surfer to own a wetsuit.

By the middle of the decade

word was spreading about the waves in Newquay and more and more foreign surfers began to visit the town. Paul Kemnitzer was a talented surfer from Rincon in California, whose parents had moved to London. From there, Paul would come down to Newquay as often as possible to surf. "Paul was a great inspiration," says Chris Jones, "he was the perfect example of a surfer from that early era when everything was so pure. The boards were big and heavy, so you had to be as smooth as you could be. Paul had been brought up surfing those always-glassy Californian waves, so he was an ideal role model."

Around this time more British surfers also started to travel, lured by the promise of warm water and perfect waves. Dave Friar journeyed to South Africa, and while he was in Cape Town he watched local stylist Donald Paarman performing a unique manoeuvre, the drop-knee turn. By lowering his back knee, Paarman got greater leverage through his bottom-turns and cutbacks; the move also looked supremely stylish. Dave was inspired, and returned to his beloved Tolcarne a few weeks later with a perfect drop-knee style of his own. It wasn't long before Friar was inspiring other surfers himself. "Dave's drop-knee cutback was a flawless technique," says Roger Mansfield, "it was so impressive I wanted to learn it too. So I watched Dave and practised until I'd perfected my own drop-knee turns." A new manoeuvre had entered the national surfing psyche.

Newquay attracted a number of top Australian surfers in the mid '60s including Dennis White, Glen Short, Pete Russell, Keith Paull and expatriate Rod Sumpter. One by one these highly influential visitors showed the locals how to surf with flair, and how to live the surfing life. They came because they were keen to check out the waves, because they wanted to visit 'the Old Country', and for one or two other reasons...as Mick Jackman succinctly explained to an inquiring journalist: "These English birds, mate, they're really great!"

British-born Rod Sumpter chose Newquay as his operational base in May 1966, instantly giving Britain its very own surfing superstar. Tall and graceful, Sumpter had a spontaneous cat-like finesse and his surfing was superior to anything previously seen in Cornish waters. "He was the complete professional package – great noseriding technique, sponsorship, the lot," noted the late John Conway, writing in the '80s. "He was living evidence of an ability to make a career out of surfing, and the first British surfer to achieve international recognition."

Rod finished fifth at the 1966 World Championships on a board sporting a huge Union Jack design. It had a big impact, and Rod subsequently helped produce many more of his 'Britannia model' boards at the Bilbo factory. Rod also pioneered the production of British-made surf films, starting with *Come Surf With Me*. His surfing prowess and international success gave British surfers a great sense of pride, and his films of Brits surfing their own waves instilled a further self-confidence (see profile, page 68).

Many who lived and surfed in Newquay

remember 1966 as the year of 'The Great September Swell'. One morning the town's surfers awoke to find a monstrous swell hitting the coast. The lines were stacked to the horizon, generated by a deep Atlantic low which had just been downgraded from a hurricane. It was the biggest rideable surf many people had ever seen. Newquay Bay was closing out at eight to ten feet, while The

below
Aussie Pete Russell takes the drop on a hefty Cribbar right-hander.
PHOTO DOUG WILSON

above
Nigel Semmens turned pro and began competing at international events in the early '80s.
PHOTO PETE BOUNDS

Cribbar – the reef off the end of Towan Head – was breaking at 15 to 20 feet. Australian lifeguards Pete Russell, Rick Friar and Johnny McElroy took up the challenge, along with their American colleague Jack Lydgate. The four surfers paddled out from the lifeboat slipway, and passed the town's main sewage outfall; they all looked back in disgust, as if to say, "What are we doing?" But their attention was focused on the long paddle and the huge waves breaking on the reef.

Pete Russell was an outstanding naturalfooter, already renowned for his love of big waves. "Surfing The Cribbar in '66 was a highlight that I vividly remember to this very day. Although I've surfed a lot of big days since, back home [in Australia], I've never experienced the adrenaline rush of that day. In the glassy, misty conditions, with that cliff face in the background, it was surreal."

The four surfers reached the lineup, but quickly got a wake-up call about the seriousness of the waves. "Jack Lydgate was first out," remembers Pete, "he was a superb paddler. But he went too deep and a sneaker set caught him. I can still picture him trying to paddle over a huge wall and getting absolutely creamed! His timing was way off but boy did he show some heart." Jack was cleaned up and left swimming. Without a leash (they hadn't been invented yet) his board was swept away like a matchstick and smashed against the rocks, breaking it in two. Jack's session was over before it had even begun; he caught his breath and began the long swim back to shore.

Rick Friar and Johnny McElroy approached the lineup cautiously and caught a couple of the smaller lefts. Then Johnny caught a clean inside wave which walled up for a beautiful long ride. Just before it closed out, Johnny used all his speed to climb the face and throw himself over the lip. He made it, but his board didn't. Two surfers down, two still paddling.

By now Pete Russell was way outside. Before anyone realised he was halfway down a giant left-hander. It was so big everything seemed to move in slow motion. Pete was just a dot with a trail of white foam snaking behind him as he sped across the 15-foot face. He made the section and paddled back out again. By this time the mist had cleared, and when Pete took off on another monster, Doug Wilson was able to click off a few photos from the headland. In one shot the wave looks eerily like Sunset Beach in Hawaii. This type of big-wave surfing was totally new to Britain.

Pete Russell caught another wave, but then suffered the same fate as his friends. "Then, of course, I got caught inside...and thought I was gone. I naively tried to duck under the massive wall of whitewater while clutching the nose of my board. Fortunately the wave that smashed me was the last in the set, otherwise I might not have lived to tell the tale."

All four surfers eventually made it safely back to shore. Iron man Jack, who'd learned to surf in Hawaii, gained lasting respect for his gruelling hour-long swim against the rip to reach safety. He finally clambered up the lifeboat slip, absolutely exhausted, his face etched with relief. Pip Staffieri had been watching the whole show from his van. He scooped out a big ice cream for Jack. "On the house," said Pip with a wink. Nobody in the enthralled crowd on the headland that momentous day knew that Pip was Britain's first surfer. Pip kept his secret to himself and handed Mahogany Jack the ice cream, beaming with pride.

In 1967 the first mainland British Championships were held at Fistral Beach, under the guidance of the newly-formed British Surfing Association. Rod Sumpter won the title

with ease. Over the next two years, local Newquay talents Chris Jones and Roger Mansfield would both win British Junior titles. They were captivated by Sumpter's amazing repertoire and he inspired them to raise the level of their surfing. Mansfield then won the British Open title in 1970, aged 18. The following year it was CJ who excelled, taking the English, British and European titles within a single year. Both surfers had rapidly progressed to become exponents of shortboard riding, a transition that Sumpter, 'the king of the malibu' did not make quite so effectively.

Throughout the '70s there was a continued presence of Australian-born (or raised) surfers in the Southwest who took part in competitions and kept pushing the local talent. Stuart 'Twizzle' Entwhistle was an early expert of the 360, while John Batcheledor and Bruce Palmer became British Champions in '72 and '75 respectively. But Roger Mansfield and Chris Jones represented the beginning of a line of young Newquay surfers who would rise to prominence in future national competition such as Nigel Semmens, Eden Burberry, Grishka Roberts, the late Randall Davies, Jon and Jamie Owen, Spencer Hargraves and the Winter brothers.

Other Newquay surf talents were not interested in contests, however. The bearded, long-haired Nigel Baker was an idiosyncratic personality of the early '70s whose charismatic charm turned many heads in Cornwall and southwest France. In big waves he would always shine, and one of his favourite breaks was Guethary near Biarritz. Tragically, he was

below
Smooth and stylish, Newquay naturalfoot Grishka Roberts rose to prominence in the '80s.
PHOTO CHRIS POWER

asphyxiated in a gas leak in 1976 during a stay in France. "While Nigel Baker had an arrogance that could really wind you up, he was also a very generous and caring person," remembers Fuz Bleakley. "He saved my life at La Barre in 1970 when I got into serious trouble caught in a rip. I'll always remember him and Martin Geary as the most talented surfers who never entered a contest."

Throughout the '70s and '80s the competitive rivalry between the likes of Keith Beddoe, Mick Etherington, Lee Parker, Lenny Ingram, Nigel Woodcock and Nigel Semmens would push Newquay surfing towards a new era of professionalism. By now the two main locations for the top dogs were Fistral and Watergate. The surfers' usual hangout was the undercover area near the car park at North Fistral. When the tide pushed up, the talented crew would reassemble at Watergate for some high-tide peelers.

Keith Beddoe spent many a winter abroad, and his experience of surfing reefs turned him into a versatile and fearless surfer. Lenny Ingram was also a top performer with a passion for bigger waves; he would happily paddle out for a lone session in sizeable waves. Newquay transplant Nigel Woodcock learned to surf in East Anglia and was bursting with natural talent. His gouging cutbacks and in-your-face turns were matched by a confident personality. While these surfers were always among the standouts at Fistral and Watergate, the star performer was Nigel Semmens and it was he who thrived in contests.

From his late teens, powerful naturalfooter Semmens decided that he would try his utmost to make living from surfing. "To me, surfing was always a complete, absolute lifestyle," says Nigel. "I wanted to live, eat, and sleep surfing. I realised doing contests and shaping boards were the best ways I could make a living from surfing, so that's what I focussed on."

Semmens worked for, and later went into partnership with Pete 'Mooney' McAllum at Ocean Magic Surfboards. The brand quickly became one of the biggest in the country, with a long list of top surfers on the team. In the early '80s Nigel became one of the most famous and successful surfers in the country, winning the British title in 1979 and the European title in 1981. These contest successes encouraged him, together with good friend Steve Daniel, to compete at professional contests around the world, as the era of pro surfing began.

In 1981 local entrepreneur John Conway organised the first British pro-am contest, the Newquay Surf Classic. Sponsored by Gul and Newquay Surfing Centre, this was the first mainstream event to offer prize money to British competitors. Nigel Semmens won it, in familiar Fistral juice. The success of the contest led to the staging of a European pro event in 1982, then an ASP World Tour event the following year which attracted 16 of the top international pro's to British shores.

From '84 onwards, Newquay cemented its reputation as Britain's top competition venue with the annual arrival of the ASP World Tour. The world's top pro's came to town every August, and surfers from across the country flocked to see the sport's elite in action. The event was sponsored by Fosters lager throughout the mid '80s and champions included superstars such as Tom Carroll, Tom Curren and Martin Potter. The spectacle of these surfers tearing apart the waves at Fistral inspired a new crew of local youngsters. The likes of Grishka Roberts, Spencer Hargraves and the Winter brothers would soon rise to the top and take British surfing into the modern professional era.

Newquay was now earning its popular press title, 'the surfing capital of Britain'. Further international recognition came when the BSA won the chance to stage the World Championships at Fistral in September 1986. Newquay played host to teams from 17 surfing nations in a smoothly run, seven-day event with decent surf. The event was a huge success. There was no prize money at stake, just national pride, which in surfing is priceless. Australia won the overall team title, but Britain won great respect from the visiting nations; we showed we had good waves, we knew how to surf, and we could run a good contest. After the difficulties Britain had faced in earlier years (for example, at the 1970 World Championships in Australia when we had to argue our rightful status as a fully-fledged surfing nation), this event proved that Britain had now arrived on the global surfing stage. It was an emancipating moment for British surf culture.

opposite
Spencer Hargraves, another Newquay prodigy, began his career in the late '80s and went on to become one of Europe's top pro's in the years that followed. PHOTO ALEX WILLIAMS

below
Tom Curren on the winner's podium at the 1986 Foster's Surfmasters.
PHOTO ALEX WILLIAMS

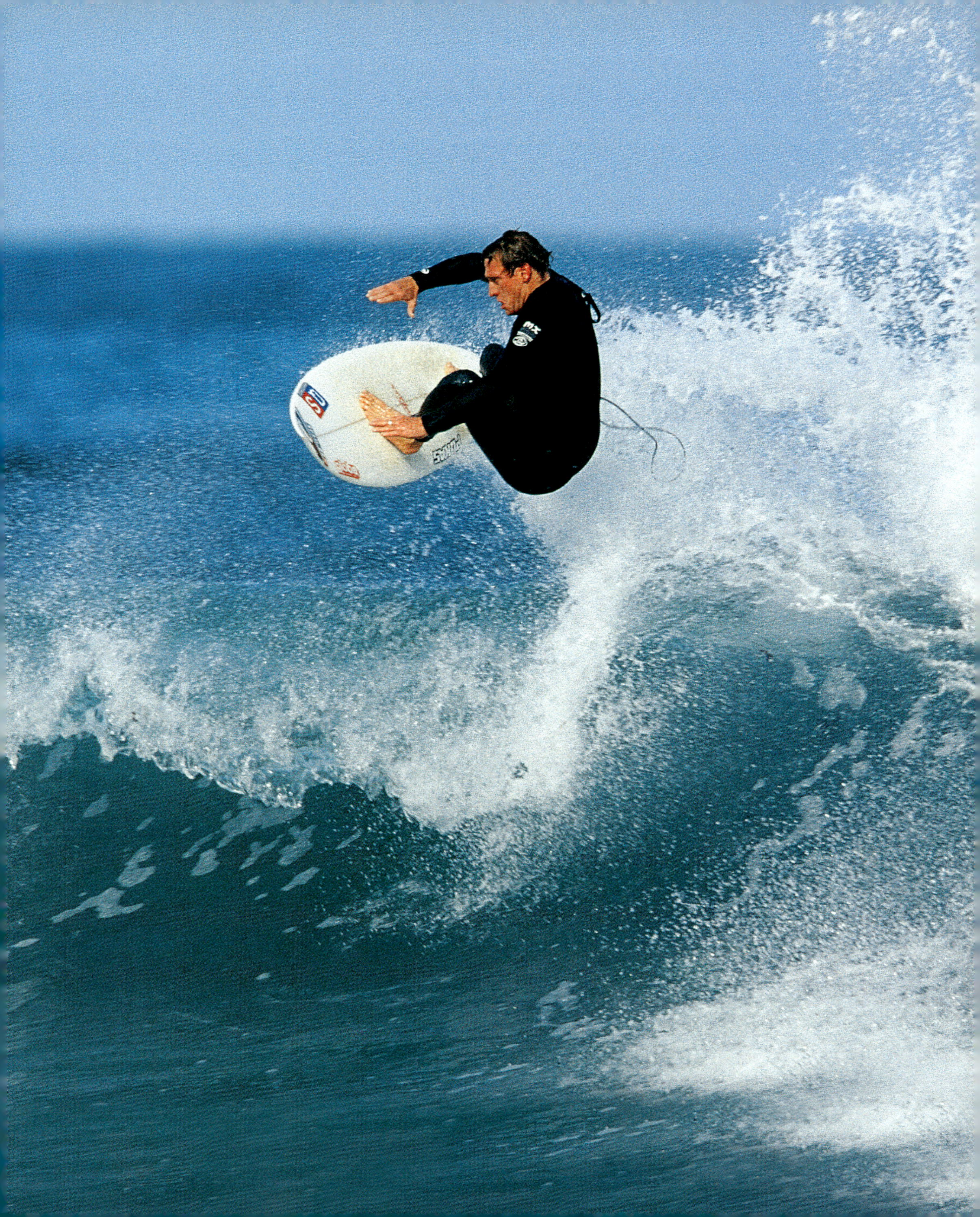

BILL BAILEY: THE FATHER OF BRITISH SURFING

Bill Bailey played a crucial role in the development of British surfing – as a Newquay lifeguard, a pioneer surfer and an expert board builder. Bill's generosity, allied to his passion and capability to shape surfboards, placed him in a unique position to facilitate the growth of a new sport within the nation. Bill was also a devoted waterman and a natural teacher, who encouraged people to live their lives to the full and follow their dreams; many went on to become surfing champions, surfboard builders, foam blowers, instructors and surf writers. Bill had a gentleness that touched the heart and he's become known within the surfing tribe as 'the father of British surfing'.

Born in 1933, Bill lived in Inglesbatch, Somerset, until he joined the Royal Air Force aged 14. For the next 13 years he trained as an engineer and pursued a career that sometimes posted him in the tropics, notably Sri Lanka, where he developed a passion for watersports. Bill left the RAF in the late '50s and his previous involvement in search-and-rescue operations and love of the sea attracted him to the embryonic surf lifesaving club in Newquay. Here he became friends with Doug Wilson, Richard Trewella and Doug Turner.

Bill was a natural technician and craftsman, so in 1961 he began building lifesaving equipment. His first big project was an Australian-style hollow wooden surf-ski, designed for two lifeguards to use with paddles. When it was finished, Bill and Richard took it out for a test run at Fistral in sizeable waves. Seated one behind the other, they fought their way out through the heavy surf. The biggest sets were described by an onlooker as "...at least two men high". Eventually they made it out the back, and sat there getting their breath back, level with the Baker's Folly house on Pentire headland and with 17 lines of whitewater separating them from the distant shore. They only caught one wave – it was big enough to dwarf the 14-foot long ski as it angled towards the bowl, and ultimately towards the beach, pushed by a seething mountain of whitewater.

The success of this venture, and the ski's ability to penetrate the surf zone, encouraged Bill and Richard to construct two 12-foot 'okanui' hollow wooden surfing boards. "This was a classic design based on Tom Blake's hollow board," says Bill. "The design stayed roughly the same from the '20s until the '60s, making it one of the most enduring surf craft. It was easy to use, paddling and punching out through the whitewater super-smoothly. It would catch waves early, giving you plenty of time to climb to your feet. It was great for cutting in a straight line, and started us off with stand-up surfing, but it was seriously limited in terms of manoeuvrability."

Bill was also a motorcycle enthusiast and had developed fibreglassing skills repairing damaged plastic fairings on bikes. This proved invaluable in 1962 when Bill saw the future of surfboards. American visitor Doug McDonald showed up in Newquay that April and rode a foam-and-fibreglass 'malibu' board in the bay. Thanks to its foam core, McDonald's 9'6" Bragg weighed just 22 lbs, far lighter than any wooden board. Since the American was leaving for home, he was keen to sell his gear and Bill bought both his surfboard and his van. At the time Bill was working as one of the earliest Newquay lifeguards, stationed during the summer tourist season on Great Western Beach. From now on he would often been found living in his yellow Ford van on 'the Slope'. From a small garage in the town, Bill also began shaping fibreglass surfboards.

By 1963 Bill's shaping ability was recognised by key individuals in the local community. Fresh back from his first trip to Biarritz he got an order from the local council for six lightweight fibreglass rescue surfboards. The council had been persuaded by their own lifeguards to invest in more advanced lifesaving equipment to replace the outdated Hicks rescue reels then being used on the town's beaches. With half the money paid in advance, Bill was able to research and purchase the materials necessary. This enabled him to design and build a mould for blowing high-density polyurethane foam blanks. The first blank was blown in a old caravan which doubled as his workshop at his home in Redruth. Things didn't quite go according to plan. The foam expanded quicker than anticipated

opposite
Bill always found time to go surfing, before or after work, or on his days off.
PHOTO DOUG WILSON

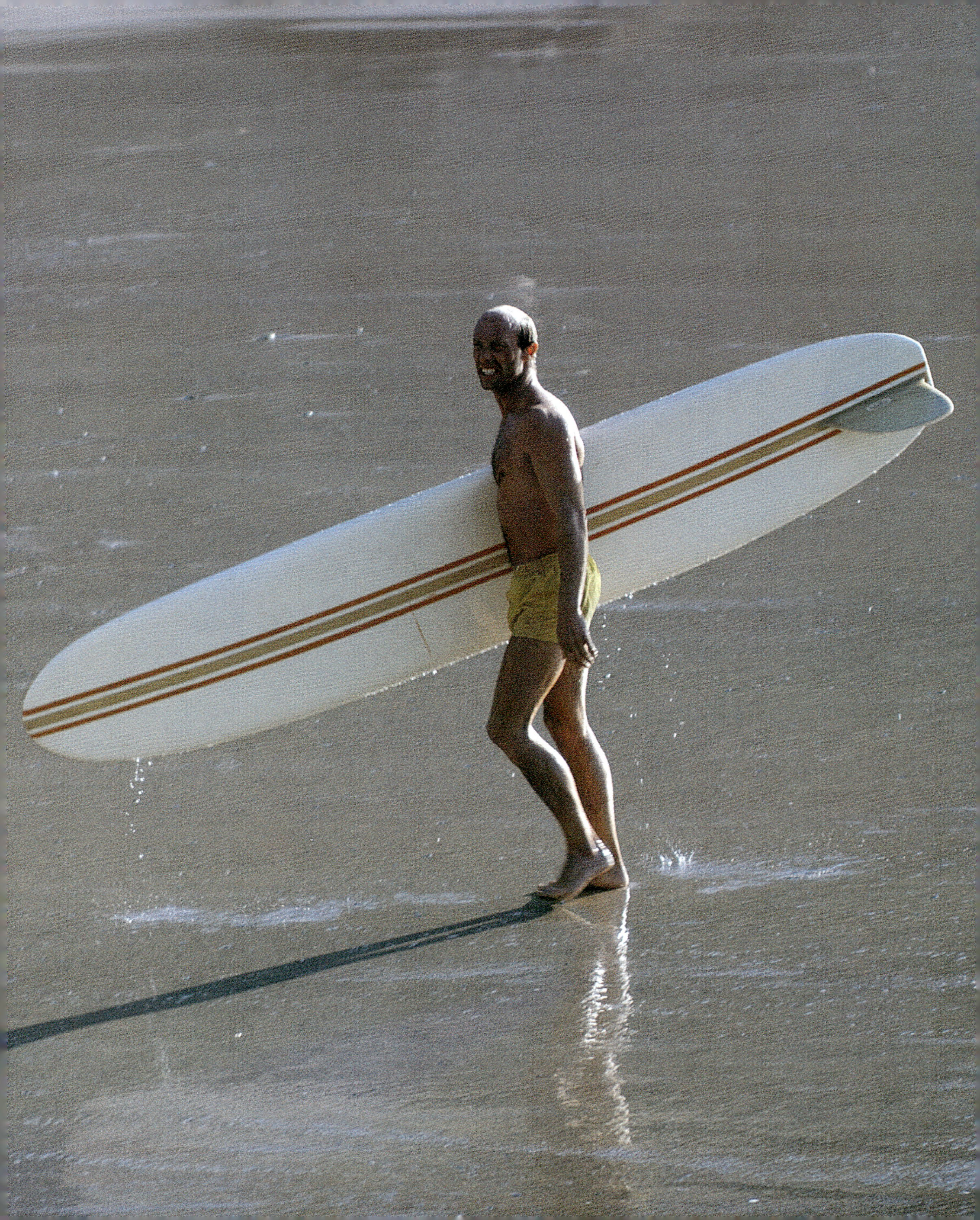

above
Bill (far left) clowning around at the Bilbo factory with Mick Jackman, Bob Head and Terry 'the bass player'.
PHOTO DOUG WILSON.

and came out of the mould two feet short and six times too thick! Newquay youngster Paul Holmes was there and assisted as best he could. "We had to stand on top of the mould to try to keep the thing from bursting through the ceiling of the caravan! Toxic fumes mixed with the damp Cornish scent of Bill's makeshift workshop. It was bizarre – California warm weather technology coming to cold, wet Britain." Bill subsequently got the mix right and his success at blowing foam was a vital step forward.

Paul Holmes ordered a board from Bill later that spring. "At 30 quid it seemed like a fortune," recalls Paul. "To get the money I had to do a whole lot of newspaper deliveries. Even then it took Bill months to make the board. Three times a week I would call by to see how it was coming along. Bill would scratch his head, puff on his pipe and say, 'Mmm, you might be able to get it…maybe next week.' It drove me nuts with frustration. Finally he finished my board. And it was worth the wait – a beautiful 9'6" with red rail wraps and four red pinstripes both sides. I was so ecstatic to get it home that, with sweaty palms, I dropped it on the back path. I took a big chip out of the gloss coat on the rail…but Bill quickly fixed it up for me."

By 1964 Bill was building surfboards commercially, while still working the summer months as a lifeguard at Great Western. 'Ding Dong', as Bill was often called, spent most of his time at his wooden lifeguard hut on the Slope. From the terrace in front of it, he puffed thoughtfully on his pipe and watched the sea. The aroma of tobacco mixed with the smell of paraffin from the stove and stench rising from a bucket of old wet T-shirts Bill used for surfing. It was a distinctive odour to say the least! Around Bill's hut on the Slope, the embryonic surf community in Newquay began to grow.

Bill was warm and generous and widely admired for his homegrown surfing skills. He was also keen to educate people about waves and surfboards. Aspiring surfers learned quickly from his counsel. He had an almost spiritual understanding of the sea. He would often say, "You'll know which wave to catch because the wave will talk to you." And in a wider context, he would explain, "We might call our planet Earth, but never forget that it's really two-thirds water." Here was a tribal philosophy starting to manifest. Bill's relationship with the ocean was different to that of the local fisherman who made a living from the sea. This attitude profoundly influenced the lifestyles of the up-and-coming generation of surfers. The luckiest would have a surfboard built by Bill, but only if they had the right attitude and were strong swimmers. He was, after all, a dedicated lifesaver and he wasn't going to provide a board for someone who wasn't ready for the experience.

In 1965 Bill went into partnership with Bob Head, Doug Wilson and Freddie Blight to set up the European Surfing Company. This business relationship between British and Australian surfers would act as a template for future collaborations between these two surf nations for decades to come. The Bilbo brand quickly took off, and from then on Bailey would always be found at the Pargolla Road factory, shaping boards, blowing foam and designing new surf equipment. Bailey was not only disciplined from his time in the Forces, but he was also skilled in aeronautics, and familiar with resins, foams and fibreglass. Add his knowledge of waves and it's no surprise that Bill thrived at Bilbo. But the innovation and the productivity of this industrial scene were far removed from his previous occupation, simply watching the ocean as a beach lifeguard.

Bailey's RAF engineer career had instilled the philosophy, 'There are no problems, only solutions waiting to be found'. Bill applied this to the developing surfing industry with ardent fervour. He created a moulded fin-and-box system; finally a surfer could detach and change fins for travel or experimentation. Bill also drastically improved the composition of foams and refined specific moulds for the process. He organised fibreglass cloth rolls to be perfectly manufactured for the glassing process. He pioneered the production of Britain's first commercial moulded surfboard. And aesthetically, his laminations in translucent colours were legendary. Bill also encouraged the refinement of wetsuit design for surfers' needs, and launched the first commercial skateboard production in Europe at Bilbo.

When up-and-coming junior surfer Chris Jones came knocking on the door looking for work in '65 he was channelled in the direction of the shaping bay. Bill meticulously trained Jones as his apprentice. Within a couple of years CJ had become a main production shaper and simultaneously one of the most respected surfers in the country. It was a winning formula for Bill's number one team member, and ultimately proved to be Chris' lifelong working commitment.

Bill also encouraged young bellyboarder Roger Mansfield to become a surfer. He watched over and advised 'The Grem', whose parents soon bought him his first surfboard, a custom Bill Bailey costing £27. Subsequently, he enjoyed free surfboard exchanges with Bill, and became the youngest member of the newly created Bilbo Competition Team.

The '60s had been an intensive and creative decade for Bill. His own life had undergone many transitions – he and his wife Lil started a family and raised two sons. With new interests capturing his attention, Bill left Bilbo at the end of the '60s. The shaping bay was in CJ's safe hands and Bill was satisfied that he had done everything a British shaper could do in the commercial longboard era. For Bill, the new shortboards offered little opportunity and interest. It marked the end of Bill's commercial surfboard building, but not his fascination for working with chemicals or solving technical problems. He took on a series of demanding new job opportunities, repairing Canberra planes at RAF St Mawgan and sinking shafts at Wheal Jane tin mine near Redruth.

Ultimately Bill left his family farm in Cornwall when he had the opportunity to launch a new commercial venture producing polyurethane foam on an industrial estate in the outskirts of Paris. This lasted several years, after which he moved to the island of Corsica for four years to develop a polyurethane-polyester factory. It was hard work, but flush from the sale of some land in Paris, Bill and his wife were able to spend some time sailing around the Mediterranean on their 45-foot ketch *Punch Coco*. They enjoyed a simple, self-sufficient life, living in Turkey for a considerable amount of time.

In the mid '90s Bill returned to his family home in Cornwall to be closer to his father and brother who had both fallen ill. He was still bubbling with ideas, and was happy to step back into the shaping bay to build a few vintage surfboards at Chris Jones' factory in Newquay.

Bill Bailey and his boards hold a special place in British surf culture. "He is our most prized shaper," says Paul Holmes. "He always did great work, whatever he made. But what was so important in the early days (when there were few guidelines or examples to follow) was the fact that he was such a great theorist. He knew how to make empirical observations about local waves and riders, and adapt the equipment to suit both."

DOUG WILSON

ROD SUMPTER: THE KING OF THE MALIBU

Watford-born Rod Sumpter was Britain's first surfing superstar. He spent his teenage years surfing in Australia and California, and by 1964 he was effectively the World Junior Champion. When he moved back to his homeland two years later, he brought a whole new level of professionalism to British surfing. Throughout the decade he competed alongside the best surfers in the world. The same summer that Bobby Moore lifted the World Cup at Wembley, Rod styled to fifth place in the final of the World Surfing Championships in San Diego…with a Union Jack plastered across his board. He flushed our surfing shores with national pride and a belief that maybe one day we could create a world champion.

The Sumpter family were part of a wave of emigrants who left for Australia on the Assisted Passage Scheme (otherwise known as 'the 10 quid ticket') in 1952. They were eager to escape the post-war gloom of Northern Europe and begin a fresh life Down Under. The family set up home at Avalon near Sydney, and the two boys – Rod and David – were instantly drawn to the beach lifestyle. They started out riding wooden bellyboards, then found their feet on the 16-foot hollow plywood boards ridden by members of the Avalon surf lifesaving club. When one of the lifeguards wiped out, the boys would dash into the water, grab the board, and try to ride one or two of the inside waves before the lifeguard swam in. As surfing became more popular, the boys pestered their father to buy them a board. Rod's dad finally caved in and he bought them a balsa board to share in 1957.

By 1962 Rod had become an excellent surfer. His loose lanky style was almost identical to that of future World Champion Nat Young, two years Rod's senior. He evolved a flowing, elegant style that mimicked his great hero Midget Farrelly. Success in contests soon followed, and Rod won the Australian Junior Title in 1963.

Rod began his career in surf film the same year, thanks to pioneering filmmaker Bob Evans. "Bob was the first person to make surf films in Australia," remembers Rod, "we used to go on trips with him and I featured in several of his films like *Surfing The Southern Cross* and *The Young Wavehunters*. Bob had a great influence on me."

Other filmmakers would also have a big impact on Rod. When Californian Bruce Brown commissioned Sydney-based Paul Witzig to shoot the Australian footage for *The Endless Summer*, Witzig immediately signed up Nat and Rod, the two hottest youngsters in the country. The film set out to capture that ethos of perpetual sunshine and the search for perfect surf. Witzig took the pair on a west coast surfari and the surfers got to demonstrate their silky footwork and deliver that vintage line, "You shoulda been here yesterday!" *The Endless Summer* duly became a global hit, the first surf film to reach out to a mass audience beyond the surfing heartlands.

Rod became fascinated with film-making and he figured it could take him to some interesting new places. So he wrote to Bruce Brown in California, to ask if he could get involved in his next film too. The Golden State was where it was at in the early '60s, and 16-year-old Rod recognised the big smiling face of opportunity winking at him. He persuaded his parents to buy him an airline ticket and flew to Los Angeles. Bruce Brown offered him a place to stay and Rod spent most of the summer of 1964 at his house. "I learned a lot from Bruce," says Rod, "he was a superb filmmaker, always in the right place at the right time."

While staying at Bruce Brown's house Rod met the flamboyant and outspoken goofyfooter Corky Carroll. The same age as Rod and sharing a similar attitude, Corky had just burst onto the Californian contest scene and was picking up all the Junior trophies. A dedicated competitor and a master of the media, Corky became one of the sport's pioneering professionals. He was sponsored by Jantzen Sportswear, the first mainstream business to recognise the viability of the surfing image. Jantzen bagged the back page of Surfer magazine and ran a series of advertisements featuring Corky, Rod and Ricky Grigg right up until 1968. Corky opened Rod's eyes to what

Uncle Sam could offer, and the pair quickly learned the fine art of recognising and manipulating an opportunity.

Surf finesse, however, was Sumpter's strongest asset. He used it to become a member of the talent-studded WindanSea surf club, and accompanied them on a team trip to Hawaii. This provided valuable experience for his biggest challenge yet, the 1964 US Open Championships at Huntington Beach. With the famous pier as a backdrop, Rod won the Junior final, to rapturous applause. To all intents and purposes, the kid from Watford was now the World Junior Champion.

Intoxicated with surfing, Rod travelled around America, down to Mexico, and even to Peru with the US team. Bowled over by the number of fun waves he'd ridden around the world, Rod began to realise that by seizing an opportunity he could make a living from doing what he loved.

After working for a while at Hobie Surfboards in Santa Barbara, he began to wonder if there might be new opportunities up for grabs in Europe. "My dad told me he'd seen a magazine article about surfing in Cornwall, and I also heard from Gordon Burgis that there was an international event sponsored by Gold Leaf cigarettes in Jersey. It all got me pretty curious to check out my British roots."

So Rod boarded another flight across another ocean and rocked up at St Ouen's Bay, Jersey, in August 1965 to take part in the Gold Leaf National & International Surfboard Championships. With the ultra-cool WindanSea badge stitched on his boardshorts, he felt invincible. In the water his balance was immaculate and he seemed glued to the board. He easily won the contest, and loved the attention lavished on him by the local media.

Rod spent the rest of the summer checking out Cornwall and France, and he was

knocked out by the whole social environment and virgin-fresh surf scene. "The moment I arrived in Cornwall I was amazed. I remember stepping off the train at Newquay station and getting my first glimpse of the waves at Great Western. 'This is the place to be!' I thought. I ended up at The Sailor's Arms. It was great – I didn't know anyone and I was only 17, but I soon found myself among a small crew of surfers who got together every night, playing darts and talking surfing."

Within a year Sumpter had decided to move to Cornwall on a permanent basis, and he took up residency in Newquay in May 1966. Rod had quite an affinity with Britain. It was his family's birthplace and he really liked the landscape and the people. He also realised that he was light years ahead of the other surfers, and he could make a living from winning contests and using his international experience to get involved in the British surf industry. Rod marketed himself superbly, strolling into the Bilbo factory with an air of professionalism and a head full of futuristic-sounding ideas. "He knew about sponsorship, surf teams, signature models, surf clothing...the whole package," says Doug Wilson. Bilbo signed Rod up straightaway, and were soon taking him on promotional tours and paying him to shape his 'Britannia' signature model.

In the waves, Sumpter surfed with effortless style, mixing up all the latest moves: head dips, nose rides, rollercoasters and aggressive Aussie turns. "You've got to remember that this was a time when there were hardly any surfers," says Charles Williams from St Ives, "we actually searched for people to surf with, rather than avoiding them like today! Then Rod showed up, and he was just smoking hot. 'Ahh, so that's how you do it!' we figured."

Rod was left to illuminate his own path for others to follow. He raised the competition standard, maintaining his place on the winner's podium (with occasional losses to Gordon Burgis) for at least five years. Through his international contacts, contest appearances and films, Rod connected British surfing to a bigger global arena. But despite his pivotal role in '60s surf culture he was not renowned for his interpersonal skills. Rod had an acute sense of how marketable he could be, and like many whose reputation is built on performance he was governed by a sense of aloofness. It all added to the mystique. Rod had supreme confidence and self-belief, aware he could win anything and cash in on his skill and reputation as a global surf star. Remaining something of an enigma was just part of the package.

In 1971, after dominating British competition for half a decade, Rod achieved a heroic third place at the Makaha International in Hawaii. It was his last big result before stepping away from the international scene. By this time the Aussie-inspired shortboard charge had well and truly taken grip, and Rod had lost interest in what had become a shortboard dominated ocean. He was very much a smooth longboard stylist who did not enjoy the aggressive approach.

For a while Rod turned his back on the ocean. He

below
Rod with his Britannia Model board, 1966.
PHOTO DOUG WILSON.

got married, relocated to Sussex, and had a son, John. But surfing would always be ingrained in his soul, and it wasn't long before he felt the lure of the ocean once again and moved back down to Cornwall with his family.

Looking for something fresh in the mid '80s, surfers rediscovered fun in an old familiar place – on the nose. Longboarding came back into fashion, and Rod was encouraged to make a comeback. He began competing again, and his swan song was a phenomenal performance at the 1988 British Championships at Thurso in Scotland. Heat after heat he charged his way through the grinding six-foot barrels at Thurso East, eventually winning both the Longboard and Masters divisions.

Rod kept himself busy during the '80s and '90s setting up 'SurfCall' – a pioneering telephone surf report service – and working for a regional TV company as a cameraman.

Without Rod Sumpter, British surf culture would have no doubt continued to evolve, but at a much slower pace. He had a profound influence on a whole range of things: contest surfing, freesurfing, board making, sponsorship, film-making and magazine publishing. More than anything, Sumpter loved surfing, and in his heyday, surfing loved Sumpter. "Total love is a very important thing to me as a surfer," mused Rod in a Surf Scene interview in 1984. "It's all about the love of the sea and the beach, a place where people caught by the bug are simply 'going surfing.' When I see some of the 13 and 14-year-olds, I know they're destined to treasure hordes of memories more enjoyable than anything else they may ever do."

above
Rod in full flow at Fistral, 1967.
PHOTO DOUG WILSON.

4 | Kernow's corners

SENNEN AND THE SOUTH COAST: WAY OUT WEST

Shrouded in Celtic melancholy

and rich in tales of smuggling and wrecking, West Cornwall is at the end of the line, where the train stops and the crowds thin. The area was once a centre of Cornish tin mining, but the industry collapsed in the 19th century, leaving behind it Britain's first post-industrial landscape. Vast swathes of the countryside were stripped of trees, strewn with mine waste, and dotted with disused engine houses. But despite the somewhat bleak and windswept environs, West Cornwall has been home to a hardy group of surfers since the '60s, inspired by a range of quality breaks that face in all directions.

While the surf scene in St Ives spread eastwards to Hayle and beyond, surfing in the Penzance and Sennen area was pioneered by John Adams, Mike Carr and Tony Hole. John, a young entrepreneur, was passionate about contemporary music; he owned The Winter Gardens in Penzance, a dancehall he'd bought for a knockdown price after it was damaged in the 'Ash Wednesday storms' of 1962. He first found out about surfing from a Porthtowan lifeguard who was also a part-time musician. "One night we had a 10-piece dance band playing called the Blue Rhythmics, and one of the guys was a lifeguard," says John. "I got chatting with him because I'd done a bit of bellyboarding and I wanted to check out the malibu boards they were riding there."

Inspired by the surf scenes at Porthtowan and St Ives, John and his mates ordered three Freddie Bickers boards from Newquay in 1964.

Sennen, two miles from Land's End, was merely a fishing village with no car park back then, and it was considered off-limits by most beachgoers due to its lethal rips and powerful waves. John, Mike and Tony broke the taboo and became the original Sennen surfers. They were soon joined by Chris Tyler, Joe Crowe, Mike Cattran, Ollie Cocker and Keith Prowse. Ollie was a professional diver who made a living collecting sea urchins and crayfish. He already supplied the local divers with 12mm wetsuits so it was an easy transition to start making 5mm suits for the surfers.

In 1964 the Sennen crew formed a surf club and John Adams was elected Chairman. He came up with the idea of having an annual surf dance at The Winter Gardens. "I'd organise a film show and everyone would dress up and have a good time. It quickly became the big event of the summer...I suppose it was the precursor to the SAS Ball. We used to publicise it by putting on a fancy dress procession through Market Jew Street [in Penzance]. There were guys dressed in gorilla suits and Tarzan outfits, and silver surfers coasting on the roof of a VW van! I gave half the takings to Sennen Surf Club, which resulted in the club becoming the richest in Britain. The members got a great deal, 'cos then we could afford our own Christmas party with everything paid for."

With wetsuits and wheels, the Penzance crew surfed all year and scoured the area for waves. John and Mike were young, single, successful businessman, and John's sports car was the slickest the area – a blue MGB which did 0 to 60 in 11 seconds. Drainpipe trousers were out, while flares and patterned shirts were in, all available from Mike's clothes shop, Modern Man. With Beatles-style haircuts to complete the look, John and Mike were a cool duo.

Since they had transport, John and Mike were one up on the St Ives boys who were younger and not yet driving. "We'd nose around, explore, and drop hints about the secret spots we'd seen," says John. "Charles and James Williams were the most talented surfers around at the time, and sometimes we'd take them with us." Perranuthnoe and Praa Sands, on the south coast, were two of the new breaks they began surfing on a regular basis. On a solid southwest swell

below
West Cornwall pioneers John Adams (left) and Dave Swift hang out between sessions.
PHOTO: TONY HOLE.

72 | THE SURFING TRIBE

with offshore northeasterly winds, Praa offered a thrilling session towards high tide.

Hungry to find more spots, Adams and Carr explored ever further along the coast of South Cornwall. "One day, when there was a good swell on the south coast, we drove down Porthleven. We were amazed to see incredible waves breaking next to the harbour. We'd never actually seen a reef break, only pictures of them in Surfer magazine, so we were just amazed," says John. "But it was pretty extreme and we weren't quite ready to ride it yet. So we kept surfing our usual winter spots, Praa Sands and Porthmeor. We surfed St Ives a lot in the winter months. Even on the strong prevailing southwesterlies it was clean and sheltered. There was a real scene, and you could leave your board in the lifeguard hut with Keith Slocombe. All the St Ives boys were anchored to Porthmeor. We told them we'd found this amazing new reef break and the Williams brothers started grilling us about where it was, but we wouldn't tell them. Anyway, after a few weeks we thought we'd better go and surf it before they found it and laid claim to riding it first!"

One morning in March 1965 John Adams and Mike Carr became the first surfers to ride Porthleven, which was cracking in at four- to five-feet with a crisp northeast wind. "We may not have ripped it apart, but we gave it a go. We realised it was really shallow… so it was a pretty intense and scary experience. Afterwards we told the St Ives crew where it was." Word about Porthleven spread and surfers from St Ives, Sennen, Porthtowan and Newquay began to travel down to check it out. During the '60s and early '70s it was treated as a secret spot and only ever ridden by a handful of surfers.

As shortboards took over the lineups in the mid '70s, West Cornwall surfers like Colin Wilson, Harvey Hoare, Mike Cattran and Rob Smith began to realise

above
An early shot of Tony Hole cruising at Sennen, circa 1964.
Photo: TONY HOLE COLLECTION.

that 'Leven offered the best barrels in the county, when conditions were right. For these surfers Sennen was the training ground, but Porthleven became the testing ground. It gained a reputation as one of the most demanding surf breaks in the country.

On the rare days when it was perfect, Porthleven enticed some of Cornwall's best surfers to try their luck. "Not many people rode 'Leven, even by the mid '70s," says St Agnes local Steve Bunt. "The place always had a real mystique about it. You knew something could go wrong at any time. I was surfing there with Gareth Kent one day and it was getting dark, but still four- to five-foot perfection. I raced one through the inside, and the reef sucked dry and I had to bail. I got dragged across the reef and came up in the harbour, but I couldn't see my board anywhere. When Gareth got out we searched up and down the rocks, but it was really dark by that time and we couldn't find it. I was gutted 'cos it was my prize possession, a really nice Tigger Newling shape. I came back the next day and looked for it as far up as Looe Bar and south to Rinsey Cove. A couple of weeks later a mate of mine told me that a local fisherman had found a board 20 miles out in the English Channel. He said the guy often drank in the pub next to the harbour. So I went down there, walked up to the bar, and asked an old guy sitting there if he knew the fisherman who'd found my board. 'That's me,' he said, 'I got it in me garage.'"

Tigger Newling from Treyarnon Bay was another Porthleven devotee in the mid '70s; he set the standard for charging the reef, riding the big-wave boards he'd started shaping after a long winter sojourn in Hawaii. "The largest and cleanest I ever saw it was on a big south swell in 1976," says Tigger. "It was big, offshore, scary and super-clean. The reef was just about holding the size with the channel not quite closing out. As far as I recall it was just me and my brother Mike out there for quite a while. At the age of 15 Mike was already developing a taste for big waves. I had some of my best waves ever that day. I remember paddling into a huge pitching outside peak. It was a long weightless drop. I reconnected at the bottom and drew out a long bottom-turn, just beyond where the lip exploded the base of the wave. I can remember feeling that my 7'10" was right at its limit, which tells you just how big and hollow it was. Up on the cliff, photographer Geoff Tydeman captured the moment on film. I hooked a snap under the lip, gaining enough speed for the inside section which was bowling in front of me. I pulled in, grabbed a rail, and a beautiful spacious tube opened up. When I flew out into the channel I heard the surfers on the cliff yelling and hooting at me. I started the paddle back out with a big grin on my face. It was such an intimate surfing arena that day. Unforgettable."

Porthleven also became Newquay surfer Nigel Semmens' favourite spot. "I first surfed Porthleven in the late '70s," says Nigel, "I remember Lenny Ingram taking me there when I was 17. I had a little flat 5'10" fish. Straightaway I knew it was the best and most challenging wave I'd ever surfed in Cornwall. I still think it is. I love the way it jacks up so quickly as it moves from deep to shallow water. Nothing is easy about Porthleven. You've got to be technically precise. It makes you grow up as a surfer and teaches you how to ride waves properly. You can't do what I call 'skateboard surfing', with little flicky turns. You've got to bottom turn, bury a rail, and surf properly. Riding 'Leven gives you a solid style. It's good to surf a wave that puts a bit of fear into you. Then you don't play around, you respect it, and that adds a cutting edge to your surfing."

A separate crew of surfers formed

into a significant group further up the south coast at St Austell Bay in the late '60s. Ron Berry, Mike Wingfield and brothers John and Graham Nile were at the heart of this dedicated group, whose local spots were Pentewan and Caerhays. When those breaks were flat, they thought nothing of making the journey to Watergate Bay or Constantine on the north coast, where they gained fame as 'the South Coast boys'.

Larger-than-life goofyfooter Graham Nile was easily the best rider from St Austell. The burly, shaggy-haired power surfer came from a family of bakers, famed for their pasties. He was already a good water polo player when he took up surfing, and quickly progressed to become an awesome competitor.

In the early '70s Graham started shaping and opened a surf shop in St Austell. His contest prowess was a major asset, putting him in touch with global shaping trends. In 1972, fresh from representing Britain at the World Championships in California,

opposite
A perfect peak at Porthleven, Cornwall's best reef.
PHOTO: ALEX WILLIAMS.

below
Tigger Newling charges a solid wave at Porthleven on a winter's day in 1976.
PHOTO: GEOFF TYDEMAN.

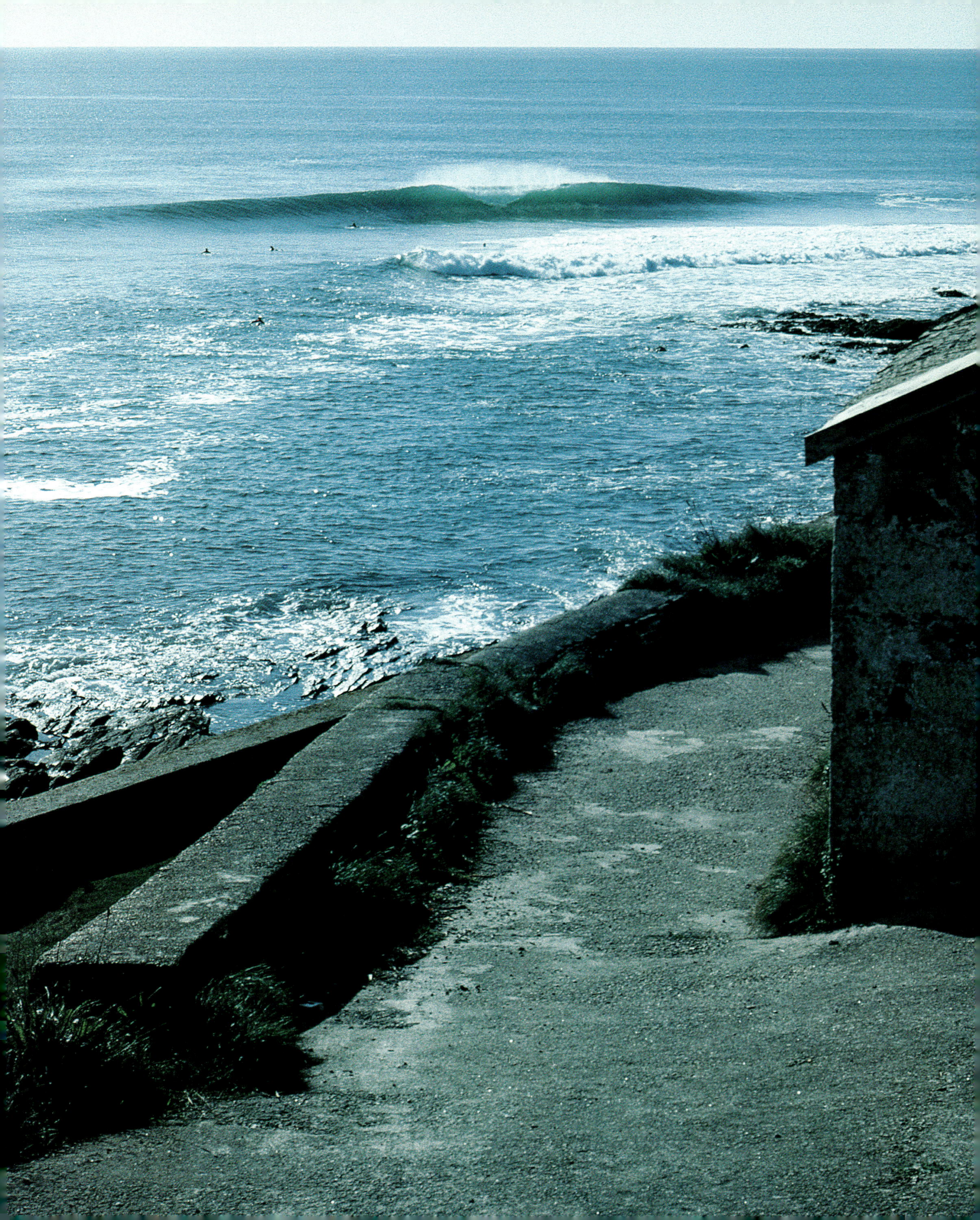

Graham became hooked on a new concept. "The big news in design is the swallow tail," he proclaimed in Surf Insight magazine. "It's a speed shape with the wide-point forward, a narrow tail, a single fin, very little rocker, an even thickness all through its length, and soft down rails. The advantages these boards give are outstandingly good handling, tremendously quick response to small shifts in stance, and tight turns especially on the backhand. The overall feeling is greater control and freedom to manoeuvre."

In 1973 Graham reached the Open final of the European Championships at Putsborough, North Devon, riding one of his favourite twin-fin fishes. A big crowd watched the action from the low cliffs overlooking the break. Cornwall, Wales and Jersey were each represented in the all-British final. Graham's fitness paid off. He pushed Tigger Newling into second place, followed by Steve Harewood and Pete Jones. It was a proud moment for Graham, and a satisfying victory as the waves were a decent size.

Three years later Nile finally claimed a long overdue British title. His peers all felt he deserved it. "He had the moves, the style and the power," says Steve Daniel, another 'South Coast boy' who hailed from Bantham in South Devon. Steve would later make his mark as a top competitive surfer and he learned a lot from Graham. "He was an all-round waterman, and he took the time to push us younger surfers. He was a major influence on us all."

Situated at the very tip of West Cornwall,

the village of Sennen was known for its bohemian surfers and laid-back lifeguards in the '70s. Mousehole fisherman Chris Tyler became immersed in the growing Penzance / Sennen surf scene and developed into one of the top surfers in the area. While on a trip to Morocco he was photographed surfing at Anchor Point and one of the shots appeared in Surfer magazine, a rare accolade for a Brit. Chris had a vision to open a 'surfing village' in West Cornwall, to give visitors to the area a taste of the surf scene. He bought some land at an old RAF camp near Land's End with business partner Ron Bishop. Here they created the infamous Skewjack Surf Village, complete with chalets, caravans, a pool, a restaurant, a bar and a discotheque. "The swinging '60s had ended and I started Skewjack because I wanted to keep the party going!" explains Chris.

In 1971 Chris invited The Times to send a journalist down to Skewjack to write an article about its first summer season. It was a huge boost for business. Young holidaymakers from Bristol, Birmingham and London soon arrived in droves.

Tyler employed many of the top local surfers to work at Skewjack, either as lifeguards or surf instructors (the first in Britain). Surfers such as Steve 'Jmo' Jamieson, Duncan and Michelle Macintosh, John and Nick Briant, Phil 'Piglet' Rowley, Mike Cattran, Martin Lloyd, Pete 'PT' Urquhart, Graham Shephard, Harvey Hoare and Colin Wilson all either worked at Skewjack or were part of the social hub.

In 1976 Skewjack featured on the BBC's Holiday Show. The locals dubbed it 'Screwjack' for its brazen advertising claim of 'two girls for every boy', a line from Jan & Dean's famous song Surf City. "There were so many girls coming down...it was pretty outrageous really!" remembers Harvey Hoare. "It was basically a Club 18-30 ahead of its time." The party night of the year was the last Friday of the season – wild fancy dress, drunken debauchery, followed by fuzzyheaded dawn patrols. Skewjack kept the momentum at full-throttle. "The whole scene was great because there was so much going on," remembers Chris Tyler's son, Essex. "We had custom car shows, contests, live music...all sorts of things. Quite a few people who came down for a week really fell for the place and ended up moving down to the area."

The '70s was Skewjack's golden era. St Ives surfers Charles and James Williams also became part of the Sennen scene when they worked there. But the local standouts were always Harvey Hoare and Colin Wilson. The pair were good friends, both fond of their surroundings but driven by different motives. Harvey was an explosive twin-fin maestro. The regularfooter had a lanky Mark Richards style and a flair for tube-riding. As a surf instructor and lifeguard, Harvey had time for everyone. But beside the busy summers, it was the peace and quiet that kept him rooted to the far west. "I never really got into the fashions or fads, I was always a jeans and t-shirt man. I just wanted to surf empty waves," says Harvey.

In contrast, cool-headed Colin Wilson was the consummate professional. A stylish and determined surfer, he was driven to win events. "I could always handle competition because I understood that it was as much about dealing with losing as winning," says Colin. His frequent travels and focussed approach earned him the British Open title in 1980 and the British Senior title in 1985. Colin was also one of the

below
Sennen standout Colin Wilson, who won the British title in 1980.
PHOTO: UNKNOWN/BSA ARCHIVES.

top board builders in West Cornwall, shaping 5-Star Surfboards in the late '70s and early '80s. "It was a really refreshing time for board design because we went through single-fins, wings, channel bottoms, twin-fins and tri-fins all in a short space of time."

Colin went on to become the administrator of the British Surfing Association for 12 years and a devoted team manager. "Running the BSA was just an extension of my passion for surfing, and a way to make a living from the sport. But it was never easy trying to keep everyone happy! Most of the time, I just had to do what seemed best for British surfing overall." Colin was the man who started the push to get the BSA re-housed into a stylish purpose-built International Surfing Centre on the sand at Fistral Beach.

Throughout his prolific surfing career Colin Wilson kept riding waves with a loose and lively flowing style. In turn, he and Harvey inspired a new generation; by the mid '80s, Ross White, Rob Smith and Rob Vaughan were bringing a vertical approach to West Cornwall surfing, aided by their skateboarding skills. Chris Tyler's boys, Essex and Cassius, were also unmissable in the lineup with their incandescent white hair and free-flowing radical style. Growing up at Skewjack, Ess and Cass both started surfing at six years of age on 4'11" swallowtail twin-fins. They quickly became two of the finest surfers in area, alongside goofyfoot tube-riding legend Janus Howard.

While Skewjack was a highly successful venture in its heyday, it was eventually overtaken by the march of progress. A new generation of young holidaymakers wanted en suite rooms not bunks, and guaranteed sunshine not hit-and-miss Cornish weather. Visitor numbers slowly declined until Skewjack finally closed in the late '80s. Ironically this was at a time when surfing was exploding in popularity, and shops like Innervisions in Penzance – run by John Ogbin – were cashing in on the surfwear boom.

As the professionalism of the '80s pervaded British surfing, many of the top surfers in West Cornwall chose to step away from the limelight and lock into a more humble and modest lifestyle. An underground, anti-commercial attitude has always been a defining feature of the area's surfers, who continue to live by the free-surfing ethos established way back in the heady days of the '60s.

above
Clean lines down Sennen way.
PHOTO: ALEX WILLIAMS.

MID AND NORTH CORNWALL: THE BADLANDS TO THE BORDERLANDS

Where the chimneys of old tin mines poke up like fingers above heather-covered cliff tops around St Agnes and Porthtowan, a thriving surf scene has grown up over the past 50 years. In the early '80s local surfers tagged the coast 'the Badlands', partly in reference to its barren landscape, partly in an effort to deter outside visitors. But the Badlands has never been a closed community, more a hive of open-minded and innovative surfers. A steely surf industry has also prospered in the area, centred in St Agnes.

Further north towards the Devon border, Bude also has surfing roots that stretch back to the 1950s. Bude's well-established surf scene reflects a rich surf lifesaving heritage, and the fact that the area is blessed with a host of top quality reef breaks.

Porthtowan's surf community owes a lot to Tom Wilkinson, who founded its surf lifesaving club in 1955 after meeting top Australian surf lifesaver Alan Kennedy. Tom was a telephone engineer from Redruth, but Porthtowan was his spiritual home and he was a passionate ocean swimmer. He used the beach frequently and recognised the need for greater water safety as seaside tourism flourished in the '50s. Tom signed up to be a voluntary lifeguard and duly became captain of Porthtowan SLSC.

In autumn 1956 the Surf Lifesaving Association of Great Britain held their inaugural National Championships at Porthtowan, hosted by the new club. At the time, the Single Ski event was the closest activity to surfing; lifeguards would soon experiment at standing up on these boards. The ski event was a race where competitors would sprint down the beach, clamber on their skis, then paddle out through the surf. Beyond the breaking waves they would paddle around a marker, then catch a wave in, surfing their skis sitting down. The first to the line in '56 was local Porthtowan lad Lawrence 'Larry' Johns.

By the late '50s, Porthtowan SLSC owned two Australian-made hollow wooden paddleboards for competitive racing. Larry was the club's star performer, and he occasionally rode waves standing up, just for the thrill of it. "In the early days, Larry Johns was the best waterman at Porthtowan," recalls Mike Hendy, one of the younger members of the SLSC at the time. "He was a natural in the waves. As early as 1958 I can remember seeing Larry riding a paddleboard standing-up, angling across a wave in perfect conditions. It was an inspiring vision."

In 1961 the club obtained two fibreglass-coated hollow wooden paddleboards with glassed-on skegs, built by Keith Slocombe in St Ives. Although these were still paddleboards they allowed better attempts at stand-up surfing. The St Ives connection extended to James Williams, who became a paid lifeguard at Porthtowan in 1962, alongside Larry.

Towards the end of that year, 17-year-old club member Mike Hendy borrowed some money from his parents and ordered a foam-and-fibreglass malibu board from Barry Bennett in Sydney, Australia. The cost, including the shipping, was £75 – a substantial amount of money at the time – but Mike was one of the keenest members of the Porthtowan crew and he wanted the best board he could get his hands on. The 10-foot board arrived several months later, in August 1963. At the first possible opportunity Mike took his new board down the beach, rubbed some paraffin wax on the deck, and paddled out. The rest of the crew looked on, electrified. As soon as they saw how well the board went, everyone wanted a go. "It was the first proper surfboard we'd ever seen," recalls Frank Johns, Larry's brother. "We simply called it 'the real one' because it was made in Australia." Frank was an young engineer who was keen to help build some surfboards for the surf lifesaving club. Using Mike's board as a template, the club pooled their resources and bought the materials needed to build their own surfboards. Over the course of the next year or so they built 15 boards; these were the second batch of foam-and-fibreglass boards to be built in Britain (the first batch having been made in St Ives the previous year).

Tris Cokes, who grew up near the beach in Porthtowan valley, was another member of the SLSC

78 | THE SURFING TRIBE

who learnt to stand up on one of the club's boards in 1963. That same year, Australian lifeguard Bob Head, who worked in Newquay, showed up and impressed everyone with his surfing. Bob was a big guy who liked to put in a few powerful turns. The display was enough to encourage Tris to buy a custom-built Friendly Bear from Bob the following year.

By 1965 the number of surfers at Porthtowan had grown and they'd linked up with another group at St Agnes, five miles up the coast. There were now also embryonic surf scenes at Perranporth and Portreath, where surf lifesaving clubs had formed in '57 and '58 respectively.

In 1966 Porthtowan's fervent crew put on a contest, the Cornish & Open Surfing Championships. This annual event soon became the biggest gathering of the clans in the Cornish calendar, and it went on to become the second-longest running surfing competition in Britain (after the Channel Islands Championships). James Williams, a naturally gifted surfer based in St Ives, rode with style to become the first Cornish champion. The Open event attracted newly-arrived international surf star Rod Sumpter and his Australian friend Glen Short. They put on a stunning show. Naturalfooter Glen was quick and agile, mimicking the style of the great Midget Farrelly; he could perch on the nose hanging five for ages. But Rod Sumpter, the consummate competitor, showed his class with some equally cool moves, and he took the Open title to rapturous applause.

The Cornish & Open fired up the local surfers, none more so than hot teenage surfer Tris Cokes. Inspired by Sumpter and Short's brilliant surfing, he put in the hours and progressed rapidly. The following year he convincingly won the Junior Surfing division at the SLSA National Championships at Widemouth Bay, Bude.

By 1970 Tris was one of the standout surfers in the area, and he'd also become a skilled board builder,

above
The paddle race, one of the events at the 1966 Cornish & Open Championships at Porthtowan.
PHOTO: DOUG WILSON.

below
Tris Cokes, a standout at Porthtowan in the late '60s and '70s.
PHOTO: UNKNOWN/TRIS COKES COLLECTION.

having made numerous boards with his SLSC mates over the years. With the demand for boards growing, Tris figured it would be a good move to start his own surfboard label in Porthtowan, so that year he set up Tris Surfboards with local lifeguard Pete Chapman. The following year Johnny Manetta, a recent arrival from London, joined the company. He shared digs with Tris at Toad Hall, further up the Porthtowan valley, which became infamous as a local party venue.

Tris Surfboards went on to become one of the most popular British board brands of the decade. Its success prompted the opening of Tris Surf Shop, right on the sand at Porthtowan, in 1974.

The surf scene at St Agnes

also grew up from its surf lifesaving club, formed around the same time as Porthtowan's in 1955. The club patrolled the beach at Trevaunance Cove where committed lifesavers Pete 'Flash' Roberts, Gerald Symons, Trevor Greenslade, Dave Docking, Pete 'Whitewater' Boeck and Dave Pugsley started stand-up surfing on paddleboards at the beginning of the '60s. Broad and burly Trevor Greenslade was one of the few who had the muscle to carry a 14-foot paddleboard alone, hoisted on his shoulder. By 1962 there were enough devoted surfers in St Agnes to encourage local joiner Ron Symons to build a few boards in his workshop in Peterville, at the top of the valley road from the beach.

St Agnes got its first gremmie when a young Steve Bunt learnt to stand on one of the enormous boards in 1962, aged 8. "I remember that board clearly, it was made of plywood and it had a bung you had to pull out to drain the water," says Steve. "It was a beast to ride... kind of like standing on a tanker!" A couple of summers later local youngsters Gareth Kent, Jeremy Selby and Barry Garland joined Steve in the Aggie lineup. The boys shared an Australian-made Keyo surfboard that Barry had scored in Newquay. On cold days they wore t-shirts to keep off the chill. The following year they pestered their parents to buy them Spartan self-build wetsuit kits. With parental help this group turned into a talented gang of young surfers, and they subsequently won the Junior Team title at the SLSA National Championships at Newquay in 1966. However, like many other groups of surfers in Britain at the time, the St Agnes boys soon turned away from surf lifesaving to focus on their true passion – surfing.

Like Porthtowan, St Agnes also became a breeding ground for innovative surfers and shapers. By the mid '70s Steve Bunt was in his early twenties and had started his own board company, Best Ever Surfboards. Running a surfboard business helped Steve fuel his passion to surf foreign waves. He fondly remembers an early trip to Morocco with the St Agnes crew. "My mate Steven Jones bought an old Citroen 2CV from Tigger Newling. But when he got it back to Aggie he realised there were no brakes, no MOT, no nothing. Still, what do you expect for £100! We were leaving for Morocco the next day, so I said we'd have to take my knackered Mini-van. We loaded the boards on the roof rack and drove to Southampton to get the ferry to Bilbao, but somewhere along the way the petrol tank started leaking. Out at sea, one of the crew must have noticed there was a pool of petrol under my van. An officer found us on deck and said, 'If you don't drain the fuel out, we're going to throw your vehicle overboard!' All in all it wasn't the best start to the trip."

The surf talent from St Agnes has always been strong and diverse. Martin 'Wiggins' Wright, Darren Frost, Mark 'Smoothy' Jewell and Steve Blundsen all became national junior champions in the '70s. Powerful naturalfooter Martin Wright was a major inspiration locally, before he emigrated to Australia in the late '80s. Charismatic Aussie Pete 'Chops' Lascelles moved in the other direction when he took up residence in St Agnes the late '70s. Chops was a regional champion in Queensland, as well as a skilful shaper. He'd learnt to surf on the Gold Coast where he'd developed a powerful style and an ability to clock up an amazing amount of time in the barrel.

In the '80s a new generation of Badlands surfers came to the fore, including Steve England and the Hendy brothers (Mike Hendy's sons Greg, James and Luke) from Porthtowan, Martin 'Mynnsy' Mynne from Mount Hawke, Jamie Kent and Drustan Ward from St Agnes, Rob Small from Perranporth, and Steve McNichol from Portreath. Steve England was a standout at Porthtowan and St Agnes, but his favourite haunt was Porthleven. Alongside McNichol and Frost he was part of the Natural Art surf shop team based in St Agnes. Later Steve became associate editor of

below
Aggie boy Martin Wright was one of Britain's top freesurfers in the '80s.
PHOTO: ALEX WILLIAMS.

above
When conditions are perfect, the beach breaks of the Badlands can be really good.
PHOTO: CHRIS POWER.

Carve, Britain's leading surfing magazine in the '90s and '00s. Steve looks back on the '80s as an exciting time in Porthtowan and St Agnes. "There was a lot of good surfing going on, and there were some really interesting boards around," says Steve. "I remember this guy called Mick Harlech. He was a full-on hippy, but a legendary shaper because he came out with a teardrop twin-fin years before anyone else did. One day I saw him coming down the beach with one of his boards, a bright green one. I thought 'What the hell is that!' But he absolutely flew on it. Everyone was blown away. He also did curved front fins on quads in the early '80s, and all sorts of weird concaves and channels. His boards looked like spaceships. At the time I laughed, but looking back I think he was probably way ahead of his time."

Original Porthtowan surfer Frank Johns did a brilliant job as Chairman of the British Surfing Association in the '80s and early '90s. During his term, the World Championships came to Newquay in September 1986. Quiksilver sponsored the event and the competitors were housed in 'Olympic Village' style accommodation at Perran Sands Holiday Camp. This allowed more than 150 of the best amateur surfers in the world – including a young Kelly Slater – to practise for their heats in the ever-reliable waves at the bottom of the dunes.

The Badlands has always fostered a lively, outgoing and adventurous surf crew. But despite all the big names and contest achievements, it's the anti-establishment attitude here that personifies the area. Steve Bunt's annual Buntabout captures this spirit. It's a informal community-oriented surf contest at Trevaunance Cove (or nearby Chapel Porth if conditions allow) where taking part is more important than winning. A good time is had by all and laughter reverberates around the Badlands cliff faces.

The most powerful community statement to emerge from the area, however, was the pressure group Surfers Against Sewage. After a series of shocking pollution incidents, a charged public meeting was held in St Agnes village hall in 1990, and SAS was set up to fight for cleaner seas. The campaign achieved its primary goals by the end of the millennium, and today continues to be a huge success (see Chapter 16).

Trevose Head lighthouse presides over a stretch of coastline with some of the best surfing beaches in the South West. Over the years some of Britain's best riders have emerged from the coastal villages of Treyarnon and Constantine, and the towns of Padstow and Wadebridge on the Camel Estuary.

Plymouth man Freddie Blight played an early role in the introduction of surfing to this area. He ran a ship chandlers business in Plymouth but spent much of his free time on the north Cornish coast. Captivated by the sea and aware of the inklings of a surf scene in Jersey and St Ives, Freddie decided to build surfboards for his sons Richard and Andrew. He already knew a lot about boat construction and could source balsawood, resins and fibreglass. So in 1961 he got down to work and made three balsa-and-fibreglass, the first of their kind to be built in Britain. Freddie took the planshape for the boards from a Life Magazine covershot of Greg Noll standing on a beach in Hawaii. The template was fine – the outline of a big Hawaiian gun. But the rocker and rail shape of Noll's board were not visible in the photo, and since Freddie had no personal experience of surfing, so he could only guess. He shaped the rails perfectly square, like a box, and added no rocker to the balsa blanks. Despite the boards' serious design flaws, Richard and Andrew 'Ajax' Blight happily learnt to ride them at Harlyn and Treyarnon during the summers of '61 and '62.

Around the same time a bohemian family called the Newlings bought a house on the beach at Treyarnon Bay. Chris 'Tigger' Newling takes up the story of the summer of '62. "I'd just turned 11, and I was absolutely amazed to see Richard and Ajax riding their malibu boards around Trevose. I was itching to have a go, so one day at Harlyn I asked Ajax if I could ride his board. He pushed me into a small clean wave, I hopped to my feet and balanced until the board beached at Freddie's feet. He looked down at me with amazement. 'You're a natural, kid!' he said. He was just as stoked as I was."

Later that year Tigger persuaded his parents to buy Ajax's red balsa board. Freddie offered it to Tigger because he was already thinking about making new boards for his sons. The third balsa board was sold to a shop in Newquay; it was bought by local lifeguard Doug Wilson, who subsequently tracked down the pioneer board shaper and introduced him to the newly-arrived Australian lifeguards. Freddie was fascinated to examine the Aussies' boards at close quarters. Straightaway he began to think how he could copy the boards' refined curves to make similar boards for his boys. Using his knowledge of boat building, he came up with a solution. He borrowed John Campbell's Australian-made Barry Bennett board, made a mould, and built four replica boards (two for his sons, and two for Aussie lifeguards Ian Tiley and Warren Mitchell). These were the first moulded surfboards to be built in Britain.

One summer's evening in 1963, Tiley, Mitchell and the other Newquay lifeguards put on a special display of surfing in front of an audience of hotel guests and spectators at Watergate Bay. The owner of the beach, Ralph Doney, had paid the visiting surfers to put on a show for the tourists. Searching for the theatrical element, Ralph arranged for the riders to surf at dusk carrying flaming torches. The Newling family went along to watch and Tigger was captivated. "We watched the whole thing from the cliffs. It was a perfect summer's evening with glassy three-foot waves rolling in. The surfers rode the waves holding their flaming torches aloft. It was a totally unforgettable spectacle."

Back home at Treyarnon, Tigger dedicated himself wholeheartedly to surfing, but his crude balsa board limited his progress. Thankfully, the following summer his grandmother, who lived near Sydney in Australia, bought and shipped over a pair of nine-foot fibreglass boards for the family.

Gradually the whole Newling family became involved in the surf scene of the '60s. Tigger's father, John Newling, ran the Trevose Head Surf Club and later became Secretary of the BSA. Tigger started competing, with considerable success; he won the British Universities title, then the British Open title in 1973, and he was twice runner-up at the European Championships. Tigger's sisters Sarah, Rachel and Alison all surfed. Sarah, like Tigger, started at a young age and won a string of national titles in the late '60s. Tigger's younger brother Mike followed suit, learning to surf at the tender age of six on a specially designed miniature Tigger Newling model called 'The Radical Gnome'. In his teens, Mike regularly battled Westward Ho surfer Tadek Drogomirecki for local junior titles, and he won a bronze medal in the Junior division of the European Championships at Seignosse in 1975. After emigrating to Australia in the late '70s, Mike competed on the IPS World Tour and built a reputation as a core member of infamous 'Newport Plus' crew alongside Tom Carroll and Derek Hynd.

Inland from Trevose, the old airfield at St Merryn became a hive of activity for the local surf industry. The owner of the airfield, Bob Partridge, was happy to rent

below
Tigger Newling ponders what to do with his clapped out 2CV...
PHOTO: UNKNOWN/TIGGER NEWLING COLLECTION

out its disused buildings cheaply. Tigger Newling and Adrian Phillips both set up board building workshops on the airfield, producing Jolly Good Surfboards and Fluid Juice Surfboards respectively. Bob was a pilot who flew scenic flights during the summer, and he kept his small plane on standby in a hanger. He would occasionally pull Tigger out of his shaping bay and take him for a few circuits over the beaches, scaring Tigger witless with his radical flying style. This daredevil behaviour was par for the course around Trevose.

The Trevose Head story extends to a committed band of locals including Roger Bennett, Nick Kavanagh, Adrian and Beverley Williams, Gary Gauss and James Trout. A later generation included Petroc Dann, 'Slim' Lacey, Mike Dodd, the Reese brothers, John Copley and early surf photographer Chris Ghazillian.

The Newlings and these other early surfers inspired another phenomenal English talent, Paul Russell. Although the Russell family lived in Leicester, they spent their annual summer holidays at Treyarnon Bay, where Paul started surfing aged seven. As a grom he watched and learnt from the older boys in the lineup, particularly Tigger. When he was 14 his family changed their summer holiday destination to Hossegor in France. There Paul became friends with French surf stars Thierry Fernandez, Jean-Luc Poupinel and Eric Graciet. Paul's dad Eddie had been a professional football player in the '50s, and he instilled a strong competitive urge in his son. By the time he was in his late teens, it was clear that Paul was going places as a surfer. The trophies were soon stacking up on his mantelpiece: consecutive British Universities titles, two English titles, two British titles (Junior in 1980, Open in 1985), and two European titles. Super-fit, super-competitive and tactically brilliant, Paul Russell was a contest machine.

In Paul's eyes, the most important and challenging events were the alternating biennial European Championships and World Championships. From 1980-88 he finished as the highest placed European surfer at four consecutive World Championships, an incredible feat. "The Europeans and the Worlds were the big ones for me," says Paul. "I used to get so fired up for those. I think I surfed the best I've ever surfed. You push yourself to a level you thought you'd never get to...you just get totally focussed." One of the prize scalps Paul collected was that of Tom Curren, later a three-time World Champion.

Paul was a key member of the Alder surf team in the mid '80s, alongside Carwyn Williams, Simon Tucker and Mike Raven. Alder boss Bob Westlake kitted the team out in matching bright red wetsuits, along the lines of a Formula 1 motor racing team. He brought together the best riders in the country at a time when British surfing was pushing into the new professional era. But while Carwyn couldn't wait to turn pro, it never appealed to Paul as he was set on following an academic career as an oceanographer. Later he became a lecturer at the University of Plymouth and a world authority on beach studies.

The Plymouth connection has been a prevalent theme in the history of Trevose surfing. When the south coast is flat, the Trevose area is the nearest stretch of the north coast for Plymouth surfers. In the '80s,

above
Paul Russell's contest nickname should have been 'gluefoot'. He never fell.
PHOTO: ALEX WILLIAMS.

above
North Cornwall is home to a handful of reefs and points which can really deliver on their day. Mike Raven races a section at a reeling left point.
PHOTO MIKE SEARLE.

Constantine became the favourite break of South Devon regulars such as John Copley and Steve Daniel. The duo could often be found tearing up the punchy high-tide waves alongside hot locals like Chris Rea, Rob Erskine and Steve Nicholls.

In the mid '80s, innovative board builder Johnny Bamford set up a small factory in Wadebridge making sailboards and surfboards under the brand name Lightwave. "It was essentially a custom windsurfer operation, but all the workers were surfers at Trebarwith Strand," says Alex Dick-Read, who worked at the factory in his teens. "The windsurf boards being made were epoxy, so guys like Ben Bamford, Alex Murray and Bill Attlee used that knowledge and started making really good epoxy surfboards. The concept was way ahead of its time." Some 15 years later the epoxy boom hit surfboard manufacturing globally. Meanwhile Alex had relocated to Bude, where he edited the highly successful surf travel magazine, The Surfer's Path.

The seaside town of Bude, close to the Devon border,

became a fashionable Victorian resort in the mid 19th century, served by a branch line of the London & South Western Railway. As swimming and bellyboarding became ever more popular in the 1950s, volunteer lifeguards stepped forward to patrol the town's beaches. This small band of lifeguards formed an informal club in 1953 and affiliated themselves to the Australian Surf Lifesaving Association. It was the first club of its kind in the country, and also the first to obtain hollow wooden paddleboards from Australia.

In 1955 a visit from inspirational Aussie surf lifesaver Alan Kennedy prompted the Bude volunteers to form an official surf lifesaving club (the second in the country, after Brighton). St Agnes and Porthtowan followed suit and the four clubs made up the core of the new Surf Lifesaving Association of Great Britain in the late '50s.

Like so many clubs around the country, Bude SLSC nurtured a generation of strong and skilful watermen. Two of the best were Tim Highams and Mike Martin. They occasionally tried riding the club's 14-foot paddleboards standing up, and sporadically surfed the town's waves in the late '50s.

In the early '60s Tim and Mike became aware that better surfing equipment was available, so they ordered three foam-and-fibreglass boards for the club from Australia. When the boards arrived, the lads became keener than ever to surf. Since the waves were often better at Widemouth Bay, a mile south of Bude, they switched their beach hangout. There the surf scene blossomed.

Widemouth was put on the map of top British surf breaks in 1967 when Bude hosted the SLSA National Championships. The organisers used the reliable west-facing beach break for the surfing events, and scores of surfers from up and down the country sampled its punchy waves.

By the 1970s, the roll call of Bude's regular surfers included Dave 'Doc' Sweet, Barry Walker, Paul Jury, Keith Perkins, Mike Jennings, Shane McGrath, Mike Sergeant, Lawrence Loader, Pete Vickery, Pete Ash, Roger Tout and Roger Adams. Visiting Aussie surfers John Quigley, Doug Walter and Alf Burnley were also part of the scene, adding their foreign expertise to the local industry. The top shapers in the area were Roger Tout, Paul Jury and Martin Pennington, and their boards filled the racks of the town's first surf shops, Zuma Jay and Surf Spot.

Spontaneous and stylish, Paul 'Ju' Jury was the outstanding local talent of this era. He was a free-flowing surfer, adventurous and enterprising, and rarely fazed by heavy waves. On land he was a larger-than-life character; confident, charismatic and popular. In his quest for thrills, Ju travelled to Hawaii where he surfed the North Shore and worked for the Willis Brothers making boards. After Hawaii, Ju moved onto Australia where he cut loose on the East Coast point breaks and working for Byrne and Pipe Dreams.

Back in Bude, Ju's business links with the Willis brothers and Phil Byrne allowed him to make boards using their brand names under license in Britain. Ju also had his own label, General Surfboards. Every time he went away on a trip, he'd return home with new ideas about board designs or surf retailing. Throughout the '80s he devoted his time in Bude to his board factory and his shop, and he also organised a few local contests. His widespread networking later brought top Californian shaper and surfer Clyde Beattie to Bude. Together, Ju and Clyde shaped some truly cutting-edge equipment. "They were always coming up with new ideas," says local Mike Raven. "Considering the designs and materials that became popular later, they were way ahead of their time. They were using epoxy resins, and taking risks with razor-thin lightweight boards."

Pete Ash was another notable local surfer who pioneered many of the rocky reef breaks around Bude. He grew up surfing spots like Crackington Haven and Widemouth, but while driving up and down the coast he spotted several excellent reef and point setups.

In the '80s, a new generation of top cats appeared on the Bude scene including Mike Raven, Robert and Nigel Moyle, Paul Westway and 'Rabbit' Hill.

Young goofyfooter Mike Raven was the most talented surfer among the new crop. He approached Paul Jury for sponsorship and soon struck up a friendship. "Ju was a huge influence on my life and my surfing," says Mike. "He was a guru and a father figure. He got me my first proper wetsuit, helped me out with boards, and also helped me get a really good sponsorship deal with Alder." Powerful, agile and lightening fast, Mike Raven became one of the country's best contest surfers in the late '80s. He won the British Junior title in 1986, and rode to victory on the EPSC European tour in 1987 when he was 17.

In later years, Mike and Ju often travelled together and their quest for the perfect wave eventually took them to the Philippines. There they surfed the hypnotic hollow rights on the island of Catanduanes. Tragically, during an intense eight- to ten-foot session at a spot called Majestics, Ju hit his head on the reef and the injury was fatal. Ju's death was an intensely traumatic experience for his travel partner Mike. The one consolation was that Ju had died doing what he loved – surfing perfect hollow waves. "Ju was a classic character and a brilliant surfer," says Mike, "he will always be fondly remembered."

North Cornwall, like many other rural areas of the county, tends to produce unpretentious surfers who are content to surf their own breaks beneath the cliffs, riding the waves purely for thrills rather than points or money. Newquay, with all its hustle and hype, may only be an hour's drive away, but the surfers who populate Kernow's corners usually prefer to stay right where they are and enjoy their own secluded spots.

below
Hot '80s freesurfer Ben Bamford was a regular in the lineup at Trebarwith.
PHOTO: ALEX WILLIAMS.

TIGGER NEWLING: COUNTER CULTURAL ICON

opposite
Tigger at 15: fresh-faced and stoked on surfing.
PHOTO: BEVERLEY MELLOR.

below
While working in Hawaii for several months in 1976, Tigger got the chance to surf some world-class breaks on Maui.
PHOTO: UNKNOWN/TIGGER NEWLING COLLECTION.

Chris 'Tigger' Newling from Treyarnon Bay was a trendsetter, a pure spirit admired by his contemporaries as one of Britain's most innovative and stylish surfers. Born in London in 1951, Tigger was the eldest of five children. His parents loved Cornwall and the family often went camping at Treyarnon Bay during the summer months in the late '50s. In 1960 the Newlings went the whole hog and bought a house at the beach. Over the next two decades the whole family threw themselves into surfing and became major players in the nascent British surf culture.

Tigger began surfing on malibu boards, but it was the shortboard revolution of the late '60s that unleashed his dynamic surfing gift. In his late teens, Tigger honed his skills in the often empty lineups around Trevose Head, making the most of the uncrowded conditions. His radical style – inspired by moves he'd seen in Australian magazines and films – took surfing to new levels above, below and inside the curl. He would periodically show up at contests like the Cornish & Open, English or British Championships, where he'd thrill the crowds with a risky go-for-broke approach. Tigger realised speed was the key to high-performance surfing, and he always wanted to go faster and more vertical.

Tigger loved travelling and he was among the first to explore parts of Ireland and northern Spain. However, the country he always longed to visit was Australia, and he finally got his chance in 1970 when he accompanied Chris Jones, Roger Mansfield and the rest of the British team to the World Championships at Bells Beach in Victoria. "We landed in Sydney, surfed Manly and North Narrabeen, and hung out with Snowy McAlister and David 'The Mexican' Sumpter [Rod's brother]. Then we headed down to Victoria and rode Bells and Winkipop with all the Aussie and American stars – Nat Young, Wayne Lynch, Michael Peterson, Rolf Aurness, David Nuuhiwa and Margo Godfrey. Then Chris, Roger and I jumped in our old stationwagon and headed back up north. We made it as far as the Gold Coast, scoring perfect Angourie along the way. It was a fantastic trip."

Tigger's most outstanding domestic contest performance was in 1973 when he won the British Championships at Freshwater West, Pembrokeshire, held in booming six- to eight-foot surf. Pete Jones recalls paddling against the killer rip to get out to the peak during the semi's, and watching Tigger firing on all cylinders. "He was dropping down these huge waves, getting totally barrelled and doing awesome sweeping, carving turns. He absolutely took it apart, surfing with so much confidence."

Like many other surfers of the era, Tigger tried his hand at making boards at a young age, partly out of curiosity and partly out of necessity. "Designing and building my own boards was really the only way to get the equipment I needed in the early days," he remembers. His started his first surfboard building enterprise, Tig Surfboards, when he was 17, working from a greenhouse at Rosmerrin. Over the years he gradually built better and better boards, and he was always eager to check out new designs. "During that trip to Australia in 1970, I saw the boards Michael Peterson, Wayne Lynch and Nat Young were riding – those really wide 'egg' shapes with big Greenough-style single fins. I liked the design, so I built some of those when I got home, and they worked pretty well for me."

By 1973 Tigger's board shaping skills had advanced considerably, and he proved it by winning the British title on a board he'd designed and shaped himself. "I won the British Champ's at Freshwater on a 6'6" by 19" rounded pintail. Obviously we were all riding single-fins at the time, but that board would look quite normal today if you put three fins on it."

Tigger's real shaping breakthrough came when he went to Hawaii in the winter of 1975. After surfing on Oahu for a few weeks, he heard about a job working for Lightning Bolt Surfboards on Maui; he applied for it and within days was on an inter-island flight. "Lightning Bolt gave me some work and I got to feel out Gerry Lopez's beautiful shapes as I finished them, out the back of a shop in Kahului. I rode a few of them at spots like Honolua Bay, Hookipa and Maaleaa, the legendary freight-train right. Dick Brewer was also living on Maui at the time, and I got to ride some of his boards too. I learned to surf hollow waves properly on that trip."

Tigger returned to Cornwall in May 1976. His skill as a board builder had improved vastly from the time he'd spent with Lopez and Brewer, and he felt confident to set up his own commercial label, Jolly Good Surfboards, based in an old chapel on St Merryn Airfield. "I remember shaping a 7'10" Brewer-style gun after returning from Hawaii, and I got a chance to try it at Porthleven later that year. That board absolutely revolutionised the way I could ride 'Leven. It was huge that day, scary big. I would have called it 12-to 15-feet. It was by far the biggest I'd ever seen it. But after Hawaii I didn't feel intimidated. I had some of my best rides ever that day. But I needed every inch of that 7'10"."

For the Newlings the mid '70s was a turbulent time. Tigger's parents divorced and put the family house at Treyarnon up for sale. The consensus among their sons and daughters was that a radical new start was the best plan. The family already had relatives in Australia, and the idea of living in the Lucky Country certainly appealed. One by one the Newlings emigrated, most of them – including Tigger – ending up living in the Newport area of New South Wales.

In Australia, Tigger continued surfing at a high level, but he began to focus his energy into his academic studies. It paid off when he graduated with a first class honours degree in Anthropology from Sydney University. In later years Tigger formed a successful film production company and was also a part-time lecturer in film studies at the university.

In his heyday, Tigger Newling was a breathtaking performer who wanted to flow with the waves when he rode them, rather than fight against them. "Waves don't have hard edges," he declared in Surf magazine in August 1974, "so neither should the way surfers ride them. You can pull off all kinds of radical stuff, but if it doesn't flow, it's ugly. The lines you draw along a wave express your understanding of the sea and your personality – it's a dance, with the wave as the music.

5 | Devon takes off

ENGLAND'S OASIS

above
Bob Powers, North Devon's first commercial board builder, waxes up one of his creations at Saunton, circa 1965.
PHOTO: BOB POWERS COLLECTION.

The striking Devon coastline from Westward Ho!, across the mouth of the River Taw, through Saunton Sands, Croyde Bay and Woolacombe, represents solid surf territory and rich wave-riding heritage. On big swells the surf zone extends further to the peeling pointbreak of Lynmouth, considered one of the longest and best left-handers in England.

The earliest account of surfing in the area dates from 1957 when, according to North Devon pioneer Barrie Charlesworth, an unknown Australian rode waves off Combesgate.

It was another seven years before the waves were ridden on a regular basis, when Alan Kift purchased a fibreglass board from Cornwall and began riding it at Woolacombe. Alan was a volunteer lifeguard and a keen paddleboarder. Following a sales trip to Newquay he came home with a beautiful Friendly Bear malibu board, shaped by Bob Head.

Fellow surf lifesaving club member Barrie Charlesworth was an energetic 17-year-old back in 1964, and Alan frequently lent him his slick new board. Immediately Barrie was gripped. A few months later Alan sold Barrie the board, and the youngster's surfing flame was permanently set alight. "At this time the surf lifesavers were surfers, and vice versa," says Barrie. "Our commitment to the beach put us in the perfect situation to pioneer wave-riding at these locations." Characters such as Ossie Gammon, John 'Fuzzy' Pridham, Paul Latham, Peter Sandy, John Howard, Mike Lock and Nigel Charlesworth were the original members of the surf lifesaver / surfer group that followed the lead of Kift and Charlesworth.

The arrival of board maker Bob Powers in late 1964 enabled the North Devon crew to get their hands on a steady supply of modern malibus, and this allowed surfing to fully take off. Bob was an expert joiner from the Midlands. He and his wife Audrey had gone on holiday to Newquay in 1962, and he'd met Bob Head who was working as a lifeguard and shaping boards in Mawgan Porth. Captivated by the surfing he witnessed, Powers asked the big Aussie how the boards were made and made some mental notes. The following summer, Powers proudly returned to Newquay with his own board (made using refrigeration foam) for Bob Head to try.

A year later, in 1964, Powers and his family moved to Mortehoe, near Woolacombe. There they opened a bed and breakfast, and Bob built himself a workshop where he meticulously shaped boards to fulfil the requirements of the stoked locals.

Over the next two years he fuelled the rise of the sport in North Devon, building more than 80 boards. He refined his designs through his constant experimentation with new materials and techniques. But the market was still small, and sales were erratic. Reluctantly, in 1967 he decided to hang up his planer and concentrate purely on his cabinet making.

As one board manufacturer shut down, another soon moved in. Tiki Surfboards had been set up a year earlier by business partners Tim Heyland and Dave Smith at Abergavenny in South Wales. On their frequent travels to North Devon they noticed the demand for boards was growing, and decided to relocate to Braunton. Over the winter of 1968 they built 110 Tiki boards to supply the North Devon and South Wales markets, and their business blossomed.

Another board builder who set up in the area at the end of the '60s was Clinton Fitzgerald. 'Fitz', as he was known, made boards under the labels Surfboards Inc and West Coast, and got started by buying Bob Powers' surplus tools and materials. Smooth-surfing Fitz was something of a local hero, and the boards he shaped at his modest premises at South Street in Woolacombe were highly popular.

Fitz was a keen traveller, and he was all ears when Barrie Charlesworth returned from a trip to South Africa with tales of perfect waves (as well as a cutting-edge shortboard template for Fitz). After taking a trip there himself, Fitz fell in love with South Africa and he eventually emigrated there live and surf. Tragically, some years later, he was electrocuted in an industrial accident while wet-and-drying fibreglass furniture. But his legacy in Devon will never be forgotten.

In subsequent years other shapers appeared on the scene. Kiwi Roger Lynden took over Fitz's old factory and started production of his weird and wonderful Celtic Surfboards in the early '70s; Kevin Cross founded the deliciously-named Creamed Honey brand with Bruce Palmer, the 1975 British Champion. By the late '70s North Devon had become a hotbed of board design as fresh ideas and equipment were tested and tailored.

For the expanding British surfing industry, locating in North Devon allowed good access to urban markets. The success of Phil Jay Surfboards in Barnstaple encouraged its owner to open an outlet in London. Jay Surf Shop in Wandsworth duly became the first dedicated surf shop in the capital.

In the mid '70s a new type of board came onto the market – the moulded board, popularised by Chapter Surfboards. The company was founded by Mervyn Beard, an original member of the Saunton crew, who'd learnt to shape while working for Tiki Surfboards. In 1976 Mervyn and John 'Flipper' Stacey developed an improved method of manufacturing moulded boards, and quickly reached an output of 25 boards per week. Experimental moulded boards had been around for a few years, but Chapter used new methods and superior resins to produce a range of mass-produced boards at highly competitive prices. By the following year, steadily rising demand allowed the company to

below
Tim Heyland was one of the standouts in North Devon in the late '60s and '70s.
PHOTO: UNKNOWN/ BSA ARCHIVE.

move to bigger premises in Knowle. Chapter went on to produce a full range of quality moulded designs, all carrying the characteristic arrow logo; these ranged from an easy-to-ride nine-foot 'Golden Oldie', to a short twin-fin model based on Mark Richards' design. The company offered a refreshing quiver of exciting shapes way before the retro movement was popularised. Mervyn later took over as sole proprietor of the business, and continued its growth by diversifying to produce custom surfboards at the end of the decade.

As well as being innovators on the manufacturing side, Chapter also had some fresh ideas about marketing. In 1980, a few years before mainstream professional surfing began in Britain, the company set up 'Team Chapter'. They used sponsored team riders, including hot local talent and 1984 British Champion Richard Carter, to ride and promote their equipment. Within a short space of time, many other board and clothing brands copied this formula, with three or four team riders fronting their labels.

North Devon is home to

a range of different types of wave, from mellow rolling beachbreaks to offshore mysto bommies. When surfing began here in the early '60s, the favoured spots were Woolacombe and Saunton. For the small band of North Devon pioneers, these mellow beachbreaks supplied exactly the kind of fun waves they were looking for. Yet, every time a clean solid swell rolled in, the crew watched and wondered about distant unridden peaks and pointbreaks.

For many years Croyde Bay was regarded as too dangerous to surf at size, due to its fast-breaking waves and strong rip currents. But by the mid '60s several individuals were surfing it on a regular basis. Tim Heyland, Barrie Charlesworth and Alan Reddington were among the first to challenge Croyde's steep-faced, barrelling waves on a solid swell. Others followed their lead and within a couple of years there was a thriving social surf scene centred on the Beach Club, run by Doc Warren and John Brockwell. It wasn't long before Croyde became considered one of the prime beach breaks in Britain.

The local crew were always keen for a new challenge, and on really big swells they noticed lines marching around Morte Point and on up the Bristol Channel. One morning in 1967, several of the original gang found their way to Lynmouth. Beyond the picturesque village they were stoked to see overhead waves spinning down a long cobblestone point. Alan Kift and Barrie Charlesworth were the first out the back, and Alan was in position when a set rolled through. He paddled for the first wave but just missed it, leaving Barrie to take the next wave and claim the honour of becoming the first surfer to ride this now legendary break.

Along the coast to the west, across the Taw Estuary, the seaside village of Westward Ho! also had its own enclave. Here the outgoing Pete Griffey started surfing independently to the crew further north in the early '60s. His enthusiastic lead drew in Steve 'Pixie' Godfrey, and in 1969 they founded the Westward Ho! Surf Club and built a clubhouse on the beach.

In every surfing community, the barriers are gradually pushed back as ever more challenging waves are tamed by those with the skill and courage to take them on. Tim Heyland was one such trailblazer in the late '60s and '70s. An athletic, powerfully-built surfer, he'd learned to surf in Brazil (his father was stationed there as a diplomat) before returning to Britain and setting up Tiki Surfboards in 1967. By the early '70s, with surf trips to Hawaii and California under his belt, Tim had a confident and ambitious approach to surfing the North Devon area. In 1971 he paddled way out to sea from Saunton to ride Downend Point. This bigger wave, breaking close to jagged rocks, had not previously seemed surfable in the period before leashes. Tim broke the ice, opening the door to a new surf spot and other big-wave breaks.

A few winters later, as a giant swell battered the coast, Tim and Barrie Charlesworth launched themselves off the point and paddled for an hour to reach Oyster Falls, a distant offshore reef which only broke on the biggest swells. It had never been ridden, and that morning it was breaking at 15-foot-plus. When the two surfers reached the lineup they realised they had the wrong boards for the job; trying to tackle this powerful ocean peak simply wasn't feasible on the equipment they had. So they turned around and began the long paddle back in. But the mystique had been glimpsed and others would take up the challenge later.

Local charger Anthony Sullivan, just back from a trip to Hawaii, decided to give Oysters a shot when a big clean swell hit the North Devon coast in the winter of 1983. He paddled out alone on his biggest gun and took the drop on several waves. Oysters had finally been cracked.

Devon was the birthplace of a new

administrative entity in the late '70s. Talented local surfer Stuart Matthews, through his role as national coach for the BSA, recognised that competitive

above
A fun looking peak rolls through at Croyde.
PHOTO: ESTPIX.

English-based surfers were not getting the full support they deserved. While competition surfers from the Channel Islands, Wales and Scotland were starting to enjoy the benefits of coaching, sponsorship and properly-funded national teams, the English were dependent upon the BSA for their national identity and any national competitive opportunity. Stuart canvassed many key players in the surfing community and laid the organisational framework for a new body, the English Surfing Federation. The ESF was launched at Braunton in April 1979, with the support of several knowledgeable members of the surf community such as Eddy Russell, Andy Schollick, Bob Groves and Peter 'Mooney' McCallum. Stuart was subsequently elected as the first ESF Chairman.

The ESF set to work, and later that year it held the first independent English Championships in Newquay. Rising star Nigel Semmens used his local knowledge to win the Open title, and a few months later he led the English Team at the European Championships in France. England had finally arrived as an identity in its own right in the world of surfing. Over the following decades English teams were to prove the most dominant in Britain, and one of the consistently strongest challengers for the European crown.

In the '80s the ESF nurtured several North Devon talents who went on to make an impact on British surfing. Croyde local Ester Spears rode through the ESF's administrative ranks to become a surf judge, coach, team manager, writer and photographer of the highest calibre. Pete Oram, Richard Carter and Neil Clifton all became English Champions and key members of the English Team. Richard and Neil were renowned as outstanding underground surfers, but didn't focus too heavily on foreign contests (although several team managers wished they had). Nevertheless, Neil's liberated backhand performance surfing for the British team at the 1988 World Championships in Puerto Rico is fondly remembered in surfing folklore.

By the late '80s Croyde was firmly placed on the surfing map. It had grown to become North Devon's answer to Fistral Beach in Cornwall. But being only a three-hour drive from the capital, it was far more accessible. Love them or loathe them, the so-called 'London set' soon spotted North Devon's potential as a holiday destination. For the locals this brought mixed blessings. On one hand, house prices went up and the crowd problems got steadily worse. On the other, there were opportunities and jobs aplenty with the ever-increasing number of surf shops, board companies, hotels, campsites and surf schools. While some lamented the unstoppable commercialisation, others knew that a dawn patrol or a magic session at a secret spot would still put a smile on their faces.

below
Richard Carter, one of several top surfers North Devon produced in the '80s.
PHOTO: ALEX WILLIAMS.

SOUTH DEVON: LAID-BACK LOCALS

Surfing in South Devon began at Bantham, the sandy bay at the mouth of Devon's River Avon, 10 miles east of Plymouth. On a lined-up southwest swell, the rivermouth here produces a long peeling right-hander which is the best wave in the area, South Devon's answer to Malibu.

During the '50s the beach became a popular summertime spot for holidaymakers, but the fast-moving currents at the mouth of the river were notoriously dangerous for bathers and claimed many lives. The local Maitland, Hurrell and Swan families responded by setting up a surf lifesaving club at Bantham in 1960. They built a wooden lookout hut on top of a World War Two pillbox which served as the club base. South African lifeguards were employed to work the summer season, and surfing soon followed.

The demand for surf equipment prompted local boat builder Geoff Lawton to try his hand at making boards for South Devon pioneers Stuart Charles, Barry Trout, Chris Vermingle and Colin Merry. They in turn inspired other surfers like Dan Connolly, Will Houghton, Duncan and Cathy Norris, Tim Spencer and John Copley. As the years passed, small surf scenes also grew up at Whitsand Bay, Wembury and Paignton.

By the late '60s the need for surf kit extended to Exmouth, where Exe Marine surf shop opened, and to Exeter, where Circle One started making boards and wetsuits in 1969.

South Devon's most famous surfer is Steve Daniel, who emerged from the Bantham talent pool in the early '70s. The loose and expressive naturalfoot quickly rose through the ranks to became an elite British performer, mentored by the likes of Graham Nile. With sponsorship from Gul, Steve tested out the first wetsuits designed specifically for British surfers. Whatever the wetsuit colour, Steve's bright surfing matched it.

Smart and forward thinking, Steve opened his own surf shop, Marine Sports, in 1975 on the Barbican in Plymouth. The cutting-edge shop instantly became a focal point for the area's flourishing surf tribe.

Steve was an ambitious contest surfer who was captivated by the idea of competing in world-class waves. When Hawaiian contest organisers Randy Rarick and Fred Hemmings set up their embryonic professional world tour in the mid '70s, Steve and close friend Nigel Semmens jumped at the chance to take part. The pair travelled extensively and entered IPS (International Professional Surfers) contests in Hawaii, South Africa and Australia.

Steve built up friendships with top international surfers like Jimmy Blears, Mark Richards and Shaun Tomson, and his connections enabled him to bring back the latest board designs for his shop. These included fishes and stingers, the first Lopez Lightning Bolt from Hawaii, and the hugely popular MR twin-fin in 1977.

Always armed with the latest board design, Steve was a great adventurer. In January 1978 he pioneered surfing in Fuerteventura with now internationally renowned South Devon surf photographer Alex Williams. "Tenerife was already on the map as a fairly cheap surf destination, but other islands like Fuerte' were unknown territory. I got the idea of going over there from some German windsurfers. Trouble was, there were virtually no flights. In the end me and Alex got a flight on a Spanish army plane from Tenerife, loaded up with boxes of ammunition and machine guns!

"The best session we had was at Shooting Gallery," continues Steve, referring to the left reef just outside Corralejo which offers a mercilessly shallow tube ride. "Alex was taking photos so I was out alone in this heavy swell with no idea what the reef was like. It was a seriously intense session!"

Steve's enthusiasm was always evident at Bantham where he inspired countless grommets. South Devon standouts Charlie Harrison, Wayne and Mark Henry, the Cohen brothers and Tom Underwood all learned to surf on boards from Marine Sports, and all were steered in a positive direction by Steve.

In 1981 Steve finally won a long overdue British title. But the biggest story that year came from Down Under – Simon Anderson's thruster. It was the fin set-up that revolutionised performance surfing. Naturally, Steve had the first ones available in Britain at his shop.

Another exceptional South Devon surfer is Rob Beling, who appeared on the scene in the '80s. Warm, modest and articulate, Rob typifies the kind of cultured soul surfer everyone admires – able to win contests hands down, but inherently anti-competitive. He is an inspiring member of the British surfing tribe, blessed with unlimited natural talent. Fluid surfing is what Rob is best known for, especially when he's styling along the waves at Bantham on his forehand. "The key to good style is perfect trim – moving with maximum efficiency and minimum energy expenditure," says Rob, who draws inspiration from the movement of animals such as dolphins and gliding birds.

Thanks to surfers like Rob Beling and Steve Daniel, plus others who emerged later like Martin Connolly and Eugene Tollemache, South Devon has developed into a surfing area of national significance.

above
Bantham lines.
PHOTO: ALEX WILLIAMS.

below, left
Steve Daniel came to prominence in the early '70s.
PHOTO: ALEX WILLIAMS.

below
Veteran stylemaster Rob Beling.
PHOTO: ALEX WILLIAMS.

TIM 'TIKI' HEYLAND

above
Travelling has always been in Tim Heyland's blood, but he had to work like a Trojan in the '70s to save up for winter trips to places like Hawaii. PHOTO: UNKNOWN/ TIKI ARCHIVE.

Englishman Tim Heyland is a legendary surf explorer and surf industry pioneer. In the '60s, '70s and beyond he pushed the boundaries with innovative shaping ideas and fearless surfing performances. Today, he and his company Tiki are still going strong and he's rightfully proud of his achievements.

Tim's father was in the diplomatic services and the family spent many years in Syria before moving back to London in the early '60s. One morning, Tim was walking through Kensington when he saw a billboard ad for Australian peaches showing a surfer. It looked thrilling, and the image stuck in the teenager's mind.

When his father was posted to Brazil in 1963, the family moved house again, and Tim decided to make a surfboard for himself out of solid hardwood. "It was pretty crude – two planks sandwiched together and hacked into shape with a machete." Despite the rudimentary nature of his equipment Tim learned to surf in the warm Brazilian waters, and later got his hands on a fibreglass board. His interest in surfing grew, and by the mid '60s he and a couple of friends had started importing a few boards from California. "Back then the import duty in Brazil was 200 percent," says Tim, "so we used a speedboat to rendezvous with the cargo ship carrying the boards. They were so heavy that the

American guys just threw them overboard, then we fished them out. It was classic."

When the Heyland family moved back to London again, Tim passed the time swimming, boxing, playing rugby and working as a linguist. But he yearned to get back in the waves. Interested to see what he might find at the annual London Boat Show, he went along and by chance met a keen surfer from Devon, Dave Smith. The pair got talking and realised they both shared a passion for riding waves and an interest in making boards. They stayed in touch and their friendship later blossomed into a business partnership. In 1967 they set up a small board-building factory in a disused wool warehouse at Abergavenny in South Wales, and Tiki Surfboards was born. The warehouse was cold and damp but the rent was exceptionally cheap.

As they didn't have a blank supplier, Tim and Dave set about blowing their own foam. "To make the mould, we used four-foot wooden blocks and wedged them between the moulds on the floor and the oak beams that supported the roof," says Tim. "The roof would rise two inches under the pressure as the foam blew!" Enlisting the help of Cornishman Ian 'Porky' Morcom (who'd learnt the trade at the Bilbo factory in Newquay), they improved the process and started producing their own brand of foam blanks, Castle Foam.

In 1968 Tiki relocated to Barnstaple in North Devon,

attracted by the growing market there. Croyde, Saunton, Woolacombe and the surrounding reefs became their often-private testing ground. The demand for boards was high, and over the first winter Tim built 110 radical Australian-inspired eight-foot vee-bottom shortboards. "Dave had agreed to glass them all," says Tim, "so I just worked really hard shaping them, and that meant I would have the cash to do a surf trip by the end of the year."

Early in 1969, Tim headed off to Hawaii where he spent 10 weeks surfing on the North Shore. He travelled with another North Devon surfer, Mike Saltmarsh. On Oahu, Tim made friends with locals Paul Strauch, Rell Sun and Fred Hemmings. But the waves were another matter. "I knew straightaway that I had the wrong equipment for my first session at Sunset," admits Tim. "It was big and shifty – even Waimea was breaking that day. I couldn't believe the size of the waves, but I had to paddle out. If I turned it down, I knew I'd regret it for a long time. I paddled out, waited for a set, and took off on a monster...but my board wouldn't hold on the bottom-turn. I got smashed. The force was unbelievable. I'd never felt anything like it. It certainly taught me a lesson about board design! But it also gave me the confidence to tackle heavy waves later."

After Hawaii, Tim travelled on to California where he hooked up with business partner Dave, who'd been spending time surfing the fabled cobble points at Rincon and Malibu. While he was there, Tim took on some shaping work. "This enabled me to make some interesting contacts and establish my personal credentials as a board-builder," says Tim. "It also helped fund a trip to Mexico where we surfed some hot glassy peelers in San Blas."

When Tim returned to North Devon he used his contacts in the States to secure the UK distribution rights for top Californian labels Gordon & Smith, Bing and Weber. As the business grew, Tiki relocated again, this time to Braunton where it found a permanent home at Velator Industrial Estate. The company also opened a shop on South Street to sell direct to the public.

In 1972 Tiki branched out again and began manufacturing wetsuits. These were eagerly snapped up by the ever-increasing number of surfers who had to endure Britain's often bitterly cold waters. Two of Tiki's employees, Rick Abbott and Andy Schollick, later went on to set up their own wetsuit companies: RA Wetsuits and Second Skin.

By the end of the decade, the Tiki factory at Velator was producing as many as 45 boards and 50 wetsuits a week. Their blank blowing operation was also in full swing. "We were blowing foam under licence from Barry Bennett, the Australian pioneer of the process. At one point we were supplying Bennett Foam to almost all the surfboard manufacturers operating in Britain." However, six years later this aspect of the business was shut down, partly due to cheap foam imports from Australia and California, and partly because Dave realised the fumes released in the production process were affecting his health.

In subsequent years Tim continued to travel extensively, often to Indonesia where he christened two waves in West Java. Returning from adventures with his head full of ideas, he never lost his taste for experimentation. His friendship with Aussie Terry Fitzgerald – the 'Sultan of Speed' – became pivotal as prototype boards went stringerless, grew wings, added channels, and tried moon tails. They were all put through their paces in North Devon's waves.

For 40 years, Tim Heyland's epic travels, willingness to experiment with innovative shapes, and total confidence in Tiki have helped keep North Devon at the forefront of the British surf industry.

6 | Wales on board

THE DRAGON STIRS

Wales is a land of strong and colourful contrasts. Pastoral and post-industrial landscapes lie side by side, and the lilting Welsh language is juxtaposed with English. The stunning Gower Peninsula offers the antithesis to the South Wales coalfields and was the first place in Britain to be designated an Area of Outstanding Natural Beauty in 1956. Today, Wales still has an industrial heartland in the southeast, but surf rich areas like the Gower, Pembrokeshire, the Lleyn Peninsula and Anglesey remain undeveloped and open to swells. With headlands, sheltered coves, reefs and beaches, her coastline is rich and varied, and it's always offshore somewhere. Geologically, an abundance of limestone rocks provide numerous quality reef breaks, and these have nurtured some of Europe's finest surfers.

The region's first surfer was Viv Ganz, a keen young sportsman from Swansea. Viv was a top junior rugby player and tennis champion, and during the summer months he loved to go bellyboarding at Langland Bay. He worked in the family business, a shipping agency which handling boats going in and out of the local ports. One evening in 1960, he was driving home after a long day at work and decided to stop at the local cinema to watch a film. By chance, before the main feature began, there was a newsreel showing a few clips of the earliest stand-up surfboard riding in Biarritz. Instantly inspired, Viv spent the next few weeks making a surfboard, determined to stand on the waves he already rode prone. Unfortunately, due to the fact that it was made out of solid beech, the board was an complete failure. But the 29-year-old Welshman was undeterred, and after doing a bit of research he got a local carpenter build a 12-foot hollow wooden board following the plans of a Tom Blake design. Viv took his new board out at Langland for the first time in the summer of '61, but initially found it hard going. "I struggled with the weight of the board and couldn't master riding unbroken waves standing up, so I tended to kneeboard into the shore." Nevertheless, he persevered and his surfing skills slowly improved.

Two years later Viv spotted a newspaper article about Jersey's surfing lifeguards, which included a picture of the fibreglass boards the Channel Islanders were riding at the time. He wrote to The Jersey Herald newspaper to enquire about surfing, and they put him in touch with Jersey company Silva Yates, who were fibreglass specialists. Viv ordered a fibreglass-and-foam board, which was built and shipped to him for £20. Viv's wave-riding aspirations were finally realised.

Langland was a two-minute car ride from Viv's house so he surfed it as often as he could, and he had it all to himself for several months. Later that year, 1963, he was joined by John 'Fritz' Edwards and Alan Bevan. Fritz and Alan started to surf regularly after returning from an inspirational visit to Cornwall, where Fritz had purchased a nine-foot hollow plywood board from St Ives craftsman Keith Slocombe. The Welsh trio began to tap into the variety of waves on offer at Langland Bay and at nearby Caswell, which was always smaller but offered cracking lefts on strong southwest swells.

These breaks were the heart of the burgeoning Welsh surf scene. Soon others were taking to the waves, among them Andy Burley, John Goss, Mike 'Pixie' Harding, Roger Owen, Roger Stairs, Glen Thomas and Andy Davies. "In the beginning, with no-one to copy, we seemed to be learning forever," remembers John Goss. He was the first to ride Crab Island, a long, sometimes excellent righthander at the eastern end of Langland that peels over

below
South Wales boasts a multitude of top quality spots. This is Freshwater West in Pembrokeshire.
PHOTO: PHIL HOLDEN.

96 | THE SURFING TRIBE

Langland Bay '65

above
The earliest known shot of the Langland Bay crew, 1965.
PHOTO: JOHN GOSS.

seaweed-covered rocks.

The early exploits of this core group laid the foundations for the Gower Surf Club, formed at Langland Bay in 1964.

It wasn't easy to obtain wetsuits and boards in the early '60s, as there were no manufacturers or shops in Wales. The Welsh boys bought sheets of neoprene and cut out their own suits (to divers' patterns) to extend their water time beyond the summer months. They ordered surfboards from Jersey and Cornwall, where commercial manufacturing was taking off.

Keen surfers Les and Jake Reece, who worked as butchers in Mumbles, rose to the challenge and began making their own boards in the mid '60s. At first it was just a passionate hobby, but aware of the growing local demand, they stepped it up a gear and founded Wales's first commercial surf label — Sunset Surfboards.

By 1965 there were sufficient members in the Gower Surf Club to organise a trip to the Surf Life Saving Association of Great Britain's National Championships, which by this time included a surfing competition. The contest took place at Woolacombe in North Devon, and for the first time the Gower boys were able to see how they fared against surfers from other regions.

The following year, 1966, Gower Surf Club became affiliated with the SLSA of Great Britain to strengthen its sporting credibility. That August they hosted a competition at Langland, regarded as the first Welsh Championships, which was won by the cool-headed Robin Hansen.

Around the same time, small pockets of activity were developing independently outside the Gower hub, like at Porthcawl near Bridgend. Surfing was a novel activity in the area, and few people had even seen pictures of it. One morning in 1966, Porthcawl police station received a 999 call from a local woman who claimed to have seen "two men floating on aircraft wings in Rest Bay!" When the Porthcawl coppers rushed to the scene, they found local pioneers Ken and Ray Evans enjoying a mellow three-foot session.

One of the early Porthcawl surf talents was Pete Bounds, who had first tried his hand at surfing while on a holiday to St Ives in Cornwall in '64. The following summer, Pete discovered the existence of handful of surfers based at the Lifeguard Club. At the time Dale Furness was the top local rider. Pete bought his first board – a 9'8" Freddy Bickers noserider – from Lyndsey Morgan who ran the town's first surf shop, operating out of a garage. It was the first of many surfboards for Pete, who went on to become a multiple Welsh Champion, a top surf photographer, and more recently a surfing and sailing instructor.

Those with commercial interests in surfing quickly became
aware of the rapid expansion of surfing in Wales. In 1966 a stock of Bilbo surfboards was shipped from Cornwall to Capstan House, a chandlery in Swansea, the first ever retail base for surfboards in Wales. The journey involved vans and trailers, which had to take the Oust-Clevedon ferry to cross the River Severn. There was such a frenzy to buy the boards that they were all sold directly out of the back of the vans, at £28 per board, before they even reached the shop! This was a clear indication of how high the level of enthusiasm from new 'wannabe' surfers was in this coastal city environment.

A commercial surfboard building business was set up in Abergavenny by Tim Heyland and Dave Smith in 1967, called Tiki. They recruited Ian 'Porky' Morcom, who'd worked at Bilbo in Newquay, to help produce the boards. The company blew their own foam blanks, which they named Castle Foam, as an alternative to the Bilbo blanks Bill Head and Bob Bailey were blowing in the south.

To capitalise on the 'city by the sea' market in the Swansea area, Bilbo Surfboards dispatched top Newquay surfer Dave Friar to open and manage a shop in the Mumbles in 1968. The industry was becoming more competitive, and over the following decade more and more surfboard producers started appearing in South Wales, such as Pete Phillips' Crab Island Surfboards.

Competitively, Welsh surfers put themselves on the national map in 1967. Events in Langland fired up
some of Wales' best surfers to mount an expeditionary force to the Cornish and Open Surfing Championships at Porthtowan. They came in convoy, and opened Cornish eyes to the vibrant scene flowering across the Bristol Channel. Not only were these Celtic cousins friendly and sociable, they were competitive and gifted enough to create future national champions. These new links encouraged a regular flow of top Welsh surfers to the increasing number of events further south, and vice versa.

In 1968 Langland hosted a prestigious Open event which attracted James and Charles Williams from St Ives, two of the best known and most forward-thinking surfers in the country at the time. Despite their presence it was a South African surfer, Trevor Espey, who won the Open riding one of the new generation eight-foot vee-bottom boards. This looser, shorter equipment, pioneered by Bob McTavish and Nat Young in Australia, would herald a new era of more vertical shortboard surfing. Noseriding, walking the board and trim became less important as surfers began using the power of the wave as a means of self-expression.

It was an exciting time for Welsh surfing, as outside influences in performance and board design started to impact on this unique surfing clan. In the late summer of '68, Australian surf star Keith Paull paid a visit to the area while on a tour of Europe. Fellow Aussie Wayne 'Rabbit' Bartholomew described Keith as having, "The most beautiful style in surfing." Keith put on a glitzy performance of rollercoasters and bottom-turns in a clean three-foot swell at Langland, sharing waves with the already established local standouts Robin Hansen, Howard Davies, Roger Bateman, Ernie Page and the new 'immigrant' from Cornwall, Dave Friar.

Pete Jones, a competitive swimmer from Swansea, was drawn into the expanding surfing scene just as shorter boards started appearing in 1968. Guided by the solid group of proficient surfers and keen competitors at Langland, PJ went on to become a leading force in Welsh competitive surfing over the next 15 years and was in his element when shorter boards opened up the possibilities of a plethora of hollow reef breaks on the Welsh coastline. The barrelling Gower beauty, Pete's Reef, is respectfully named after its pioneer.

While Llangennith, the Gower's swell magnet, became the heart of competitive surfing in South Wales, strong local scenes thrived in Port Talbot, Porthcawl and Llantwit Major. In 1969 the Porthcawl and Rest Bay locals formed Crest Surf Club. The name was an abbreviation of their local surf spots: Coney, Rest, Esp, Sker and Trecco. The club was renamed the Welsh Coast Surf Club in 1971, the same year that Bob Blyth opened a second surf shop in Porthcawl. A new wave of local standouts emerged, including

opposite, top
By the early '70s there were surfing hotspots all along the South Wales coast. Newport local Wendell takes off at Sker, near Porthcawl.
PHOTO: PETE BOUNDS.

opposite, bottom
Pete 'PJ' Jones was the first to surf this reef on the Gower, and it bears his name to this day.
PHOTO: PHIL HOLDEN.

99

Mike Conlan, brothers Wyn and Steve Davies, Duncan Thomas, Dai Halpin and Paul Conibear.

The sport of surfing gradually spread throughout Wales, reaching the western beaches of Pembrokeshire, Anglesey, the Lleyn Peninsula and Aberystwyth. Pembrokeshire is a beautiful county with minimal development, unspoiled sand dunes, red sandstone cliffs and several national parks, so it was no surprise that it became a popular 'surf safari' destination. In 1973 the newly-formed British Universities Surfing Club staged their annual inter-university competition at Freshwater West. The surf was big and clean at the exposed beachbreak, and Tigger Newling from Treyarnon Bay in Cornwall won the title. Already a well-known board shaper, Tigger was studying Building Construction at Bristol Polytechnic at the time, and he excelled in the contest, applying his gymnastic torque to the Atlantic juice. Tigger returned to Fresh' West in September to win the 1973 British Championships, held in solid offshore surf.

The same southwest swells that hit Pembrokeshire also sweep north to deliver waves to Cardigan Bay, the Lleyn Peninsula, and the southwest coast of Anglesey. In this part of Wales a separate microcosm of Welsh surfing society developed in the late '60s. This was largely due to the ease of access to waves for the increasing number of people from northern England who had taken up the sport. Surfers like John Baxendale and Des Thompson often made round trips of up to 300 miles to surf Anglesey and Hell's Mouth on the Lleyn Peninsula, and in 1968 a group of them banded together to form the North East West Surf Club.

Inevitably, several surfers settled in these locations and then a few locals caught the bug. According to Cardigan Bay local and West Wales pioneer Tony Jeffs, "The spread of surfing came mainly from Anglesey and the Lleyn during the late '60s and '70s, and not from the south."

The university town of Aberystwyth embraced the sport in the early '70s and developed a lively surfing community. Prince Charles even surfed here in 1973. Aberystwyth's outstanding possession was The Trap, a well-formed peak near the harbour. Those who surfed it in good conditions were irresistibly tempted to spread the word, and inevitably the secret filtered out.

Rhyll High School on Anglesey was perfectly positioned to notice the arrival of surfers. In 1969 the school formed its own surf club, under the guidance of an eccentric English teacher and surfer named Bez Newton. Unfortunately, the County Education Authority objected. So Bez privatised the club, affiliated it to the BSA, and renamed it Sol Y Mar Surf Club. Bez was full of ideas and keen to reach out to the wider world. For starters he wrote to famous Hawaiian power surfer Barry Kanaipuni, and asked his permission to be an Honorary President of the club.

The club hosted a new contest in 1974, the North

below
PJ (right) and Phil Evans on the North Shore of Hawaii in '76.
PHOTO: PETE JONES COLLECTION.

above
PJ, fully covered and going full tilt at Aberavon, winter 1976.
PHOTO: PETE BOUNDS.

Wales Open, which marked the arrival of Anglesey as a legitimate surfing area. It was won by the then-reigning Welsh champion Pete Bounds, who was keen to embrace surfing in lesser known areas like northwest Wales.

Sol Y Mar Surf Club frequently invited the top British performers of the time to their contests, such as Tigger Newling and St Austell's Graham Nile. Surfers would compete, hold honorary positions, and even be invited to travel abroad on club expeditions. Newquay surfers Nigel Semmens and Keith Beddoe were among those to hook up with the club when they organised a trip to Morocco in the mid '70s. The fabled right points of the Taghazoute area were still considered new surfing territory back then. Sol Y Mar-ions also claim to have discovered the waves at Playa de las Americas on Tenerife in the '70s, now a well-known and crowded surfing hotspot.

This dynamic and influential surf club even converted its club magazine into a commercial publication, Surf, which it endeavoured to sell nationwide. Edited by Bez, Surf was an interesting and popular magazine which ran from 1974 to 1978.

Nothing could stop Bez. In the sea, he combated

his short-sightedness by wearing wacky-looking surf goggles. He was a free-thinking bohemian who loved travelling, and when he tired of teaching he took up writing. His first book was *The Natural: Adventures of a Surfing Super Stud*, written in 1978. Although in parts it's a shocking read, it remains the first ever British surfing novel. Four more books followed: *The Patriarch*, *Islander*, *Exile* and *Captive*, all published by Mayflower Books.

Despite having a membership of more than 300 in its heyday, the Sol Y Mar Surf Club eventually disbanded in the early '80s after Bez and a significant number of its driving force left to live overseas. Bez emigrated to Australia, and sadly died there some years later, but he'll be remembered for his important and flamboyant role in early Welsh surfing.

Welsh surfing came together as a single force in January 1973

with the formation of the Welsh Surfing Federation. Denzil Smith from the Swansea lifeguard scene became the WSF's first President, and Ron Williams from the Welsh Coast Surf Club became its Secretary. The new WSF organisation gave surfing in Wales a distinct national identity. This was also thanks to the energy and commitment of Pete Jones, Paul Conibear and Ken Price, as well as the recognition Linda Sharp was achieving for women's surfing.

The WSF keenly supported the development of a highly competitive inter-club contest scene. The original Gower Surf Club competed regularly with Langland Board Riders, Gower Lifeguard Surf Club, Welsh Coast Surf Club, Aberavon Surf Club and various smaller clubs that developed in more outlying regions. This grew into a strong trait among Welsh surfers. Whenever they crossed the Severn Bridge they always stuck together (and invariably drank their English challengers under the table); but at home they were divided into all manner of clubs and crews. In the space of just 30 miles, numerous different surf communities can still be found, each guarding their own waves and having their own sacred patch.

In 1979, with Sports Council funding, the BSA appointed Mike Cunningham to be its full-time Administrator with its headquarters in the heart of Swansea. The BSA started to develop specialised coaching programmes, and Mike worked hard to get Sports Council funding to bring the World Championships to Britain. It paid off, eventually.

above
Kiwi shaper Craig Hughes helped Wave Graffitti become the leading Welsh board brand in the late '80s.
PHOTO: PHIL HOLDEN.

below
Porthcawl's Brad Hockridge waxes up.
PHOTO: ALEX WILLIAMS.

Throughout this period outstanding domestic and international contest performances

from Pete Jones, Pete Bounds and Linda Sharp broadcast the fact that Wales was a hotbed of surfing talent.

Multiple Welsh Champion Pete Bounds was a contest machine. He had a laidback temperament, but under pressure he was a heat tactician who knew how to keep calm and make the most out of every wave he caught. He also seemed to be able to mask his determination behind his waist-long hair and a thick moustache.

Pete was a keen traveller and became a true 'barefoot adventurer' in the early '70s as he hated wearing shoes. After exploring the potential of North Wales and East Anglia, he headed west to California and Baja. This set the stage for some serious travelling in the mid '70s throughout Europe and South America. After representing Britain at the World Championships in South Africa, Pete embarked on an epic trip overland through the Middle East and onto Java and Bali, then virgin surf territory.

When Pete represented Britain again at the 1982 World Championships at Burleigh Heads, Australia, he was joined by a new Welsh prodigy, Simon Tucker. By this time a new crew of Porthcawl surfers had risen through the ranks, among them Tucker, Brad Hockridge and Mark Schofield. Powerful naturalfooter Schofield nailed two consecutive British titles in '82 and '83 and was a surf talent to be remembered. He always looked silky-smooth on the wave face, no matter how critical his turns or how challenging the sections. Mark was the epitome of surf finesse and Welsh charm. But it was Simon Tucker's rivalry with Langland-based Carwyn Williams that captivated the surf media throughout the '80s.

Simon and Carwyn's first national showdown came at the British Junior Championships in 1981. They pushed each other to the edge, and further. Simon took the title and Carwyn was runner-up. Welsh surfing had a lot to look forward to from this pair.

above
Clean lines at Manorbier in Pembrokeshire.
PHOTO: PHIL HOLDEN.

Simon was explosive, but reliable. He rarely fell during a heat. Carwyn was flashy and spontaneous, but unpredictable. Regardless of whether or not he was recovering from a late night out, the Swansea surfer looked like he could take his surfboard to any part of the wave he wanted. In 1983 Carwyn became Welsh, British and European Junior Champion.

In 1986 Simon Tucker won the Open title at the British Championships, and two years later he turned pro, sponsored by Devon-based Alder Sportswear. But it was not to be the route for Simon; he maintained his job at British Steel, raised a family, and devoted himself to his home coast. Simon's foreign contest ambitions were focused on representing his country at the World Championships. Carwyn, also sponsored by Alder, took the opposite career path. He was ambitious to represent himself and make it as a professional. He was prepared to camp on the beach if he couldn't afford a hotel. It paid off, and he won the European Pro Tour in '85 and '89.

As well as being an incredibly gifted surfer, Carwyn also had a strong gut feeling for the kind of boards he wanted to ride. So he looked to Kiwi shaper Craig Hughes (Viv Ganz's son-in-law) of Crab Island Surfboards, who later teamed up with John Purton to form Wave Graffitti Surfboards. Craig's refined boards helped harness Carwyn's talent as his career progressed. Carwyn's eccentric manner, combined with his dynamic surfing, established him as a popular character on the ASP World Tour when he qualified in 1989. This notoriety brought with it a recognition and respect for Welsh surfing from a wider audience. But, cruelly, Carwyn suffered a serious knee injury in a car accident a couple of years later which prevented Wales' first pro surfer from realising his World Tour potential.

While Carwyn was taking on the world, Simon Tucker, Chris French, Ian 'Cat' Thomson and Matt Stephen fought the home corner in the late '80s. At the same time another Gower surfer, Chris 'Guts' Griffiths, caught the longboard bug. He had the spark and style to become a professional longboarder, with an incredible ability to smack a lip almost as vertically and radically as a shortboarder. With his powerful attack and big-wave gusto, Guts helped fuel the longboard renaissance in Europe in the late '80s and beyond.

"Everyone loves Welsh surfers," is a phrase often heard on travels. Wales has created one of the most popular clans in our surfing tribe, and their top surfers have always known how to rage on the dance-floor as well as in the lineup. Welsh surfers also have a lot of respect for their peers. "Surfing in Wales has a great heritage," says Carwyn. "I grew up always respecting the locals, who were by rights the best surfers in the lineup."

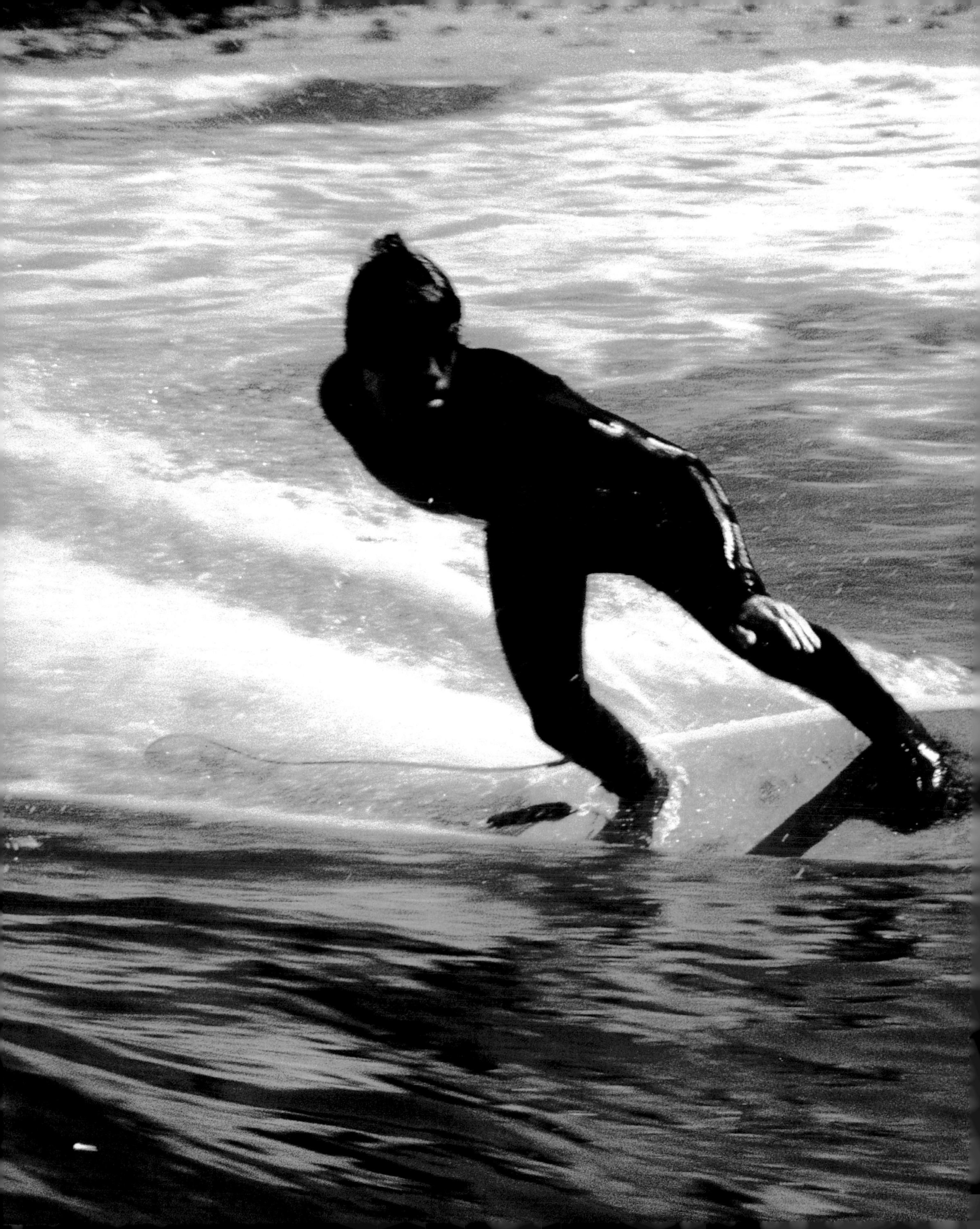

Porthcawl's Mark Schofield won consecutive British titles in the early '80s. PHOTO: PETE BOUNDS.

PETE 'PJ' JONES: A PASSION TO BE THE BEST

Warm, articulate and charismatic, Pete 'PJ' Jones radiates Aloha spirit. He is the Gerry Lopez of British surfing – a legend and pure stylist. As a former European, British and eight times Welsh champion, PJ has inspired generations of surfers and acquired heroic status. But PJ's kind-hearted attitude and pure stoke outshine all the trophies buried below his surf shop in Llangennith. His longevity is testament to the surfing lifestyle he leads and his flowing surfing is still as smooth as silk.

PJ's rise to surfing fame started one hot day during the summer of 1967. The chirpy 17-year-old was already a keen competitive swimmer, and he was hanging out by the Lifeguard Club at Langland watching the waves. His best mate Phil Hayward had just purchased a nine-foot Tiki, which he'd proudly brought to Langland for its maiden session. PJ naturally accepted a go, and surprised himself by standing up first time. "It was like an electric shock through my whole body," says PJ, recalling his first hit of stoke. He surfed on borrowed boards as often as he could for the rest of the summer.

The following spring PJ drove to the Tiki factory in Abergavenny (shortly before it relocated to North Devon) and bought the shortest board in stock. "I didn't have a roof rack and wanted something that would fit inside my Minivan, so I just asked for the smallest board they had." That turned out to be a pig-shaped 7'7" reverse teardrop single-fin. PJ was unaware that shorter, more manoeuvrable boards were about to become the flavour of the future. "In '68 my board was the shortest at Langland, and I remember all the locals saying it was too radical to ride." But PJ soon learned to 'rollercoaster' his board and got straight into the new style of involvement surfing, staying close to the pocket of the wave.

PJ was totally hooked and he surfed every day he could for the next three years. "I was quite competitive through swimming and I thought that if I got the latest designs then I could really get into it." The rising popularity of contest surfing in Wales, centred initially on Langland, infected the young PJ. With a super-fit physique and a good attitude, he was able to flourish in competitions. He entered his first contest in 1968 and won his first Welsh title four years later in 1972. This was the start of a run of eight victories at the Welsh Championships, an achievement that was to make him the most recognised face in Welsh surfing at the time.

PJ's refined wave judgement and graceful poise made him a pleasure to watch, but he was a pragmatic guy who knew that contest success could open up a world of travel at a time when money was scarce. In 1972 he got the chance to compete at the World Championships in San Diego with his great hero, Hawaiian Gerry Lopez, a surfer PJ described as, "the ultimate model of wave-riding elegance." Many British surfers of the era would describe PJ in the same way.

PJ's performance at the 1976 Smirnoff Pro at Sunset Beach

has gone down in the annals of popular British surf culture as being nothing short of heroic. For the modest PJ it was "just another contest", but to take part in a competition at a big-wave venue like Sunset was undeniably a great experience. Cornishman Graham Nile and PJ had been invited to compete in the amateur division of the event, regarded as one of the sport's most prestigious contests at the time. When the pair first set eyes on the sizeable waves at Sunset, they wondered what was in store for them. "We'd just arrived and we went to the podium to check in with contest organiser, Rabbit Kekai," remembers PJ. "He told us the contest was postponed because they were expecting a better swell tomorrow. It was already really big, so we were like, 'Oh no, it's gonna be enormous!'" The next day the waves were indeed massive, but PJ charged. It was his big opportunity to shine with the top dogs, and he wasn't going to let it pass. He paddled out and went screaming down a couple of ferocious West Peak beasts, beating locals like Mark Liddell to progress through to the next round. In the end he made it as far as the semi's, where his plucky charge was halted by Buttons Kaluhiokalani and eventual winner Dane Kealoha.

The following year PJ fulfilled his destiny to win the European Championships, taking a deserved victory at Freshwater West in Pembrokeshire. The waves were big and clean, and PJ put on an unforgettable display of radical yet stylish turns. He always seemed to be able to get the most out of the single-fins of the era, jamming them on a rail through kinetic, flowing moves. To put the icing on the cake, his wife Carol gave birth to their son James the very same day.

A year later PJ added the British title to his trophy haul. The reigning Welsh Champion was also Wales' first European and British champion – a triple whammy.

PJ's consistent performances earned him a place in the British team, not just for one year but for an entire decade, from 1972-82. He attended no fewer than five World Championships, representing his country in California, Hawaii, South Africa, France and Australia. He gave his all at every event, and in doing so inspired the younger surfers in the team to follow his lead and aspire to be the best.

As surfing in South Wales became more popular, PJ took the initiative to open a surf shop in Llangennith in 1978. In the decades since he's expanded the shop (relocating to bigger premises twice), pioneered and run a daily surf report, guided his son to become one of the top surfers in Wales, written a book, become a grandfather, and travelled extensively.

PJ's life journey truly began the moment he stood on a surfboard. "Once I started I knew surfing would be important in my life. But I didn't have much money and hence no means to get to better waves. So I competed to win the opportunity to travel abroad. This worked for me, and I eventually surfed some of the best waves in the world." Yet, as PJ remembers with a twinkle in his eye, "It all goes back to that first ride at Langland."

opposite
Once asked by a journalist to describe himself, Pete Jones jokingly replied, "A short, hairy surfer from Swansea." In fact this humble, modest man is one of the country's all-time greats and an inspirational figure to generations of Welsh surfers. PHOTO: ALEX WILLIAMS.

below
PJ in action at the 1981 European Championships at Thurso East. PHOTO: ALEX WILLIAMS.

CARWYN WILLIAMS: SURF HARD, PARTY HARD

In the early '80s, after Pete Jones had blazed a trail for Welsh surfers, another amazing talent emerged from West Glamorgan – Carwyn Williams. Born in 1965, this prodigal surfing son from Langland Bay barnstormed his way to national recognition as a dynamic competitive surfer in 1983. In that one season he won the Welsh, British and European Junior titles, the opening gambit of a dramatic but at times self-destructive career. The highs of this rollercoaster ride were epic surfing performances when he took on and beat world champions. The lows were career-threatening injuries. But through it all, Carwyn remained one of the best-loved characters in British surfing, a surfer with boundless energy and enthusiasm who caused mischief and havoc wherever he went.

The '80s were a decade of change for the world's top performers as professional surfing captivated the international surf media and became its main focus. In Britain, talented individuals such as Nigel Semmens, Steve Daniel, Paul Russell and Grishka Roberts had already attempted to make a living from surfing, following Ted Deerhurst's pioneering example in the late '70s. But all wannabe professionals need commercial assistance and quality equipment. Carwyn's talents were undoubtedly enhanced by the world-class boards provided by his shaper, Craig Hughes of Wave Graffitti. The marketing potential of the young ripper was also recognised by Britain's largest surf clothing label at the time, Alder. The Devon-based sportswear company set him up as their surfing frontman and tapped into a big new market in Wales in the process. Still in his teens, Carwyn had the backing and the talent to go all the way to the top.

After winning the Junior title at the 1983 British Championships in Scotland (kitted out in an unmissable white wetsuit), Carwyn set his sights on winning the Open division of every contest he could enter. He knew that sponsorship and travel was the real prize.

The young Welshman was fired up by his rivalry with Simon Tucker and Paul Russell, the two top Brits at the time. The contrasts couldn't have been more striking. Paul Russell, the British number one in the mid '80s, was a cool-headed contest machine who knew all about tactics and preparation. Carwyn was the exact opposite. Like a live wire, he would paddle straight out for his heat, surf as hard as he could, come out of the water and head off to find the nearest party.

In 1984 Carwyn turned pro

and turned his attention to the newly-formed European Professional Surfing Association (EPSA) tour. Thanks to a string of good results he finished the season ranked second in Europe, a huge boost to his confidence. For the next five years he spent the summer and autumn months in Europe competing on the EPSA tour. During the winter he would head to Australia, where he trained and entered as many pro contests as he could. His determination was rewarded when he won the EPSA tour in 1985, and again in 1989. He might have won it in 1986 too, had he not spent most of the season nursing a broken wrist, the result of "a foolish skateboarding accident" by his own admission. Injury would again feature later in his career, the unfortunate price for his no-limits lifestyle.

Carwyn's biggest ambition was to break into pro surfing's upper echelon, the ASP Top 30. To do this involved a lot of travelling, both to train and to follow the World Tour, where he'd compete in the trials prior to the main event. Always strapped for cash, Carwyn did it the hard way, often sleeping under the stars and surviving mainly on a diet of vegetable soup. He spent the first six months of 1987 touring the coast of New South Wales and Queensland in his 'mobile home', a '69 Morris Minor. In the autumn he returned to Europe and competed in all the pro contests in France and Spain, at night sleeping in his battered '79 BMW. If he didn't have the cash, Carwyn didn't mind that the beach became the hotel.

By slogging it out on the World Tour, and spending months training at prime surfing locations around the world, Carwyn honed his repertoire and maximised his fitness. Frequent exceptional performances built up his international reputation and spread the word about

opposite
Throughout the '80s, you'd always find Carwyn in southwest France during the late summer and autumn.
PHOTO: ALEX WILLIAMS.

Wave Graffiti
RIP CURL
CARWYN
RIP CURL WETS SUITS
Torquay, Vic. Australia
WAVE GRAFFITI
RIP CURL
WILL
WAVE GRAFFITI

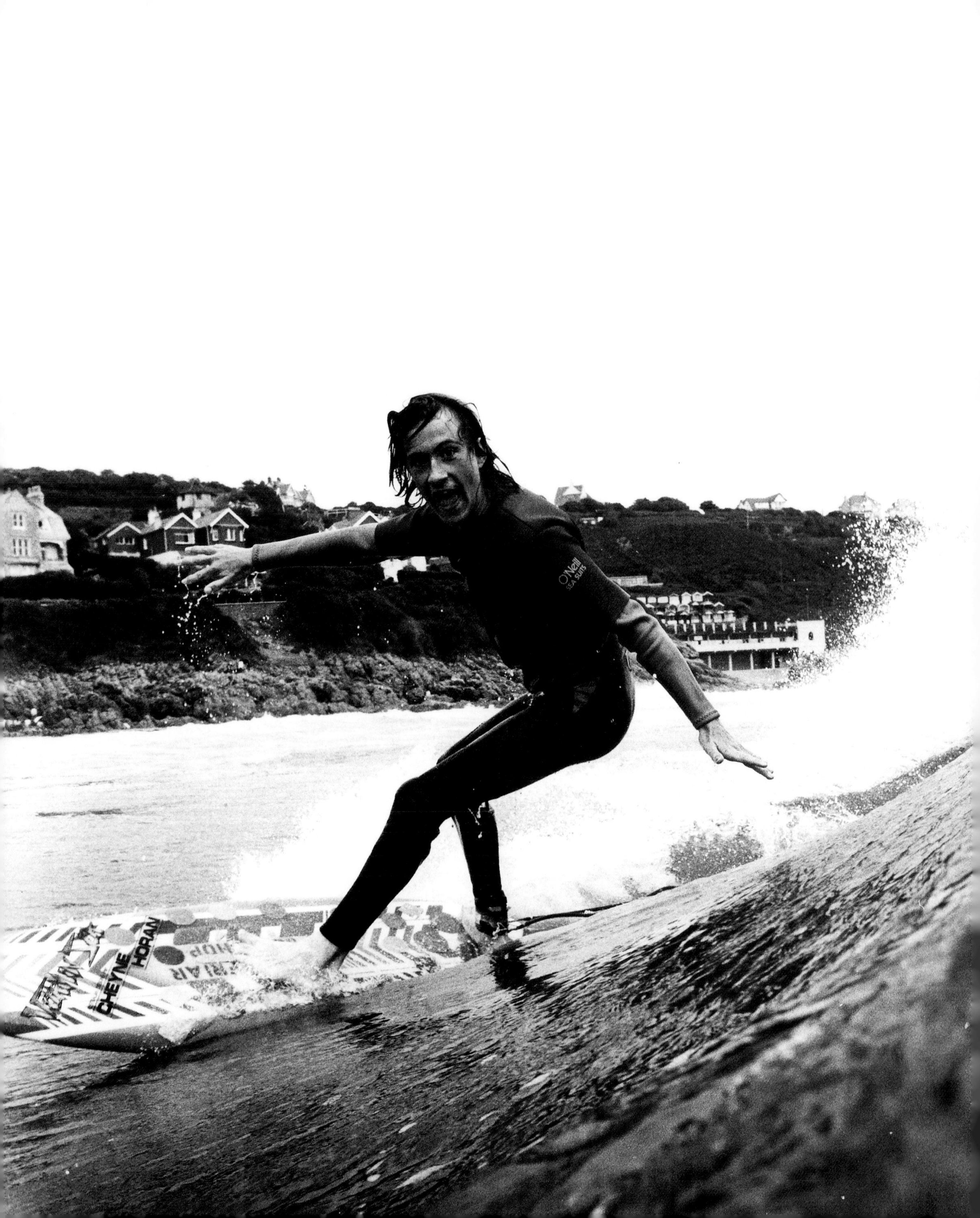
O'Neill
SEA SUITS
CHEYNE
HORAN

In November '87, Carwyn flew out to Hawaii for the winter season. He gained notoriety for his resourcefulness as a financially struggling pro when it was discovered that he was living in the car park at Sunset Beach, in a rusty Chevrolet stationwagon he'd bought for $250. As a virtually unknown *haole* on the North Shore, Carwyn had a tough time getting waves at first. It didn't help that on his first session at Sunset he got pitched by a solid 10-foot lip and landed on Hui local Johnny-Boy Gomes. But the ever-smiling Welshman always made a good impression, socially and in the juice, and he soon made many friends.

One of the most memorable moments of that trip was totally unplanned. He found himself surfing gnarly Third Reef Pipe all alone one evening, after the five other guys in the lineup all snapped their boards in the space of half an hour. He rode some epic waves, barely able to believe that he had the lineup all to himself.

Later, walking up the beach, Carwyn stopped to chat with the owner of a beachfront house at Off The Wall. It turned out that the guy needed help redecorating his million-dollar pad, but was having trouble finding a painter willing to work the hours. He mentioned that he even had a couple of spare rooms. Carwyn wasted no time volunteering his services, and spent the rest of the season living like a king in the best house on the North Shore!

The high point of Carwyn's competitive career occurred in France in 1988.
In epic six- to eight-foot barrels at his beloved Hossegor, he beat the reigning World Champion Damien Hardman man-on-man in the Rip Curl Pro. It was the biggest upset of the year.

Thanks to that performance and other solid results, the Welshman made it into the elite ASP Top 30. Finally he was up there with the best in the world, and getting the respect he deserved. "Carwyn is the complete surfer in anything from two foot to 20 foot," commented Aussie pro Robbie Page in a magazine interview, "and he proved it by beating Hardman in perfect Hossegor barrels. Whatever he does, he does it for the love of the sport. He'd give you his last piece of bread as long as you smiled when you ate it."

The Aussies took Carwyn under their wing on the World Tour and he became great friends with contemporary greats like Mark Occhilupo, Tom Carroll and Gary Elkerton. Photos of Carwyn regularly appeared in Tracks and Surfing Life, proving his popularity Down Under.

However, Carwyn's whirlwind success story came to a shuddering halt in the summer of 1990. He was involved in a near-fatal car accident in France and severely injured his right knee. Carwyn's leg was so seriously damaged that the French doctors thought he would never surf again. Eight months later he had reconstructive surgery and went into a period he called 'the big struggle', aware that he might be out the water for years, if not for life. After an initial period of depression familiar to every athlete who sustains a career threatening injury, Carwyn began an intensive programme of physiotherapy. He trained for six hours every day until his knee was strong enough for him to resume surfing. It was a miraculous recovery considering the damage sustained.

When he resumed competing, his top turns were just as vertical as they'd been before, and he made a spectacular comeback on the EPSA circuit.

The ASP tour was another matter, however, and Carwyn was denied the opportunity to pick up where he'd left off before his injury. For two years in a row he missed out on a slot in the Top 30 by one place. This left him feeling bitter and confused about his direction in life. But he had always been a generous surfer, often sharing his sponsor's goodie bags with surfers less fortunate than him, and inspiring countless Langland groms. Carwyn decided to redirect his energies away from being a competitor, and instead try to help other young people achieve their ambitions. By this time he had moved his base from Langland to the somewhat sunnier environs of Hossegor. With the support of his main sponsor, Billabong, Carwyn became a team trainer for some of the best young international talent, particularly from Australia. Today, he's still at it. His house-cum-hotel is where he shares his wisdom about all aspects of surfing: diet, exercise, performance and attitude...as well as some hilarious travel stories. So while Carwyn may no longer be aiming for the number one spot, his protégés certainly are.

"Carwyn has always done it his way," says long-time friend, Welsh shaper and photographer Paul Gill. "That's always been without rules or regard for personal preservation or financial gain. He's one of the surfing world's greats. And he's made us proud to say that we're Welsh surfers."

opposite
By his mid teens, Carwyn was already a standout at his home break of Langland Bay. PHOTO: PETE BOUNDS.

above
A gutsy performance at Brims Ness won him the British Junior title in '83. PHOTO: PETE BOUNDS.

At his peak in the late '80s, Carwyn was as radical and spontaneous as any surfer in the ASP Top 30. PHOTO: ALEX WILLIAMS.

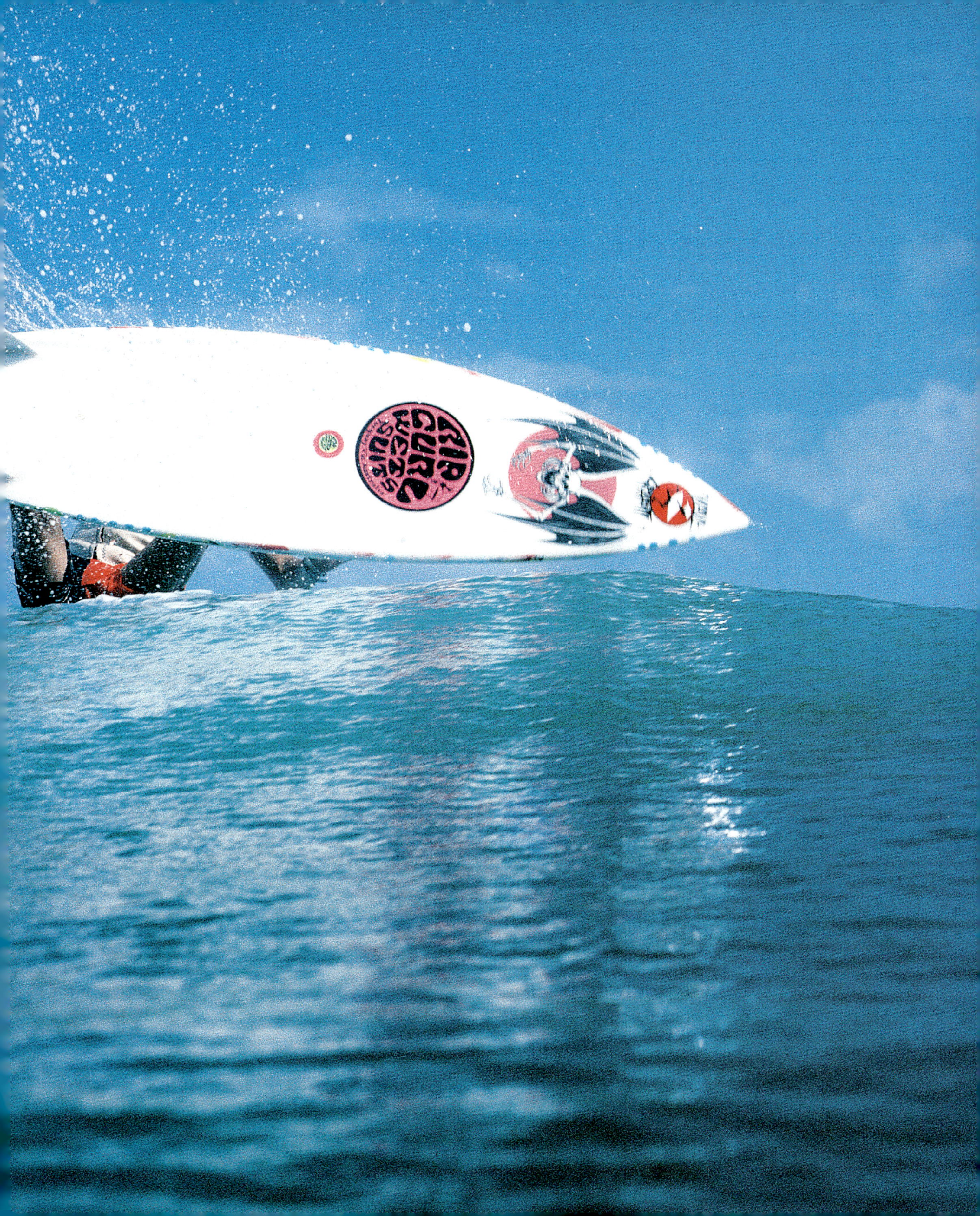

7 | England's enclaves

BRIGHTON, BOURNEMOUTH AND
THE ISLE OF WIGHT: SOUTH COAST SURF FEVER

Sea bathing began on England's South Coast in the early 19th century, earlier than in any other part of Britain. In the 1800s, the Prince Regent (later George IV) helped popularise Brighton as a fashionable alternative to spa towns such as Bath, and sea bathing was one of the key attractions. In the early days, sea bathing merely meant going for a quick dip in sea on a warm summer's day. But as time went on, some of the local folk began to enjoy going for a decent swim, and even racing one another. In 1860 a dozen or so of the keenest local swimmers banded together to form Brighton Swimming Club, the oldest of its kind in Britain. The club held races, often over 500 or 1,000 yards, for prizes that varied from a few shillings to a barrel of oysters. Various galas and social functions were also organised from the club's HQ under the arches of the promenade near the Palace Pier. On frequent occasions members of the club went to the rescue of casual bathers who'd got into trouble, and accordingly they won the respect of the townsfolk.

Among the hardy souls who ventured into The Channel for a dip in the 1890s was a half-Hawaiian half-Scottish student, Princess Victoria Ka'iulani. Born in Honolulu, Victoria was second in line to the Hawaiian throne (the islands were a monarchy with strong British links at the time). Her father, Archibald Scott Cleghorn, was a Scotsman and governor of Oahu. In 1889, at the age of 13, Victoria was sent to England to receive a private education, which would, it was hoped, prepare for her future role as the head of a modern Hawaiian state. Victoria attended Great Harrowden Hall in Northamptonshire, and then studied in Brighton in 1892. While there, she apparently took daily 'sea baths' which gave her 'renewed vigour'. The evidence comes from letters she wrote home to three of her royal Hawaiian cousins. Victoria and her cousins had all surfed while they were growing up on Oahu. In recent years somewhat fanciful claims have been made that the princess may have surfed while she was in Brighton. However, in her correspondence, Victoria never mentioned surfing. Furthermore, such a spectacle would undoubtedly have caught the attention of local folk (such as the members of Brighton Swimming Club), and the media, yet no records of this have been found. So we can only conclude that there is no substance to this theory.

By the early 20th century, Brighton Swimming Club had expanded considerably. It organised informal swims, water polo matches, swimming races (including the popular pier-to-pier swim) and summer galas. Over the years, several members of the club attempted to swim the Channel, some successfully. Inevitably a responsibility for the safety of other bathers developed, and a lifeguard section of the club was formed to patrol the beaches in the summer months. This became designated as an official surf lifesaving club in 1954. When the Brighton SLSC team attended a Surf Lifesaving Association gala at Bude in 1955, they were inspired to obtain two 14-foot hollow wooden paddleboards for water patrols back on the South Coast.

Despite the intermittent surf, a handful of Brighton men developed an interest in wave riding in the early to mid '60s. By 1965 a small group of surfers were regularly riding waves at the West Pier and nearby Littlehampton when there was a swell. Steve Wright and brothers Sean and Jerry Mahoney were three of the pioneers; all owned boards they'd bought on trips Newquay. They were soon joined by Mike Sadler, Rod Norris and Alex Ross. The lads topped up their enthusiasm for surfing with frequent visits to Cornwall.

Edward 'Fast Eddie' Hoskin was a Brighton lifeguard who watched the surf scene develop around the West Pier. In 1966 he bought a Bilbo board from Shoreham Watersports, one of the largest watersports shops in the area which had just started stocking surfboards to meet the growing demand on the South Coast. Fast Eddie took to the waves and subsequently linked up with a young crew which including Vince Ward, Tom and Terry Hanley, and 'Ajax' and 'Lumpy' Wyatt, all based around the Palace Pier.

Many of the Brighton surfers of the '60s were drawn to Cornwall, and Newquay in particular. Vince Ward spent time working in Doug Wilson's Bilbo shop, the cultural epicentre of the Newquay scene in the mid to late '60s, where visitors would not only admire Chris Jones' hot shapes but also tune in to the latest Californian bands playing on the stereo – Spirit, Jefferson Airplane and Quicksilver Messenger Service. Outgoing and popular, Vince fitted straight into the Newquay surf community. He even appeared in a few Bilbo ads, modelling the company's surfwear. The Brighton link was well recognised by the surfers in Newquay. "It was almost like an unofficial twinning," recalls Chris Jones. Through this social mechanism a strong sense of surf culture became planted into the Brighton beach scene, which by the '70s and '80s could witness dozens of surfers in the water if the waves were good.

A couple of particularly notable surfers emerged from this scene, such as second-generation Brighton

opposite
Clean lines at Bournemouth Pier on a rare easterly swell.
PHOTO: GARY KNIGHTS.

above
Brighton pioneer Sean Mahoney strikes an *Endless Summer* pose in front of the Palace Pier in 1965.
PHOTO: JERRY MAHONEY.

boy Mike Smith. As a grommet, Mike developed his talent in the lineups of Brighton and Newquay, and he became a hot shortboarder. In 1982 he took part in the Gul-Alder pro-am event at Fistral Beach in Newquay, and made it through to the quarterfinals. There he came up against renowned Australian power-surfer Richard Cram, one of a handful of pro's who'd flown over to take part. Mike surfed with determination, but he couldn't compete with the curly-haired Aussie and his scything forehand cutback. In fact no-one could, and Cram went on to win the event.

Mike was an open-minded and self-assured character who liked to do his own thing. Later the same year he flew out to Australia and little was heard from him for eight months. At Alexandra Head in Queensland, Mike met up with a crew of laid-back longboarders who were surfing the long peeling rights in a way that seemed totally cool and fresh. "It changed my mind about the magic of surfing," says Mike. "I discovered I could catch an abundance of waves and I was blown away by the length of each ride. I felt reborn."

Mike returned home in 1983 with a brightly sprayed eight-footer, which he rode with effortless skill and style. He also rode the nose, a technique which hadn't been seen since before the shortboard revolution, 15 years earlier. Out of the water Mike seemed quieter and more humble than in his shortboard days; a new side of surfing had touched him. But the moment he took to the waves with his longboard he stood out like a neon glow. Mike is widely seen as a key player who reinvigorated longboarding in Britain in the mid '80s. Without his example, it might have taken a lot longer for the global longboard renaissance to hit British shores.

Later, in the '90s, ex-pro skateboarder Jock Paterson would pick up the torch for South Coast longboarding. The agile Brighton naturalfooter was a regular competitor at longboard events and became one of the country's best.

Beach culture is a part of life on the Isle of Wight.

Wherever you are, you're just a stone's throw from a sandy beach. Roger Backhouse, Mike Hutchinson, Sid Pitman and Ben Kelly were among the first to start surfing here, around 1964. They picked up the idea after going on a holiday to Cornwall and returned with a couple of surfboards, knowing that good waves could be found on the island from time to time.

Mike Hutchinson was a woodwork teacher, and he decided to build himself a balsa board. It took him days to shape, and when it was finished he coated it in resin (in the same way that you'd varnish a wooden deck on a boat). Unfortunately, he didn't realise that he needed to use fibreglass cloth as well. The board was light and it trimmed well, but the resin coat soon cracked and the wood went spongy without a watertight coating. It must have been frustrating to say the least.

Despite initial equipment setbacks, the crew persevered and formed the Isle of Wight Surf Club the following year, 1965. The club was based at their home beach, Ventnor, although most sessions took place at Freshwater Bay or Compton Bay on the west coast, which receive more swell. Keen to promote the sport on the island, the club advertised meetings in the local paper. This drew Glyn Kernick and Keith Williams into the scene, and the club soon became the centre of surfing action on the island.

The local crew's motivation was raised further by the brief return of an island son, Rob Ward, an officer in the Royal Navy who'd travelled the globe and learned to surf while in South Africa. Subsequent postings in Central and South America had turned him into a highly competent surfer with a taste for solid waves. In fact, Rob was so hooked on surfing that he abandoned his seafaring career (and his island home) to become a global surf explorer, which earned him recognition as Britain's first committed big-wave rider.

By the late '60s, friendly links with the new surfing fraternity around Bournemouth resulted in the South Coast Surfing Championships being held at Compton in 1969. This was the first proper contest to be staged in the era and it was primarily a team event. It was co-ordinated by Bournemouth surfer and shaper Bob Groves, the man behind Wessex Surf Club. Shore Surf Club (from East Wittering), Wessex Surf Club and the Isle of Wight Surf Club battled it out in a three-way contest. West Sussex surfers Derek Adlam, Brian Butler, Ian Wood, Keith West, Terry Cole, Brian Price, Keith Kingham and Brian James had formed Shore Surf Club specifically for the contest and named it after the Shore Inn in East Wittering where they surfed and hung out. In small clean waves, the local Isle of Wight team won. Team member Roger Cooper took the individual title in convincing form.

The Isle of Wight has since been the breeding ground for a number of significant and creative surfers, many of whom ultimately migrated to the mainland to make more of an impact upon the sport. Derek Thompson, who transplanted to Cornwall, provided many of Britain's surfers with their first professionally-made ankle leash in the early '70s; Derek's Cosmic leashes saved countless long swims to the beach and dinged boards. Roger Cooper moved to South Wales where he shaped top quality boards under a variety of labels. Another shaper, Tad 'the Guv' Ciastula, moved to Newquay where he ran the hugely successful Vitamin Sea Surfboards in the '80s.

Bournemouth has grown to become the main centre of surfing on the South Coast,

and the man who played the most significant role in the sport's early development was Bob Groves. Like so many others, Bob began riding waves on a bellyboard, during family holidays to Cornwall. In his twenties he became a lifeguard at Lee-on-Solent, and in 1963 he built himself a basic surfboard (using a design in the Australian SLSA manual), which he learnt to ride at Eastoke Point on Hayling Island. Later that year he travelled to St Ives to take part in the SLSA National Championships, where he encountered the earliest surf clans of Cornwall. There Bob got some valuable advice about surfboard design from American lifeguard Jack Lydgate, and he gleaned more info from a copy of Surfer magazine which he bought at the beach cafe cum surf shop, Man Friday. Equipped with considerably more know-how, Bob returned home to make three boards for himself and friends Bill Davies and Bob Rudland.

The trio kept a close eye on the swell and surfed whenever possible. "As far as we knew, there weren't any other surfers in the Hampshire area at the time," says Bob, "so we'd surf alone at Eastoke after storms, or when a depression came up The Channel from the Atlantic." To cope with the cold water the surfers wore two-piece diving wetsuits, and had to endure the discomfort of prone paddling with the front toggles of the suits pushing into their groins. "Knee paddling was the best technique," said Bob, "but that gave you painful surf bumps...still, it proved you were a real surfer!"

As the years passed, more south coasters took up surfing and Boscombe Pier became the nucleus of activity as it received the most consistent waves. In 1964 Bob and his friends formed Wessex Surf Club, to provide a point of contact for surfers in Bournemouth,

above
The Isle of Wight has some good breaks... unfortunately, swells like this are frustratingly rare.
PHOTO: ROGER POWLEY.

below
Roger Cooper, who won the inaugural South Coast Championships at Compton in 1969.
PHOTO: BOB GROVES.

117 | THE SURFING TRIBE

above
South Coast surfer and shaper Bob Groves, who founded Wessex Surf Club in 1964.
PHOTO: BOB GROVES COLLECTION.

Poole and the surrounding area. The same year, Bob met Geoff McGratty, a watersports instructor at the Sandbanks Hotel who was keen to learn to surf. Bob helped Geoff buy a board from Newquay, and the pair became dedicated surf companions at Boscombe Pier.

Bob and Geoff were keen to find out if there were other spots along the Dorset coast, so they set about exploring the area. It wasn't long before they stumbled across a stretch of rocky coastline with a cluster of interesting-looking reef setups. Further visits on offshore days revealed the true quality of these breaks. Word quickly spread among the Bournemouth crew and the race was on to ride the new waves. "I'm not sure who was first to surf Yellow Ledge, but I was the first to surf Broad Bench," claims Bob. "It wasn't big, only about three feet, but it took me 20 minutes to paddle out because of the current. On a bigger swell it works as a pointbreak, with an easier paddle."

The Bournemouth crew had no shortage of good breaks, but the lack of consistent swell on the South Coast prompted them to go on regular weekend trips to North Devon. So frequent was this ritual that the first Wessex Surf Club contest was held at Woolacombe. Attended by 12 Wessex members, the contest was won by Tony Cope, an apprentice surveyor, who went on to become a consistent South Coast performer.

As local demand for boards increased in the mid '60s, Bob Groves and Bill Davies teamed up and began making boards. Over the next couple of years they built about 30 boards under the Groves-Davies label. However, the lure of the surfing lifestyle in Cornwall was too strong for Bob, and he moved to Newquay in 1967 where he worked for a while as manager of Bilbo surf shop. "He was fantastic to work with," recalls Paul Holmes, a fellow Bilbo employee at the time, "he was like a mad scientist, always coming up with weird and wonderful ideas for board designs."

Bob's time in Newquay provided him with a valuable insight into the commercial side of surfboard building. In 1969 he moved back to Bournemouth and started a business called Groves Foam Products, blowing foam blanks, selling DIY surfboard kits and building Infinity Surfboards. A Groves surfboard kit cost around £20 and included a 7'3" blank, resin and cloth, tape, sandpaper, a fin and a set of easy-to-follow instructions. Bob later went into partnership with Stuart Affleck and together they opened Surfline surf shop in Boscombe in 1970, which sold every piece of equipment and clothing the South Coast surfer could possibly need.

By the late '70s a large number of surfers were riding the intermittent swells on the South Coast at spots like Highcliffe, Southbourne, Boscombe, Bournemouth and the Dorset reefs.

Another boost to surfing on the South Coast came through its association with the BSA and Reginald 'Reg' Prytherch. A top water polo player, Reg owned a sports shop in Parkstone which sold waterskis and other watersports gear. He started stocking Groves-Davies surfboards in the mid '60s, and began to develop an interest in the sport when he realised how quickly it was growing. He got involved on the administrative side and worked his way up the ladder to eventually become Chairman of the BSA in 1968. His shop housed the BSA Office for several years, well into the '70s. The BSA's move away from the South West didn't go down well in surfing's heartland, however. Many surfers there were disdainful of Prytherch's bureaucratic and straight-laced approach, and questioned whether he was even a surfer at all. By the early '70s, critics of the BSA claimed the Association had become a muddled and inept organisation working far below its potential, because sadly no top-flight surfers wanted to be involved.

However, from the point of view of the BSA, things were happening. In the mid '70s, Reg Prytherch managed to persuade Prince Charles to be the Patron of the BSA. Charles had dabbled with surfing while on a tour of Australia, and he'd also ridden a few British waves at Constantine and Aberystwyth. Reg pulled off a bit of a coup when he arranged for the 1978 British team to meet the prince at Buckingham Palace, before they flew off to the World Championships in South Africa. The likes of Linda Sharp, Graham Nile, Pete Bounds, Steve Daniel, Pete Jones and Nigel Semmens motored up to London in a van and pulled up in Hyde Park where they changed into their shirts, suits and ties. Trouble was, Pete Bounds had no shoes with him, so the team quickly had to drive to King's Road to buy him a new pair. Inside the palace, Charles noted that Pete, Graham and PJ all sported heavy moustaches, the style of the time. "Are they to keep you warm in the sea?" joked the prince. The guys laughed. But the gap between their world and that of royalty was as big as the gap between the bureaucratic BSA and the needs of the everyday surfer in Britain.

Mike Cunningham took over from Reg Prytherch as head of the BSA in the early '80s, and the Association's headquarters moved to Swansea. However, Reg's involvement in amateur surfing's administration continued, and he drew praise in the mid '80s for his efforts to bring the World Championships to Britain. Mike Cunningham and Dave Grimshaw spent months lobbying the International Surfing Association to hold the prestigious event in Newquay, then Reg enthusiastically talked up the proposal at the deciding meeting in Queensland, Australia. With support from Quiksilver, the World Championships were duly held at Fistral Beach in September 1986. "Mike and Reg must take a lot of the credit for that," says Grimo modestly.

The exploits of the surfing community in Bournemouth were broadcast to a wider audience by the popular Tube News magazine between 1980 and '91. Originally produced by Roger Castle and Ben Liddell for Wessex Surf Club, the publication developed kudos as a national magazine, expanding its coverage to link up with the larger surfing communities of North Devon and Cornwall. Tube News also profiled local talents such as Guy Penwarden, Tony Cope, Steve Brown and Darryl Williams.

Bournemouth surfer Guy Penwarden was the area's top surfer in the '80s. He rarely missed a good session at the Dorset reefs and honed his repertoire there, as well as on frequent trips to the South West. He competed at national level for several years and represented Britain at the World Championships in France in 1980, before returning home to open his own surf shop, Hot Rocks.

England's South Coast doesn't get nearly as much swell as the South West, but its locals are just as dedicated to surfing, and totally committed to maximising every single ocean pulse.

above
Bournemouth surfer Guy Penwarden in action at one of Dorset's prime reefs.
PHOTO: GARY KNIGHTS.

119 | THE SURFING TRIBE

FROM KENT TO CROMER:
FINDING WAVES IN EVERY CORNER OF THE ISLE

above
Snow on the beach, and a clean empty peak out the back. A timeless image of surfing in East Anglia.
PHOTO: NEIL WATSON.

below
East Kent pioneers Paul Knowles (left) and Pete George in 1967.
PHOTO: PAUL KNOWLES COLLECTION.

With a low pressure system in the right position, the Norfolk, Suffolk, Kent and East Sussex coastline can come alive with decent waves. The history of surfing in these areas harks back to the 1960s.

Paul Knowles, a young accounts clerk who lived on the Isle of Thanet in Kent, loved the surf music coming from California in the mid '60s and he'd seen clean North Sea waves breaking at his local beaches from time to time. He found his way to the Bilbo Surfboards stand at the London Boat Show in 1965, and seeing the beautifully-finished boards on display he was inspired to have a go at surfing himself. He built himself a crude wooden board which he rode at Camber Sands and a few other spots around Kent. The following summer he drove down to Newquay in search of bigger waves, and there he bought a second-hand Australian-made Keyo malibu. Fired up by the vibrant Newquay surf scene, he returned home and started surfing the North Sea as often as possible.

By 1968, Paul and his mate Peter George were surfing on a regular basis and they started exploring the East Kent coast for waves. The lads' quest for waves took them to Joss Bay, near Broadstairs, where they bumped into Ian Stevenson, a cadet Engineering Officer in the Merchant Navy. Ian had just returned from Australia where he'd learnt to surf and bought a cool Scott Dillon board. Soon after, they hooked up with another East Kent surfer, Tony Ward, who'd been surfing Joss Bay on his own for about a year. Joss Bay, always a good mid- to high-tide break on a solid north swell, quickly became their preferred break.

The number of surfers in the area continued to grow, and East Kent Surf Club was formed in 1968 to give a focal point to the local surf community. Paul, Ian and Tony realised there was a considerable local demand for boards, so they joined forces with two recent converts – Kurt Maskelyn and Tim Keenan – and set up their own surfboard company, Island Surfboards. Together they built around 30 boards, with Kurt (a boat builder by trade) doing most of the shaping. Sadly the venture only lasted a couple of years because of a lack of capital. Kurt, Tim and Ian subsequently moved to Braunton in North Devon to follow their surfing dreams.

After other key members of East Kent Surf Club

moved away or emigrated in the early '70s, the club was reluctantly disbanded. "From the mid '70s to the mid '80s there was only a very small group of locals headed by Paul Watkins, John Clarke and John Meritt," recalls Paul Knowles. "They'd all started in their teens, and used to tow their boards behind their bikes from Broadstairs to Joss Bay. They certainly had it uncrowded in those days!"

In the late '80s, Ian Stevenson returned to Kent after living in New Zealand for a decade or so. By now the surfing population of the area was on the increase again, and Ian started the annual Big Chill surf contest. Soon there was a vibrant new surf scene at Joss Bay, and Joss Bay Surf Club was formed to fill the social vacuum left by the demise of the East Kent club.

In 1989 Paul Knowles started Surf's Up, an A5-size local magazine along the lines of Tube News, which gave this corner of England's coastline a much greater identity. Around this time, there was a huge resurgence of interest in longboarding. Surfers who rode longer boards gained the advantage of an easier paddle against the strong currents of the North Sea, and they could also go surfing much more regularly. Even on the weakest of north swell pulses, a longboarder could fade left, swing right, and maybe sneak a quick nose-ride.

The coast of East Anglia,

from north-facing East Runton to east-facing Lowestoft, can offer punchy waves in wintertime over the flint reefs and alongside piers and groynes. The coast has a unique feel, backed by the flat landscape of the Fens and characterised by traditional Norfolk crab boats and tractors (which tow the boats up the beach).

East Runton is the spiritual home of surfing in East Anglia, but Cromer – a large seaside resort with its own pier – became the best-known break to outsiders. Surfing here began in 1967 when East Runton man John Parkin built himself a wooden board. Later the same year, top Welsh surfer Pete Bounds visited the area while on a trip to explore new territory around Britain. Pete enjoyed his time in Norfolk and returned the following summer; while he was there he built and sold a few boards. This was enough to get a handful of locals riding the following winter. People began to realise that the waves around East Anglia could be pretty good in the right conditions.

Local lad Dave Farrow was another who got into surfing in the late '60s after buying a second-hand Bilbo from Cornwall, and in 1968, he thought he'd have a go at building some boards himself. Dave and his mate Robert Brownsell named their label Cougar Surfboards and started building innovative seven-foot shortboards in Dave's parents' garage. Bizarrely they sold the boards in the local village fish shop.

Lowestoft, like Cromer, is a popular seaside resort with a pier which works on swells coming down the North Sea. The peaks either side of Claremont Pier can be surprisingly good on a big swell. The first guy to take to the waves here was Maurice Butler, in the late '60s. Despite the intermittent nature of the swells, surfing caught on quickly. By the mid '70s Lowestoft Surf Club had a membership of over 100, bringing together surfers from across Norfolk and Suffolk. By this time local shaper Dave Farrow was producing boards under a new label, Karma Surfboards. He recalls the strong sense of unity and dedication shared by the early surf community. "Despite the fact that our surfing was grabbed in occasional moments, we knew every surfer for a hundred miles. Lowestoft Surf Club helped keep us in touch with everyone else's activities. It was a happening scene."

The club produced a quality newsletter called Ripple, which was the masterful work of local writer Neil Watson. Neil fell in love with surfing while on honeymoon in Cornwall in 1969. Throughout the '70s he devoted himself tirelessly to British surf journalism, contributing words and photos to Surf Insight, Surf Scene, Tube News and Atlantic Surfer.

Ultimately, East Anglia shapers Dave Farrow and Nigel Woodcock found the lure of the South West was too strong to resist, and both moved to Newquay. Nigel later became a top competitor on the national scene, and his Wavekraft label was highly successful.

The surf scene in East Anglia continued to thrive in the '80s, with big crowds at the main spots on good days. Cromer offered the dicey thrill of shooting the pier – surfing between the pier legs like '60s surfers did at Huntington Pier in California. Despite the growth of the sport, wintertime surfing in the '80s at East Runton, Cromer and Lowestoft still felt like an isolated bohemian activity that set you apart from the norm, much as it did in the '60s at more popular surfing areas in the country. The expansion of surfing to these North Sea breaks (and the local breed of dedicated surfers that resulted) is something to be celebrated. Neither ice cold water or inconsistent waves could stop British surf culture from spreading inexorably to every corner of the isle.

below
Tom Watson-Bell at Cromer in the early '70s.
PHOTO: PETE BOUNDS.

RIDING THE RIVER: THE SEVERN BORE

above
Bore riders Dave Lawson (left) and Steve King have been regulars on the Severn for decades.
PHOTO: ESTPIX.

These days river bores are ridden at various locations all around the world, but bore riding was pioneered on the River Severn in Britain half a century ago. The Severn Bore is a tidal wave which flows through rural Gloucestershire for 25 miles, from the top of the Severn Estuary to Maisemore Weir. This amazing natural phenomenon has spawned a unique and quirky clan that has helped to add more colour to our already vibrant surf tribe.

Although the Bore occurs twice a day, only the biggest spring tide Bores are rideable and it's the huge tides around the spring and autumn equinoxes (in March and September) that attract surfers.

The first person to catch a wave on the Severn was an adrenaline-seeking veteran commando officer called Colonel Jack Churchill. In July 1955 he caught a wave near Stonebench, riding prone on an Australian style 16-foot wooden paddleboard. The writer FW Rowbotham witnessed Colonel Jack's daring feat. "There was a tide of 31 feet at Sharpness. As the fair-sized bore approached, the Colonel placed his board beneath him and began to swim upstream. Moments later the leading slope of the bore slid under him and he started planing forward."

The Bore was first ridden standing-up seven years later, in 1962. Film footage of the Bore was occasionally shown in cinema newsreels, so it was no secret. Newquay's Bill Bailey remembers that American lifeguard Jack Lydgate was the first of the town's surfers to suggest a trip up to Gloucestershire to try to ride the Bore. "Jack had the idea to ride it. We'd go anywhere to ride waves in those days. Me, Jack, Bob Head and the other Australian lifeguards were all mad keen to ride it."

In September 1962, after the summer lifeguard season had ended, the Newquay crew arrived in Gloucestershire in time for the biggest tides of the year. The local police advised them not to make an attempt, and threatened arrest if they did. But the surfers went ahead regardless, and rode the Bore standing up for half a mile, by which time they were out of sight of the cops. Local youngster Dave Lawson, who lived in Rea, witnessed those first stand-up sessions and was enthralled. In later years he would become one of the top local bore riders.

However, bore surfing didn't capture the attention of a wider audience until 1967, when Rod Sumpter became interested in the idea of riding and filming the wave. Rod was in the Sailor's Arms in Newquay one evening when Bob Head told him about the Bore. "I thought he was crazy," recalls Rod, "but Bob told me he'd surfed it for 500 yards. So I found out a bit more about it, and drove it up there on the next spring tide to have a go. When I saw it I was amazed, and riding it was really easy. The second time I went up I rode it for six miles! We got some great footage for my film, and I thought, 'This is it! This is the next big thing in surfing!'"

Footage of Rod riding the Bore (filmed by his girlfriend Simonne Renvoize) featured in his first surf film *Come Surf With Me*, which was screened at coastal venues around the country in 1967. "After that I went up every spring and autumn," remembers Rod. "I thought I'd found the greatest thing ever. It took me four years to realise what it really was – mud, dead sheep and stinking water! So then I stopped going. But riding the Bore was great fun. It tested your repertoire to the limit. Everything you'd ever learned about surfing was played out in 30 minutes. The wave went from overhead to waist-high, from glassy to choppy, from steep to fat. You constantly had to dodge trees and watch out for shallow mud banks. Just everything was chucked at you! So it was a great experience. I loved it."

In 1968 Rod penned a well-written article for Surfer magazine in America about the Severn Bore. 'The World's Most Unusual Wave' turned a few heads and surfers all over the world began to check out their local rivers. Rod was the original expert in pursuing surfing novelty. After the Severn he conquered another bore in the Bay of Fundy in Canada.

The bore-riding sections in Rod's films enticed many surfers to try to ride the Severn Bore at least once. A cult of lunar cycle controlled bore-riding developed, attracting all sorts of wave riders on all sorts of crazy craft.

The Bore made another significant appearance in Alan Rich's 1976 film *Playgrounds In Paradise*. It featured a wacky section of British champ Bruce Palmer getting to grips with the Bore – mud, thick neoprene, river reeds and all.

Devon surfer Stuart Matthews and multiple Welsh champ Pete Jones subsequently took up the challenge. Their joint attempt in 1980 achieved an official record of 2.5 miles (Rod Sumpter's epic ride in '67 had been deemed as 'unofficial' because it had not been independently adjudicated).

Two years later, Cornishman Colin Wilson took a novel approach by using a board with a retractable fin to achieve a 2.9-mile ride. His record stood for six years.

By the late '80s, the river had spawned a sizeable crew of die-hard bore riders. Rea local Dave Lawson was the most experienced among them, and in 1996 he smashed the old record with an epic ride of 5.7 miles.

Recently, in 2006, another local rider, Steve King, rode the Bore for an incredible 7.6 miles. But his feat was not witnessed by a BSA adjudicator, and Lawson's ride remains as the official Guinness record.

"Preparation has always been the key," says long-time Bore aficionado Toby Stevens. "You need to wear booties because of rocks, sharp reeds on the banks and the inevitable long walk back to the car...if you're lucky enough to get a long ride! Thicker, longer boards have always been the preferred option as they keep gliding when the wave backs off in deeper water. Also, fresh water provides less buoyancy than the sea, so smaller boards tend to sink."

The three most popular stretches of the river for Bore riding are Newnham, Minsterworth and Maisemore. With a bit of planning they can all can be surfed in one day. The Bore breaks slowly and softly at Newnham, at the head of the Severn estuary. Minsterworth, the mid section, offers a shorter ride on a faster, bigger wave. At Maisemore, further upstream, surfers get the quirky thrill of surfing under bridges.

"Once you've surfed the Bore, you'll be addicted!" claims Toby. "It provides a very different surfing experience to the sea. It's a shared wave, for obvious reasons, so the drop-in rule doesn't apply. Because of this it's very much a shared experience – you can have long conversations with other surfers while you're on the wave! And there aren't many places where you to surf past wildfowl, over elver eels and under bridges."

The unique, communal experience of riding the Bore has been appreciated by surfers of all nationalities over the years, as Toby explains. "Surfers travel from all over the world to experience the Bore. Many foreign surfers said they felt the spirit of surfing was more alive on the River Severn than anywhere else they'd been on their travels."

below
The Bore has always attracted top surfers. Here's Welsh supremo Pete Jones having a crack at it in 1983.
PHOTO: PHIL HOLDEN.

8 | Northern lights

EDGING INTO THE COLD: THE NORTH EAST

The North East's earliest connection with surfing goes right back to the 18th century and Yorkshireman Captain James Cook. Cook grew up in the small fishing village of Staithes before getting an apprenticeship on a coal ship sailing out of Whitby. When he was 27 he joined the Royal Navy and slowly worked his way up through the ranks. In 1768 he was given the command of *HMS Endeavour* and embarked on the first of three epic voyages to explore the Pacific Ocean. On the third of these expeditions, Cook and his crew became the first Westerners to witness surfing, in Hawaii in 1778.

By coincidence, the stretch of coast where Cook grew up is home to some of the best surf spots in the North East. One of these, The Cove, is a long and hollow left-hander, unanimously considered to be the region's jewel in the crown. "If Cook were to thread his way through the reefs of his native coastline today, it's likely that he'd sail past some rubber-clad soul paddling into a thick brown barrel, thousands of miles from where this dance of grace and balance began centuries before," wrote British surf author Bez Newton in his 1978 novel *The Natural*.

With the characteristic grit and determination bred in the North East, Cook is an inspiration to the modern day surf explorer. From his home coast have come some of the nation's finest, among them Nigel Veitch, Gary Rogers, Gabe Davies and Sam Lamiroy. These surfers continue the lineage that stretches back to North East pioneer John Baxendale, who started surfing here in 1963.

Lancashire-born Baxendale was a student at university in Newcastle-upon-Tyne in the early '60s. He took up surfing during a visit to Cornwall in 1963, where a lifeguard at Crantock Beach lent him a board. When he returned to the North East, he built a surfboard and took to the waves at his local break, Whitley Bay. Tall and lanky, John surfed the sporadic North Sea swells alone, until finding the companionship of fellow student Colin Frazer a year or so later. After graduating, John moved back to his native Lancashire, where he built several more boards under the brand name Northumbria Surfboards. In 1968 he became a founding member of the North East West Surf Club. This club had every angle covered and gave a social and sporting identity to the growing number of surf enthusiasts scattered across northern England, particularly in Liverpool.

Further down the North East coast, Saltburn lad John Smith became interested in surfing in 1965. He'd got hold of a book called *Surfing, the Sport of Hawaiian Kings* which was packed with photos of Hawaiian surfers riding waves not dissimilar to the waves he could see breaking all along the Cleveland coast. The book led Smith and his friends Ian Davies and John Roughton on an interesting journey of discovery. Smith bought blocks of foam from the nearby ICI complex, then glued, cut and shaped the foam into a good approximation of a malibu board. The glassing process proved to be more problematic, as the fibreglass resins of the time were very volatile and one or two of the catalyst-rich 'hot mixes' caught fire. But eventually he finished the board and the three surfers were ready to hit the waves. Three men with one board and one wetsuit between them, taking turns in the cold North Sea waves at Saltburn – this determined effort marked the start of the communal sport of surfing in the region.

By the following summer the three surfers each had their own board, all built by John Smith whose production methods were improving with every board. Two new converts joined the group at this time, Tim Gladders and Alistair McCauley, who were eager to learn how to surf. "It was all trial and error," admits Tim. "We didn't really know what to do! Onlookers would ask tongue-in-cheek questions like 'Where's the

opposite
North East pioneers John Roughton, John 'The Bull' Smith and Ian Davies on the beach at Saltburn in 1965.
PHOTO: UNKNOWN/JOHN ROUGHTON COLLECION

124 | THE SURFING TRIBE

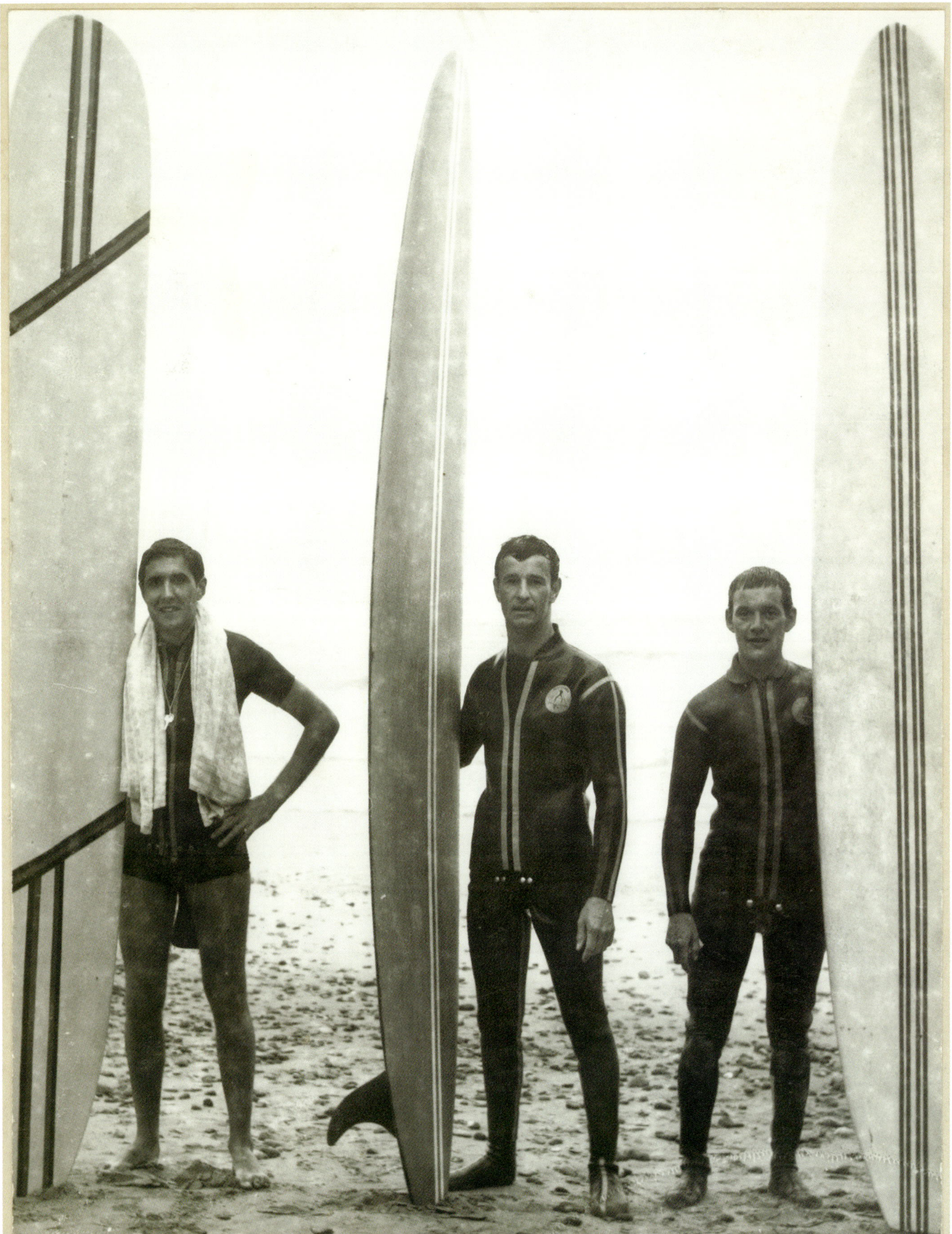

engine?' We had to work it all out for ourselves without any help, other than seeing photos in an occasional Surfer magazine. We just surfed our local beach and, if I'm honest, progress was slow. But it was a lot of fun."

In 1970 Cornish surfer Mike Hendy from Porthtowan visited the area on family business. He was amazed to find quality waves at Saltburn, and even more amazed to find a crew of local guys trying to ride them on home-made boards. Mike was a skilful surfer with a refined style. He took to the water on a borrowed board and showed the local lads what was possible in the Saltburn surf. They watched and learned, stoked by Mike's display.

On a subsequent visit to the North East in 1973, Mike was accompanied by Tris Cokes and Johnny Manetta from Porthtowan, who were eager to check out the empty reefs and points they'd heard about. In the back of the van were six Tris surfboards the guys had built; these were on their way to a sports shop in Newcastle called Denton Cycles, which had just started stocking boards due to local demand.

By the mid '70s, surfing in the North East had extended down to Scarborough, where Surfin' Scene surf shop was doing good business supplying equipment to the steadily rising number of locals. Meanwhile, up at Tynemouth, a strong scene had formed at Long Sands. Through the '70s the crew here included Trevor Steven, John Pearson, Eric Oliver, Dave Allen, Benny Howe, Paul Sallows from Western Australia, Peter and Anthony Beard, Ronny Hudson and Roger Elliot.

In the '80s, skateboarding became hugely popular in Newcastle and the crossover between skating and surfing saw the emergence of John and Davey Stores and future pro surfer Nigel Veitch.

Surf clubs were an important part of the North East scene at this time, far more so than in the South West. Clubs from Tynemouth, South Shields, Saltburn and Scarborough competed on the popular East Coast contest circuit, with Foam At The Mouth Surf Club from Tynemouth often coming out on top. The circuit offered a stepping-stone to push the talents of the region's finest.

The English Surfing Federation acknowledged the strength of surf clubs in the North East when it held the English Championships at Tynemouth in 1989, with the help of Foam At The Mouth Surf Club. This gave many of England's best surfers reason to visit a part of the country they'd never been to before. Rising young performers like Dean and Steve Winter, Randall Davies and Spencer Hargraves showed up with their fluoro wetsuits and logo-covered surfboards, alerting the youth of the North East to the rising commerciality of surfing further south. Despite the youthful push, it was the ultra-consistent Paul Russell who won the contest in the six-foot surf at Long Sands. Regardless of wave size or quality, Paul seemed to be able to find the best waves to win virtually any event at the time.

The ice-cold water of the North Sea
has always been a big barrier to winter surfing in the North East. In the '60s and '70s surfers had to endure wetsuits designed for diving, or try to source purpose-made surfing wetsuits suits from companies in the South West. In the early '80s the first locally-manufactured surfing wetsuits became available when Gavin Scott started his C-Dog brand. Scott's wetsuits utilised good thick neoprene to ward off the North Sea chill, but they were unpretentious and affordable. Many of the top surfers in the area went to him for custom suits, and before long his team included Nigel Veitch, Davey Stores and hot grommets Gabe Davies and Sam Lamiroy. This group of talented North East surfers would go on to great things in the years that followed.

Nigel Veitch burst onto the national scene in 1982 when he won both the English Junior and British Junior titles. Prior to that he'd dominated the East Coast contest circuit for a couple of years, after switching to surfing from skateboarding. The stocky goofyfoot quickly became a top performer on the national competition scene, before embarking on a tragically short career as a professional surfer (see profile, page 128). While in his prime, Veitch befriended Tynemouth youngsters Jesse and Gabriel Davies, and he had an enormous influence on them.

Gabe Davies started surfing in 1984, aged nine, encouraged by his elder brother Jesse and family friend Richard Harris. As the boys progressed they began to take their place in the lineup alongside the top surfers in the area. Nigel Veitch became a huge inspiration to the brothers, who looked up to him as a local hero.

below
Saltburn's elegant Victorian pier has been a gathering place for surfers since the mid '60s. PHOTO: CHRIS POWER.

When he was 13, Gabe spent six weeks on Australia's Gold Coast, staying with his aunt. The warm water and steady supply of waves allowed him to dramatically improve his repertoire, particularly his backhand surfing. He returned home in the spring to dominate the junior division of the North East club scene. From there he progressed on to national events, and his success in the juniors was the springboard for a career as one of Europe's best professional surfers.

Sam Lamiroy, a hot young naturalfoot from Tynemouth, emerged on the scene in the late '80s. Thanks to countless sessions at quality North East reefs he developed a powerful style characterised by trademark go-for-broke turns. In subsequent years, like Gabe, he would go on to win numerous national titles and earn a living as a top pro.

By the late '80s, the North East was finally getting national recognition as a region with quality waves. Its talented sons were winning plenty of silverware, and the South West based surf media had woken up to its seriously heavy waves. Magazine articles proclaimed that the North East had some of the finest set-ups in England...a fact the locals had known (and kept quiet about) for years. But breaks like 'The Cove' could never remain secret spots forever. On a good day this world-class left offers freight-train barrels that rival those of Mundaka in northern Spain.

The North East is now recognised as a prime surf zone for top riders from the length and breadth of the country. "Who would have thought that the coastline where Captain Cook grew up would become a regular pilgrimage for top British surfers?" marvels Saltburn surf shop owner Gary Rogers. "If the tides are right, you can even pull off the 'East Coast treble', scoring three sessions at the best reefs in one day!" That's no easy feat though. It takes the drive and determination of a character like Captain Cook to really tap into the North East's unlimited surf potential.

above
Tynemouth surfer Gabe Davies in action at 'The Cove'. Gabe burst onto the scene in 1990 when he finished second in the juniors at the English Championships; in later years he won the British Open title and three British Senior titles. PHOTO: ALEX WILLIAMS.

NIGEL VEITCH: NORTH SEA WAVE WARRIOR

opposite
Veitch, photographed for a Laser Surfboards ad in 1986. PHOTO: COURTESY LASER SURFBOARDS.

below
Even second reef Pipe didn't faze Veitch. PHOTO: UNKNOWN/COURTESY STORES FAMILY.

As a young surfer with striking features, Nigel Veitch looked like a Nordic wave warrior as he flew along the waves with his long straw-blonde locks flowing behind him. His looks, talent and bravado led to a successful professional career in the late '80s; but it was cut short by tragedy.

Veitch grew up in urban Newcastle and he was a top skateboarder in his teens, winning the East Coast Championships among other accolades. Several of his skater mates also surfed and they encouraged him to give it a try. Despite the chilly North Sea temperatures he quickly got hooked and by the age of 15 he was a regular at Tynemouth. Nigel proved to be something of a natural, and over the next few years he developed his skills at the beaches and reefs of the North East. By the early '80s he was the North East Champion, and in 1982 he won both the English Junior and British Junior titles. Backed by Gul and Laser Surfboards, this young man was clearly going places.

Veitch's dream of becoming a pro surfer took over his life. He trained with focused determination, and studied videos and books about his heroes Tom Carroll and Cheyne Horan. Veitch was looking up to the best, but he understood the subjective quality of surfing. "One of the great things about surfing is that there is no wrong or right," he commented in a magazine interview at the time. "The act of surfing is an expression of yourself, an interaction between you and the sea. Like two lovers kissing, it's not the act but the feeling which is important."

One feeling Veitch always craved was the feeling of winning. He was inspired by the examples of Ted Deerhurst, Steve Daniel and Nigel Semmens, who had competed internationally as pro surfers. But none of them had embarked on the full tour, full-time. Veitch set his goals sky high. He wanted to be the first European pro to take on the challenge of the newly established ASP World Tour. Veitch thrived on attention he got in the press. He was a showman and wanted to be remembered, even immortalised. He would do anything he could to give him an edge. He even changed his name by deed poll to simply 'Veitch' because he thought it sounded more striking.

In 1986 he set off on the World Tour. His plan was to compete for a full year, and hopefully finish among the elite Top 30. He knew the travel costs would be exorbitant but he had just landed a new sponsorship deal from Newcastle Brown Ale, and he also signalled his self-belief by taking out a hefty personal bank loan.

Veitch performed impressively on the tour as it meandered around the world with stopoffs in Japan, Brazil, South Africa, California, France and Hawaii. He battled his way through the trials at each event, and made the main event at several contests. He eventually finished the year ranked 33rd in the world. Asked in an interview about his reasons for following the tour so determinedly, Veitch said he just wanted to give a shot. "I don't want to get to 30 and think 'Oh, I wish I had tried'. I want to see how far my surfing can go."

The gutsy Geordie displayed moments of brilliance in Hawaii, as his protégé Gabe Davies remembers. "There's an inspirational photo of him on a massive wave at second reef Pipeline, which shows him as far back as any British surfer I've ever seen. He loved big waves."

Unfortunately, Veitch's achievements on the North Shore were countered by a serious knee injury he sustained over there. There's no question that if this injury hadn't happened Veitch would have kept on improving and risen up the ASP rankings.

The following year, Veitch's pro surfing dreams were shattered when his sponsor withdrew their support. What turmoil there was in his personal life at the age of 26 is not quite clear. It might have been the trauma of a career-threatening knee injury, or maybe debt. Whatever the reasons, Veitch became deeply depressed and took his own life in the summer of 1987. He walked to the edge of a cliff at Tynemouth and with the rescue services watching helplessly, he dived in a perfect arc onto the rocks below.

His parents asked Gabe and Jesse Davies to scatter his ashes in the North Sea waves he loved so dearly.

Veitch remains an icon of British surfing, remembered for his charisma and his fearless attitude in big waves. "The character traits that led Veitch to chase his dreams inspired a generation of groms, myself included," says Gabe. "His lust for life was infectious. Why such a promising life was brought to a premature end, no one knows. But few stars have burned with more fire, or shone more powerfully than the star that was Veitch."

HIGH PERFORMANCE
GADER
SURFBOARDS
Croyde N. Devon England

9 | Scotland's beauties

SEARCHING FOR HIDDEN TREASURE

The Scottish melting pot of Gaelic and Norse culture is as far as you can get from the southern heartland of British surfing. Its rugged 2,000-mile long coastline is indented with lochs and firths, and it wears a necklace of dozens of islands. Where the Atlantic meets the North Sea, powerful depressions track eastwards from the open ocean making Scotland serious swell territory.

Scotland's geographic separation, not to mention the 18-hour drive from Cornwall to Edinburgh in the '60s, delayed the growth of surf culture on its coasts. For the same cost and time spent travelling, surfers knew they could find warmer waves heading in the opposite direction to southwest France. The roots of Scottish surfing were finally planted in 1965 when Aberdeen's Andy Bennetts watched surfers in action during a holiday in Cornwall. But Andy didn't bring the new sport north of the border until 1968, when he returned from a subsequent visit to Newquay with his own Bilbo board. He started riding the waves between the Town Beach groynes in Aberdeen, where he was soon joined by local man George Law who had built himself a wooden surfboard.

Subsequently, Scottish surfing development shifted south, to the Edinburgh region. Andy was living and studying at university there, so he started exploring the East Lothian coast for waves with student mates Ian Wishart, Bill Batten and Stuart Crichton. The choice find was the beautiful north-facing Pease Bay. "On the right-hand side of the beach is a boulder reef, near where the stream enters the sea," explains Andy. "Towards high tide we noticed it created a well shaped right-hander. So that became the spot we usually tried to ride."

Newcomer Glyn Fielding joined the Edinburgh crew in 1969 and together they began to explore the coast to the south, finding good waves at Coldingham and Belhaven. Their next great discovery was on the Mull of Kintyre, where a surfari highlighted the powerful low-tide waves at Machrihanish, clean on a southwest wind. The incredible potential of Scotland's western seaboard was recognised. "You just had to look at the map and you knew that so many magic waves could be found," says Glyn.

By the late '60s the clan of surfers was growing, exploring and communicating. There was now a Glasgow surf contingent, led by George Raynes. In Edinburgh, Andy Bennetts, Glyn Fielding, Phil Mathieson, Pete Rennie and Robin Salomon formed Napier University Surf Club. It felt like the focal point of Scottish surfing. But unknown to the Edinburgh crew, another group of Scots were also 'up and riding', 130 miles to the north.

At Fraserburgh, a steely fishing town on the northeast tip of Aberdeenshire, a hardy surf clan had been surfing 'The Broch' since 1968. Swashbuckling local Willie Tait, who owned a sport fishing boat, had made a trip to California in 1969; enthralled by the surf scene at Huntington Beach, he returned home to Scotland with a 10'6" malibu board. Sadly, Willie's surfing career was later cut short when he lost an arm in a boat accident, but not before he spurred on his mates to take up surfing. His lead encouraged other surfers to order boards and wetsuits from California. Among them was 17-year-old student and lifeguard Malcolm Findlay, who always stood out in the lineup due to his mop of curly blond hair. "The idea

below
Students from Edinburgh University were among the first to ride Scotland's chilly waves in the late '60s. (Left to right) Bill Batten, Pete Rennie, Phil Mathieson, Glyn Fielding and Andy Bennetts. PHOTO: ANDY BENNETTS COLLECTION.

above
Thurso East, on a perfect offshore morning in September 1984 with Ian McKay charging down the line. Sadly, the canon guarding the castle's north wall is no longer there; it was washed into the sea by a huge swell a few years later.
PHOTO: ANDY BENNETTS.

of having fun in the sea in Fraserburgh, rather than making a living from it, was frowned upon by the older generation," recalls Findlay, now a university lecturer. "In fact, quite a few of the early surfers were going against their parents' wishes getting into it. We were almost outcasts in the community."

The Edinburgh and Fraserburgh surfers didn't cross paths until 1973 when Andy Bennetts set out on a trip around Scotland with his wife. Although Andy knew nothing about the Fraserburgh area, he had a feeling that he might find waves there. Sure enough he stumbled across perfect three-foot surf at The Broch… as well as Malcolm Findlay tearing it up alongside a dozen of his hardy friends. Andy was staggered to see that Fraserburgh had a thriving surf community. The 'lost tribe' had been found and the two strands came together.

The fusion of the Edinburgh, Glasgow and Fraserburgh crews united Scottish surfing. The first Scottish Championships were held in 1973, and the Scottish Surfing Federation was formed three years later. Malcolm Findlay's competitive zeal and powerful top-to-bottom repertoire subsequently made him Scottish Champion on five occasions. Over the following two decades, other champions included Andy Roberts, Iain Masson and the awesome Ian McKay.

In 1970, adventurous Edinburgh surfer Bill Batten

attended a wedding in Armadale, further north than any of the other Scottish surfers had travelled. He found great waves on the north shore of Sutherland and rode the right-hand rivermouth at Torrisdale and the beach break at Bettyhill. Batten didn't find Thurso, but he certainly paved the way.

Three years later a Kiwi surf-traveller called Bob Treeby explored Caithness and Sutherland counties (since merged into the Highland region). Bob discovered several world-class reef and point breaks, and documented them in an article in Surf Insight magazine entitled, 'On the North Shore in the Midnight Sun'. Pictures of hypnotic waves at Brims Ness, Balnakeil Bay and Thurso Bay forced English and Welsh surfers to re-evaluate their ideas of Scottish wave potential. Scottish surfers themselves began to realise what a treasure trove they possessed just

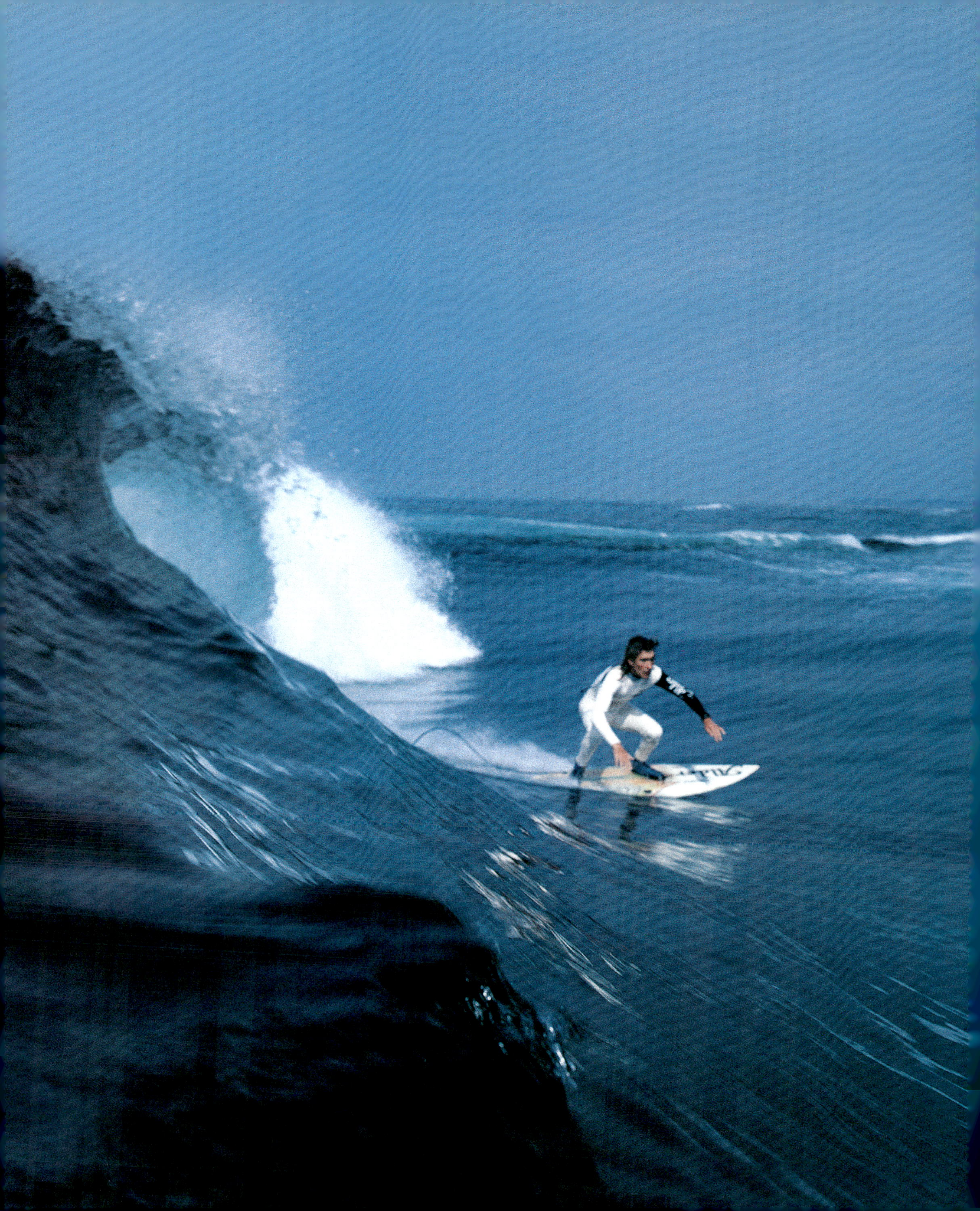

beyond the North West Highlands. Treeby wrote poetically about "the huge groundswells coming out of deep water" and "the folding greenery of mountain slopes that melt into white sand and blue sea. Here one will find uncrowded waves in some of the most fantastic scenery the British Isles has to offer."

Surfers across the country were stoked reading Bob Treeby's article, none more so than Liverpudlian Pat Kieran. In fact Pat was so inspired that within weeks he set off on a Scottish surfari himself. Once in the Thurso area, Pat struck up a friendship with new surf enthusiast Grant Coghill, who had held onto a couple of boards left behind by Treeby. Pat was awestruck by the quality of the surf in Caithness, as well as the dramatic landscape. He fell in love with the place, and later took up residence in the village of Reay. In subsequent years he surfed nearly all the prime spots in the area, becoming not only the hot local, but also the only local. Apart from occasional visits by the Fraserburgh and Edinburgh crews, Pat Kieran had the Thurso area all to himself until 1978.

Welsh surfer Paul Gill was also an early visitor to Thurso. He recalls his first impressions of the place, which he visited as a schoolboy. "In 1971 I went to Thurso on a geography field trip and saw thundering waves on the north shore. Later I got into surfing, and in 1975 I went back up to Scotland with an Aussie friend, Paul Hanning, in his split-screen VW camper. We met up with a guy called Ron Gallagher who lived up there and we surfed the Shit Pipe [the reef next to Thurso harbour] together. While we were out there I saw a perfect right barrel breaking further along the bay. We surfed it the next day – it was like Mundaka in reverse." This session at Thurso East opened Gill's eyes to the quality of British waves, and he later went on many wild adventures exploring various Scottish isles and Ireland.

The wider British audience got another glimpse of Thurso in 1979 when reigning British Champion Nigel Semmens and Steve Daniel visited. They had just judged the Scottish Championships in Fraserburgh, where they'd been impressed by the good waves, the warm welcome, and the descriptions of A-grade surf to be found around Thurso. These two well-travelled southern performers couldn't leave without checking it out. They arrived at Thurso East to find perfect four-foot waves, which they shared with the solo resident surfer, Pat Kieran. "It was like the famous Jeffrey's Bay in South Africa – precision rights…only a bit colder," remembers Nigel.

By the time the duo got back to Cornwall, the word was out: the far north of Scotland has world-class waves.

Another landmark year for the Caithness coast was 1981, when Thurso played host to the European Championships. The warm-up week was flat but Lord Thurso, Robin Sinclair, made an upbeat speech to 200 European surfers at the opening ceremony and he was adamant that the waves would come. They did, and so did international attention. Thurso was added to the global map of outstanding surf spots. Nigel Semmens won the event, taking advantage of the hollow rights on his frontside. "Winning the Europeans in those quality six-foot waves was a real crowning achievement for me," recalls Nigel.

Third place went to local hero Ian McKay. This was more of an impressive achievement than it sounds. A few years earlier, while working as a roofer, Ian fell 50 feet from scaffolding and was rendered paralysed. Doctors said he might never recover, but Ian was exceptionally healthy before the accident (he was a trained diver and a great surfer). The gritty Glaswegian made a full recovery. After a trip to Australia, he returned to push Scottish performance levels to new heights at Brims Ness, and he was one of the country's most daring solid surfers during the '80s.

Steve Clelland subsequently followed in McKay's footsteps, often escaping the brutal winters to train in Australia before returning to tackle Scotland's demanding reefs in the springtime.

In 1988 the British Championships were held in Caithness in cracking conditions. Jersey's ever-popular Renny Gould was the clear standout, but rising star Spencer Hargraves from Newquay showed his determination by eventually winning the Junior and Open titles. Another savvy competitor, Rod Sumpter, emerged from a long competitive retirement to make a comeback at the event. He charged through some hefty tubes at Thurso East to take the Longboard and Masters' titles.

Scotland's north shore remains one of the most isolated outposts of British surfing. Its waves are undoubtedly world-class, but the bitter water temperatures and lack of winter daylight mean that it's likely to stay pristine and uncrowded for many years to come.

above left
Bill Batten was the first to sample the waves on Scotland's north shore, and later became President of the Scottish Surfing Federation. PHOTO: ANDY BENNETTS.

above right
Robin Salomon (left) and Ian Wishart on an early trip to the Mull of Kintyre in 1970. PHOTO: ANDY BENNETTS.

opposite
Welsh teen sensation Carwyn Williams races a wave at Brims Ness while warming up for the British Championships in 1983. PHOTO: PETE BOUNDS.

ANDY BENNETTS: SCOTTISH SURF PIONEER

below
As well as being one of Scotland's top surfers in the '70s and early '80s, Andy Bennetts' interest in photography led to important exposure for the country's waves and surfers. PHOTO: ANDY BENNETTS COLLECTION.

Scottish surfing champion, custom car enthusiast and keen photographer, Andy Bennetts has played a pivotal role in Scottish surfing since the late '60s.

Andy grew up in Aberdeen, but it was the annual summer holiday visits to his grandparents in Falmouth, Cornwall, that ultimately shaped his future. As a young teenager he loved playing in the sea and soon became a keen bellyboarder. One day in 1965, on a day trip to Newquay, he saw a couple of lifeguards surfing on 10-foot boards at Great Western Beach. For Andy, the lure of surfing proved irresistible. Over the next two summers he learnt to surf on boards hired out at Great Western, and in 1967 he bought his own board, a Bilbo. He could now ride Scottish waves at home in Aberdeen...after he'd carried his board for two miles from the railway station to the beach!

That same year he started university in Edinburgh, and in 1969 he formed the Napier Surf Club. This small but hardy group of student surfers began to explore the East Lothian coast of the North Sea for decent waves. "There were about six of us in that early Edinburgh student group, all in our late teens and early 20s," remembers Andy. "Before we got our own cars we'd get a lift down the coast with Pete Rennie's dad. Pease Bay became our favourite break. The owner of the caravan site was a bit surprised to see us there at first, and quite bemused by our desire to surf. He pointed out the signs warning of dangerous currents. We just ignored the signs...and then learned the hard way! The currents *were* bad – we learned by experience and had to figure out how to deal with rips very early on in our surfing."

In August 1969 Andy once again made the long trek south to Newquay, this time with his Edinburgh University friends. They teamed up with a group of surfers from Aberdeen and became the first clan of Scots surfers to ride waves in southern Britain. In Cornwall the sport was absorbing the radical performance and equipment developments through its links with Australia. Andy was not slow to adopt the shortboard zeitgeist of the time and he soon acquired a 7'6" pop-out, the best his student budget could afford. Stoked with his purchase, Andy took his shortboard back to Scotland determined to raise the level of his surfing to that of the beach boys in the south. In subsequent years many more Scots would follow his lead.

"Pease Bay became our usual meeting place," says Andy. "We'd get together, swap stories, and head for another break if necessary. Trying to predict the swell was a trial and error process – we often turned up at Pease to find howling onshore conditions. Sometimes the water was so churned up it looked like chocolate milkshake. I have clear memories of those early days – being freezing cold, hanging out by the toilet block and watching huge foaming waves all the way out to the horizon. Ah, the home of the brave! But we weren't stupid, so if it was out of control we'd head to sheltered spots like Coldingham and we'd often score really decent waves."

Andy's passion for surfing was tirelessly channelled through the university surf club. He arranged contests, organised trips to explore new stretches of the Scottish coast and made contacts with the wider surfing world.

When Andy drove north on a whim and discovered the 'lost tribe' surfing The Broch in northeast Aberdeenshire he brought together all the existing strands of Scottish surfing – the crews from Edinburgh, Glasgow and Fraserburgh. The result of these new links was the staging of the first Scottish Surfing Championships in 1973. East Lothian pioneer Bill Batten won the event, which was held in five-foot waves at Coldingham. Scotland was united.

The Scots continued to run their national championships, largely co-ordinated by Andy's Napier Surf Club. Then in 1976 the Scottish Surfing

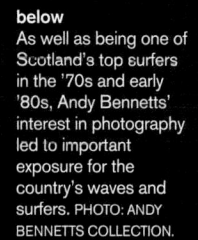

above
Pease Bay hasn't changed much since this shot was taken in the early '80s, although today surfers ride thrusters rather than bonzers. PHOTO: ANDY BENNETTS.

Federation was formed, and recognised by the BSA and the Scottish Sports Council. This made it eligible for funding as an emerging new sport in Scotland. Bill Batten became the President, and Andy took on the roles of both Secretary and Treasurer.

Another of Andy's passions in the '70s was custom cars.
All those long drives between Scotland and Cornwall, and the necessity to rely on lifts from parents and friends in the early days, seemed to fuel a major interest in 'hot wheels'. In a classic article entitled Custom Wheels in Surf Insight magazine, Andy revealed all about the hot new 'Beach comber' he had built with Ian Wishart. "Board, wetsuit, wax – the purist's essentials for surfing. But how do you get to the beach? Getting back to nature is a fine thing, but if you're without wheels in the '70s, baby, you ain't going nowhere. Still, we can get it together, by personalising the machine age. And a fully customised beach buggy fills the gap. My own Volkswagen-based buggy took 13 months and 2,700 hours of work to complete. Everything possible is chromed. When customising any vehicle the important point is to pay attention to the finest details, and the overall effect will take care of itself.

So, all you confused anti-machine age surfer stars, get yourselves together. Don't criticise, customise!"

In 1975, with more surfing time under his belt than most other Scots, Andy travelled up to Fraserburgh to compete at the Scottish Championships. In clean four- to five-foot lefts at The Broch, he won the Open title.

Through almost two decades from the early '70s, Andy served as Secretary of the Scottish Surfing Federation and was a crucial figure in the co-ordination of Scottish surfing, both nationally and internationally. This lead to his appointment as Vice-President of the BSA in the late '70s, and he went on to became Secretary of the European Surfing Federation in the '80s. Scotland was networked to a bigger surfing world and Andy was the link.

"Surfing is one of the few sports you can enjoy without having to compete against someone," says Andy, explaining his lifelong passion for wave riding. These days he runs a photographic business, but still finds time to surf his local patch between Dunbar and Pease Bay when conditions are perfect. He admits that it's hard to beat the joy of surfing in warm water in Australia and France, but notes the crowds those countries attract. Crowds will never become a problem in Scotland he observes. "It's too cool."

PART THREE
EXPLORATION, EQUIPMENT, EQUALITY AND CULTURE

A VW van, a few boards and a couple of mates – all you needed for a classic road trip in the '70s. PHOTO PETE BOUNDS

10 | Exploration

THE QUEST FOR THE PERFECT WAVE

In Joseph Conrad's semi-autobiographical Heart of Darkness, the main character, Marlow, goes on what turns out to be a terror-stricken journey through uncharted territory in Africa. Conrad, a seaman and a great traveller, said through his character Marlow, "As a boy, I always had a passion for maps. I would look for hours at maps of South America, Africa, or Australia, and lose myself in the glories of exploration. At that time, there were many blank spaces, and when I saw one that looked particularly inviting I would put my finger on it and say, 'When I grow up I will go there.'" This was written in 1899. Over a century later, those blank spaces have all been mapped. But for surfers there is another aspect of cartographic mystery – whether there are any quality waves along a certain coastline. For travelling surfers, Conrad's blank spaces equate with unridden waves, and every travelling surfer knows that there are still many jewels yet to be discovered.

While some surfers never venture beyond their home break, others are fuelled by a love for adventure and the promise of the perfect wave. Even if a long-haul surf trip results in less than utopian peelers, there is still the payoff of the travel experience – new territory, new culture, and the buzz of danger that made Conrad a sailor first and a writer second. Surfers are intrigued by the promise of the unknown, spurred on by the quintessential images of Mike Hynson and Robert August trekking over the sand dunes in *The Endless Summer* to find the 'perfect' reeling point break at Cape St Francis, South Africa.

In 1965 British surfers were presented with another challenge, pioneering big-wave surfing at Guethary in France. Alan 'Mac' McBride, Dave Friar, Richard Trewella, Terry McAlayne and David 'Moby' Patience camped at Alcyons in an abandoned villa during a huge autumn swell. "A massive set closed out the whole channel between Guethary and Alcyons," says Mac. "Terry got hit on the head and lost his board. It turned out that some anxious onlookers called the fire brigade. We suddenly noticed total pandemonium in the harbour with a fire engine racing down the hill. Terry was trying to swim in against this impossible rip. It was like a river. Moby found a rope, paddled out to Terry, and gave the signal for the fire engine to tow, but no-one had attached the rope to land!"

Travel and discovery are relative experiences. For the grommet without transport, a lift up the coast to a new spot is a true surf adventure. But what drives us all is the inquiring soul, the desire for new experiences, and the sense of anticipation. Whether a soul journey, a photo shoot, or that first trip to surf a secret spot, we are all doing the same thing – satisfying the spirit of adventure fuelled by curiosity. Even in the age of the internet, the best travel involves a critical element of

above
Jersey surfer Gordon Burgis watches a classic swell roll in at Angourie, New South Wales, in 1965.
PHOTO: BOB WEEKS.

chance and discovery.

Surf travel is also about humble acceptance of local culture.

Recall the footage of Mike Hynson and Robert August giving surf lessons to throngs of Ghanaian kids. World leaders could learn a lot from this kind of social icebreaker. No politics or false diplomacy, just the universal language of laughter.

In contrast, travelling surfers sometimes present a challenge to the cultures they visit, and this has to be handled carefully. When filmmaker Alby Falzon and surfers Rusty Miller and Steve Cooney visited Bali in 1970, they discovered that the Balinese considered swimming in the ocean a religious taboo. Uluwatu was 'the place of the living dead' to the locals, a stretch of coast populated with evil creatures and unsettled spirits. To enter the water was sacrilege. When the taboo was broken, a cultural tradition was snapped by an outside force, surfing. Falzon published amazing pictures of Uluwatu perfection in Tracks magazine, and almost overnight Indonesia became the Shangri-la for adventurous surfers.

For early British surfers, the Promised Land was France. Those who had been to the Biarritz area described a picture of perfection – crystal clear green tubes cracking close to the beach and exotic girls lying around in bikinis under huge Martini umbrellas. The southwest coast of Landes quickly became a regular sojourn for Britain's finest talents. A trip to France meant an escape from the cold water and a chance to surf with international superstars like Mickey 'Da Cat' Dora and Billy Hamilton, who could be seen surfing the famed lefthand rivermouth at La Barre in the mid to late '60s. The iconic beach break tubes, warm water, exciting waves and cheap wine still appeal to every British surfer...even if the crowds of the modern age mean there are a lot fewer waves to go around.

VIVE LA FRANCE!

above
French surfers check the possibilities at Avalanche, south of Guethary, in 1964.
PHOTO: ARNAUD DE ROSNAY.

The origins of surfing in Europe are shared between Britain and France. Their surfing seeds are similar, but in France the earliest surfers came from the upper echelons of society, while surfing in Britain had working-class roots. With Hollywood connections and aristocratic pedigree, brothers Joel and Arnaud de Rosnay became the ambassadors of French surfing in much the same way that Bill Bailey contributed to the growth of British surfing. The wealthy de Rosnays

140 | THE SURFING TRIBE

magazine in 1964 that Hollywood script writer Peter Viertel had brought surfing and the first balsa board to Biarritz in 1957, he hadn't quite told the whole story. According to research by Paul Holmes (revealed in his book *Dale Velzy Is Hawk*), the story also involves a young Californian called Richard Zanuck. He was the son of legendary Hollywood producer and studio mogul Darryl Zanuck, founder of 20th Century Fox. Richard had been a keen surfer since the early '50s, he was one of the original Californian Malibu crew, and his surfing adventures had taken him north to Santa Cruz and west to Hawaii.

"Richard Zanuck can take credit for introducing surfing to southwest France," writes Holmes. "The occasion was the filming in Northern Spain of the 1956 movie *The Sun Also Rises*; the screenplay was adapted from the Hemingway novel by Peter Viertel and the film was being produced by Darryl Zanuck. Richard was tagging along, an apprentice, fresh out of school. Screenwriter Viertel had homes in both Switzerland and Spain, but on one of his many visits to Hollywood during the pre-production phase of the picture, he remarked to Zanuck that he had seen waves just like those at Santa Monica and Malibu along the beaches of the Basque country near the film location. Zanuck needed no further prompting. When the studio loaded a charter plane with camera equipment, props and costumes, Zanuck added his surfboard."

"Peter Viertel and I drove down from Paris heading for Pamplona, and on the way down we stopped at Biarritz," says Zanuck. "It was a weekend [in September 1956] and I went out and surfed. There were a lot of people there and I was the centre of attention. They'd never seen a board before."

Viertel was well impressed by the young Californian's skill in the French waves. "After Viertel saw me surfing, he became obsessed…and surfed every day for years," says Zanuck. When filming was over, Viertel remained in Europe, living in Northern Spain with his wife, the famous actress Deborah Kerr. Zanuck left his striped black-and-white board with Viertel, who became a regular in the emergent French surfing scene. Biarritz had long been transformed from its origins as a quaint fishing village to a glitzy and glamorous resort town in the European post war tourist boom. It was no surprise that surfing took root here in the late '50s.

bought what they wanted, while working-class Bailey made what he wanted; but both had the same passion for surfing, and both were happy to share their expertise and encourage more people into the sport.

When Joel de Rosnay explained to Surfer

By 1957 Frenchmen Joel de Rosnay, Jacques Rott and George Hennebutte had joined Peter Viertel riding waves at La Cote des Basques. Within a year

opposite, top
The first ever surf trip by a British crew. This gang of eight Jersey surfers travelled down to Biarritz in 1962. Among the faces are Gordon Burgis, Peter Gould and Ian Harewood. PHOTO: PETER GOULD COLLECTION.

opposite, bottom
The scene at La Barre on a small clean day, circa 1963. PHOTO: ARNAUD DE ROSNAY.

below
From the very beginning, French surfers have always done things in style. Photo: ARNAUD DE ROSNAY.

the group had expanded to include characters like Michel Barland, Andre Plumcoq, Robert Bergeruc and the Moraiz brothers, all sharing a total pool of seven boards. Then in September 1959 the Waikiki Surf Club was formed at La Cote des Basques.

The Waikiki club became the social base of the Biarritz surfing scene. By 1961, Michel Barland and Jacques Rott were collaborating to build elementary foam-and-fibreglass surfboards, which enabled more would-be surfers to take up the sport.

In 1962 eight Jersey surfers

including Peter Gould, Gordon Burgis and Ian Harewood travelled to France, and were warmly welcomed by the Biarritz locals. The friendships they formed encouraged a return the following year. Independently Bill Bailey, Bob Head, John Campbell and Ian Tiley made the trip south from Newquay for their first experience of France in 1963. In the Channel Islands and in Cornwall the word was out: France has good waves, warm water, pretty girls and cheap wine!

In 1964 Newquay-based Aussie lifeguards Bob Head and Bill Cleary ventured to France on surfboard-customised 200cc Vespa scooters. After spending a couple of weeks of surfing La Barre, they caught the train to southern Spain, en route to Morocco. At Algeciras station they discovered to their horror that their boards were full of holes; Bob asked the station manager what had happened. The apologetic Spaniard explained that the guard on the train wanted to stop them sliding around in the luggage wagon, and thinking they were some kind of furniture he'd nailed them to the floor!

By the mid '60s the French surf scene was growing, but it wasn't as big as the scene in Britain. Rod Sumpter recalls his first trip to Biarritz: "The first time I went was with Doug Wilson and [Aussie] Dennis White in autumn 1965. It was a Bilbo promo tour, and Doug had some boards to deliver as well. I'd spent time in Jersey and in Cornwall, and I was really keen to surf La Barre. It was the classic spot. Surfing was still very new and exciting down there. It was a bit like surfing in Cornwall in the sense that only a few lifeguards did it, but it was certainly on a smaller scale in France back then. The Lartigau brothers were both good surfers, but Joel and Arnaud de Rosnay were the two really classic characters down there. They always dressed up smart and looked like film stars. They used to wind us up by taking us to expensive restaurants in Biarritz that we couldn't afford. But then they'd end up having to pay the bill because we just didn't have any money! They were great, thay really looked after us when we were down there."

Only a small number of boards were being made in France at the time, so the locals were desperate for equipment. American and British visitors could sell a board for anything up to 600 Francs. It became common for travellers to take at least one extra board to sell. Demand was high on the Basque coast and it helped fund the trip, while guaranteeing you were a welcome visitor. Contacts developed as the sport grew in each country. By 1966 Bilbo was making large orders of boards that were shipped over on cargo boats heading for Brittany. Jo Moraiz, who had opened France's first surf shop in Biarritz, would collect the deliveries and drive them south to sell in the town. Over the next two years Bilbo would build and ship hundreds of boards for the growing French market.

The prime time to visit Biarritz was after the French tourists had gone home and the first autumn swells were rolling in. An annual sojourn in September became an essential part of the hardcore British surfer's life. La Barre was the number one spot. The hollow left-hander could hold waves up to 12 feet. But it was destroyed by a jetty extension in the '70s. Initially, when the local authorities started the work, the wave improved unbelievably; but then it deteriorated in quality and stopped breaking altogether by 1973.

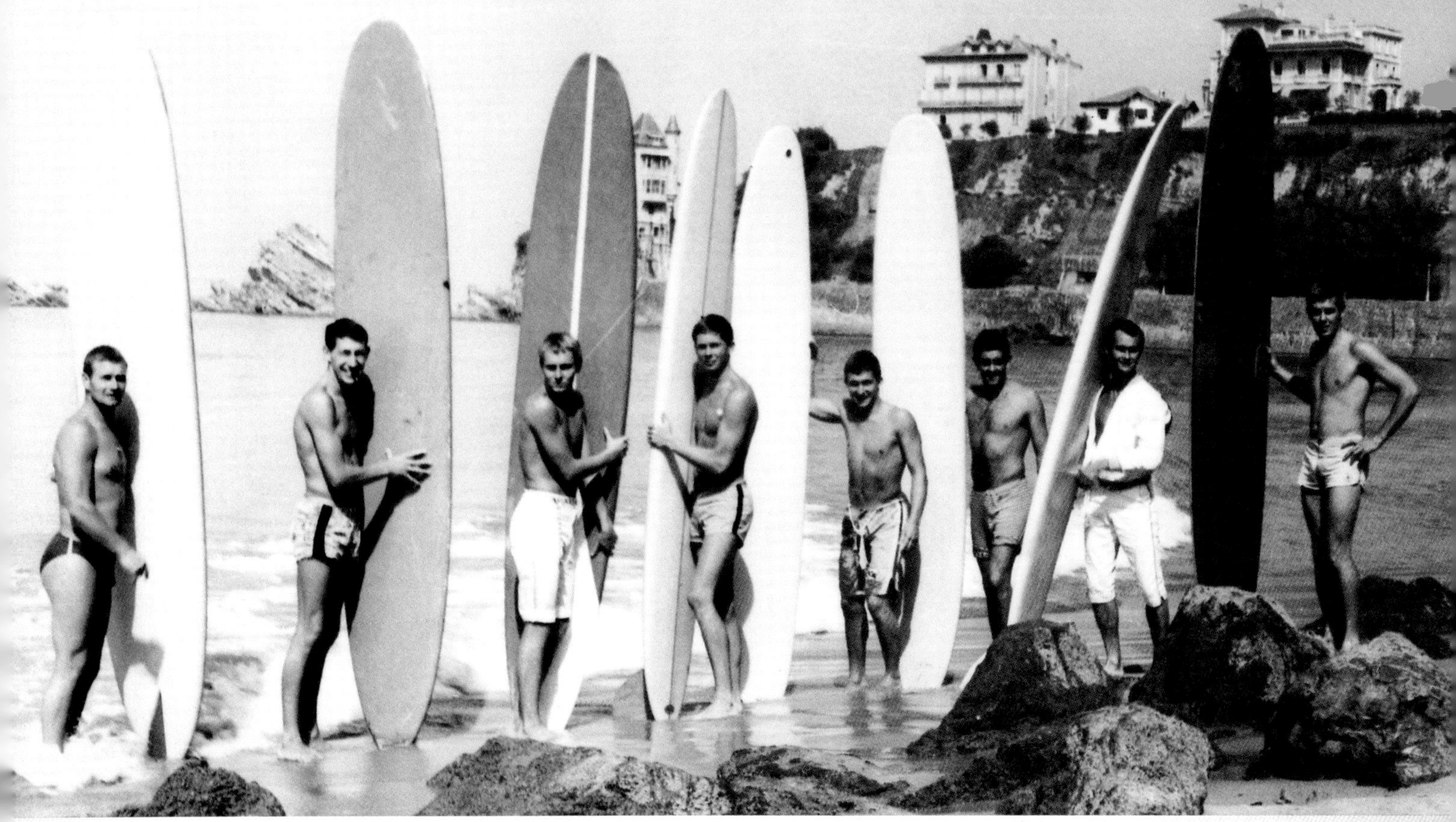

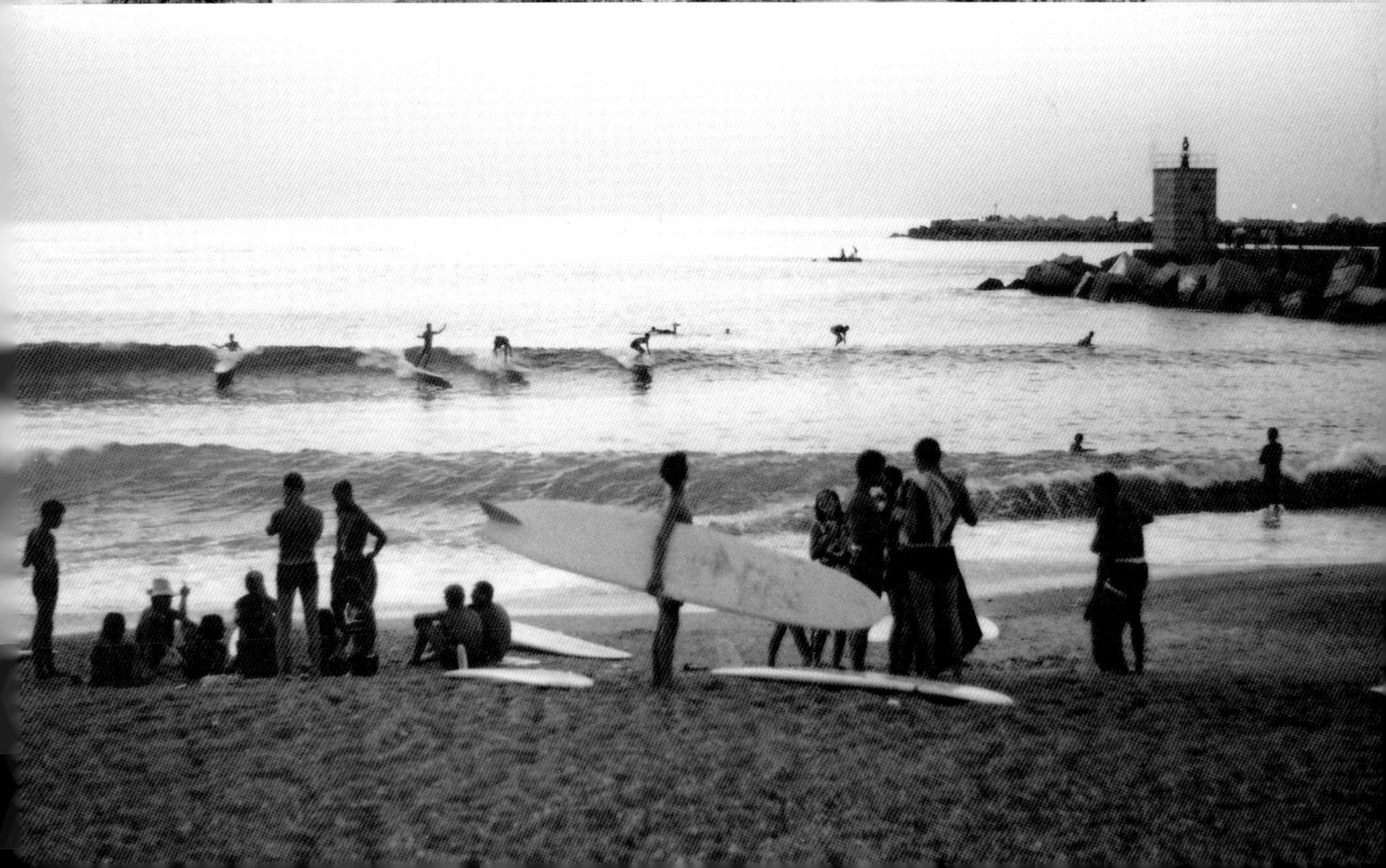

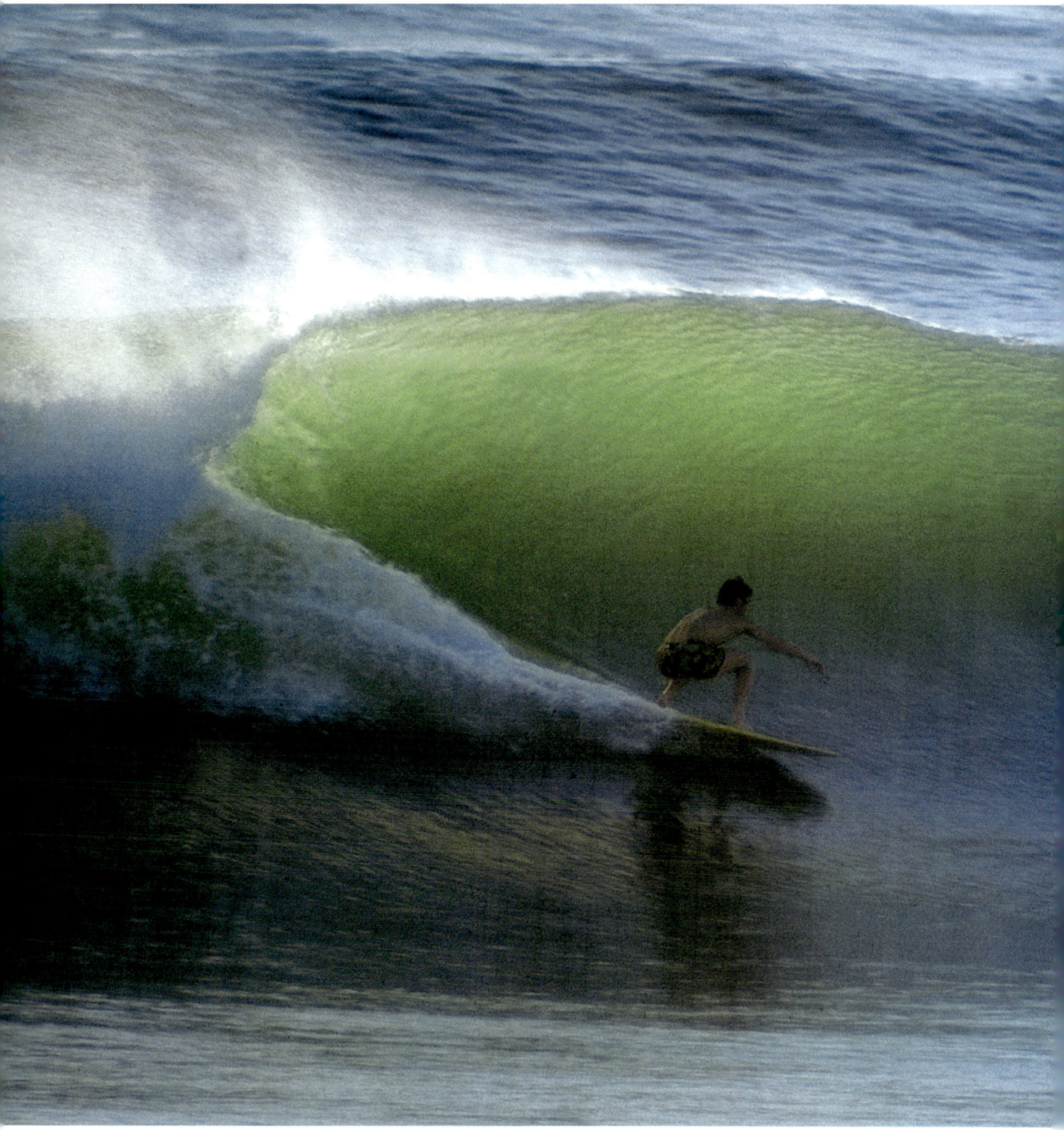

Further south, the A-frame peak at Guethary was the French big-wave break, while Lafitenia was its quality point. In the mid '70s, Hossegor began to capture the imagination, and became recognised as a world famous stretch of hollow beach break.

Occasionally French surfers would head north. Jean-Marie and Francois Lartigau (two of France's best surfers of the '60s and '70s) and the de Rosnay brothers often travelled to Jersey to compete at international events.

Teenage surfers Francois-Xavier 'Fix' Maurin and Roger Mansfield signed up to do a foreign exchange in 1967. Both were top young surfers in their respective communities, Fix later becoming a French Junior champion. They surfed together for two consecutive summers, and helped to cement a cultural link between the two surf nations.

By the end of the '60s, France and Britain had both become internationally recognised surfing nations. In 1969 the first European Surfing Championships were held in Jersey and won by local hero Gordon Burgis. A European Surfing Federation was formed with France and Britain at its core, which grew to include all the other surfing nations in Europe.

Today the heart of the European surf industry has shifted to France from its early base in Britain. And nearly half a century on, France remains a highly popular destination for British surfers.

opposite
Before it was destroyed by a groyne extension in the early '70s, La Barre was one of the best breaks in France. Here's Aussie visitor Wayne Lynch on a perfect day in '68. PHOTO: ARNAUD DE ROSNAY.

below
A band of early Brit travellers camping at Guethary. PHOTO: DOUG WILSON.

THE MAGIC OF IRELAND

Unravel Ireland's convoluted coastline and you'll find some of the finest waves in Europe.

Below moss green hills and towering cliffs lie spitting peaks and reeling points. However, Ireland's early surfing hotspots were not Easkey or Lahinch, but places like Portrush on the Causeway Coast, Rossnowlagh in County Donegal, and Tramore way down in County Waterford.

Irishman Ian Hill, a keen swimmer and water polo player, was bellyboarding at Bude in North Cornwall when he first witnessed stand-up surfing. It was October 1963. The following Easter he returned to Cornwall and bought a Bob Head malibu board for £20. Back home, Ian explored the coast from Ballycastle to Magilligan and rode quality waves at Tullan and Bundoran, alone. When he ran out of surf wax he turned to Surfer magazine, and learned that he could melt paraffin wax onto the deck of his board to get some traction.

The country's first high-profile surfer was Kevin Cavey, who affectionately became known as 'the daddy of Irish surfing'. Kevin first discovered surfing in a Reader's Digest article in 1962. It inspired him to try to ride a skimboard made by a local County Kerry farmer. This was a total failure, so Kevin built his own board out of marine plywood. But this too was flimsy and fell apart in the sea, so he could only kneel on it. His next construction was a balsa board which finally allowed him to stand up. His first successful ride was at Gyles Quay in Dundalk in May 1965.

Soon he was hooked, and thanks to an uncanny sense of balance he progressed rapidly. Keen to travel abroad, he saved up enough money to buy an airline ticket to Hawaii, and set off in early '66 to truly get his teeth into surfing. Undaunted by the power of the waves, Kevin surfed a variety of breaks on Oahu including Sunset Beach. From Hawaii he flew to California where he surfed spots like Rincon and Huntington Beach with his friend Jim Duane. While in California, Kevin met Pat McNulty who came from an Irish family and worked for Surfer magazine.

After returning home Kevin founded the Bray Island Surf Club, drumming up interest in the venture by hiring a stand at the Irish Boat Show in Dublin. Pat McNulty had given Kevin a huge poster of Greg Noll at Waimea Bay which he used as a backdrop on his stand. The poster caught the attention of another keen surfer, Roger Steadman, who had just moved to Dublin with a fibreglass board he'd bought from Cornwall. The pair joined forces and Kevin followed Roger's lead by ordering a Cornish-made Bilbo board from the European Surfing Company.

In the spring of 1966 Kevin embarked on a long surfari around Ireland with his brother Colm, Patrick Kinsella and an American Vietnam war veteran, Tom Casey. At Rossnowlagh they met Vinnie and Mary Britton, whose sons Brian, Barry, Conor and

below
Irish pioneer Kevin Cavey (far right) with Jurek Delimata, Pat Kinsella and Roger Steadman in 1967.
PHOTO: KEVIN CAVEY COLLECTION.

146 THE SURFING TRIBE

William were already keen surfers. The Brittons were to become one of the most prominent families in Irish surfing.

On his travels Kevin met another Irish pioneer, Desmond 'Bow' Vance, at Portrush on the Causeway Coast. The core group of surfers on this north-facing coast included Davy Govan, Alan Duke (who later won the Irish title four times), Martin Lloyd, Dave and James Campbell, Alistair McCartney and John Bloomer. For many of them, their surfing life involved a weekend dash to the Causeway Coast from homes in Belfast; if it was flat, they'd jump back in their cars and head for the more exposed west coast.

The unification of the disparate surfing groups resulted in the creation of the Surf Club of Ireland. It was based at Mount Herbert in Bray, to the south of Dublin, and clearly signalled that Irish surfing was an all-island affair. "Surfing in Ireland has always been a cross-border sport, like Irish rugby," explains Barry Britton. "Irish surfing competitions and teams have always included surfers from both northern and southern Ireland, and over the years our champions have come from both areas."

Kevin Cavey's international reputation resulted in an invitation to attend the 1966 World Championships in San Diego, California. There he met the enigmatic Duke Kahanamoku, as well as British-born up 'n comer Rod Sumpter. Kevin surfed out of his skin to reach the quarterfinals of the contest, while his new pal Rod went all the way to the final, finishing fifth in the world.

Back home, Kevin started to make frequent trips down to Tramore, and his infectious enthusiasm convinced many locals and lifeguards to try surfing. Meanwhile, over on the west coast, Roger Steadman was turning folks onto wave-riding in and around Lahinch. This created a demand for boards, and it wasn't long before the pioneers put two and two together and began making

above
The Peak at Bundoran, showing its class.
PHOTO: MIKE SEARLE.

below
How do you get five Irishmen in a Mini? Team Ireland at the European Championships in 1970.
PHOTO: KEVIN CAVEY COLLECTION.

147 | THE SURFING TRIBE

boards. Kevin and Roger formed the C&S Surfboard Company, with a shamrock for the logo; further north Alan Duke and Davy Govan (following Bow Vance's lead) made boards called Portrush Specials, identified by a Celtic symbol.

By the mid '60s a trickle of adventurous Brits had started to explore the Irish coast, among them Tim Heyland. But it would take many years for the average British surfer to become aware of the existence of quality surf and native surfers in Ireland.

Tigger Newling from Cornwall made his first trip to Ireland in 1967, aged 16. "I went over with my mates Nick Kavanagh and James Trout in my dad's old Land Rover," says Tigger. "The drive across Ireland took hours and we arrived at Strandhill tired and befuddled from breathing the Land Rover's exhaust fumes. But we soon perked up when we saw lines of awesome green surf curling across the bay! For the next few days the conditions were some of the best I've ever seen. On the last morning we rode glassy 10-foot waves breaking for 400 yards with perfect shape. Leaving those waves was a slightly devastating experience, but we wanted to take part in the Irish National & International Surfing Championships at Tramore, so we had to go."

When the boys arrived at Tramore they were glad to see there were waves there too, and more besides. "The contest was part of the town's annual shenanigans," continues Tigger, "there were wrestling contests, donkey derbies, banquets, brawls, music and dancing...it was brilliant, there was so much going on. We met up with Rod and David Sumpter, Chris Cannings, Johnny McElroy and Alan Rich. They'd come over from Cornwall to enter the contest and to shoot the last section of a film Alan was making. Kevin [Cavey] had also invited Des Thompson and John Baxendale from the North East West Surf Club. It was a great gathering, one of the best contests I've ever been to. Eamon Matthews eventually won the Irish event and Rod Sumpter won the International. After four amazing days of surfing and partying, we decided to move on while we still had our health! We joined the Australians, pooled our resources, and explored southwest Ireland in convoy. Alan Rich wrote an article about the trip which was later published in Surfer magazine. There was a classic photo of Nick, James and I standing by the Land Rover with our boards on top."

In 1969 Irish surfing took another leap forward with the formation of the the Irish Surfing Association, headed by Bow Vance. Representatives from the Surf Club of Ireland, the South Coast Surf Club and the North Shore Surf Club (the three largest clubs) got together to draft a constitution and set some goals. In August that year Ireland sent a five-man team (Davy Gowan, Alan Duke, Bow Vance, Eammon Matthews and Dave Kenny) to Jersey for the inaugural European Championships.

Just three years later the European Championships came to Ireland. It was the first time most European surfers had visited Ireland and expectations were high. As fate would have it, the surf at Lahinch was disappointingly small and only the Junior event was run (won by carefree Welshman Dai Halpin). But a solid swell hit at the very end of the event, rewarding those who had hung around with classic eight- to 10-foot waves at Spanish Point and other reefs in the area. The sessions would be talked about for years, and the European Championships returned to Ireland in 1985.

The regular contest gatherings provided a solid platform for rubber-limbed Hugh O'Brien-Moran to become one of Ireland's best competitors; he won the Irish Open title four times and later became a standout in the Masters division at successive European Championships. Success also followed for Grant Robinson and six times Irish champion Andy Hill, whose pioneering father Ian had settled in Portrush.

Ireland has now gained international recognition for its once secret wealth of waves. Surfers come from all over the globe to rent a cottage, sip Guinness, dodge the rain and anticipate powerful waves. Naturally the country's surfing population has grown considerably, with many new surf shops and board manufacturers popping up around the coast. Recently there has been considerable coverage of the incredible sessions in huge waves at Aileen's, a dramatic reef nestled beneath the Cliffs of Moher on the west coast. Countless pages in the British and Irish surf press have been devoted to this new big-wave movement, and many of the images are truly astonishing. Yet for most surfers, it's the emerald-coloured peelers and unique cultural flavour that make Ireland so magic.

above
Southwest Ireland has plenty of good spots, as this visiting crew discovered.
PHOTO: PETE BOUNDS.

opposite top
Brit surfers Eric Peters, Tom Watson-Bell, John Parkin and Gary Russell check out the wildlife while on an Irish surfari in '71.
PHOTO: PETE BOUNDS.

opposite bottom
Portrush surfer Andy Hill in action at The Peak, Bundoran.
PHOTO: ALEX WILLIAMS.

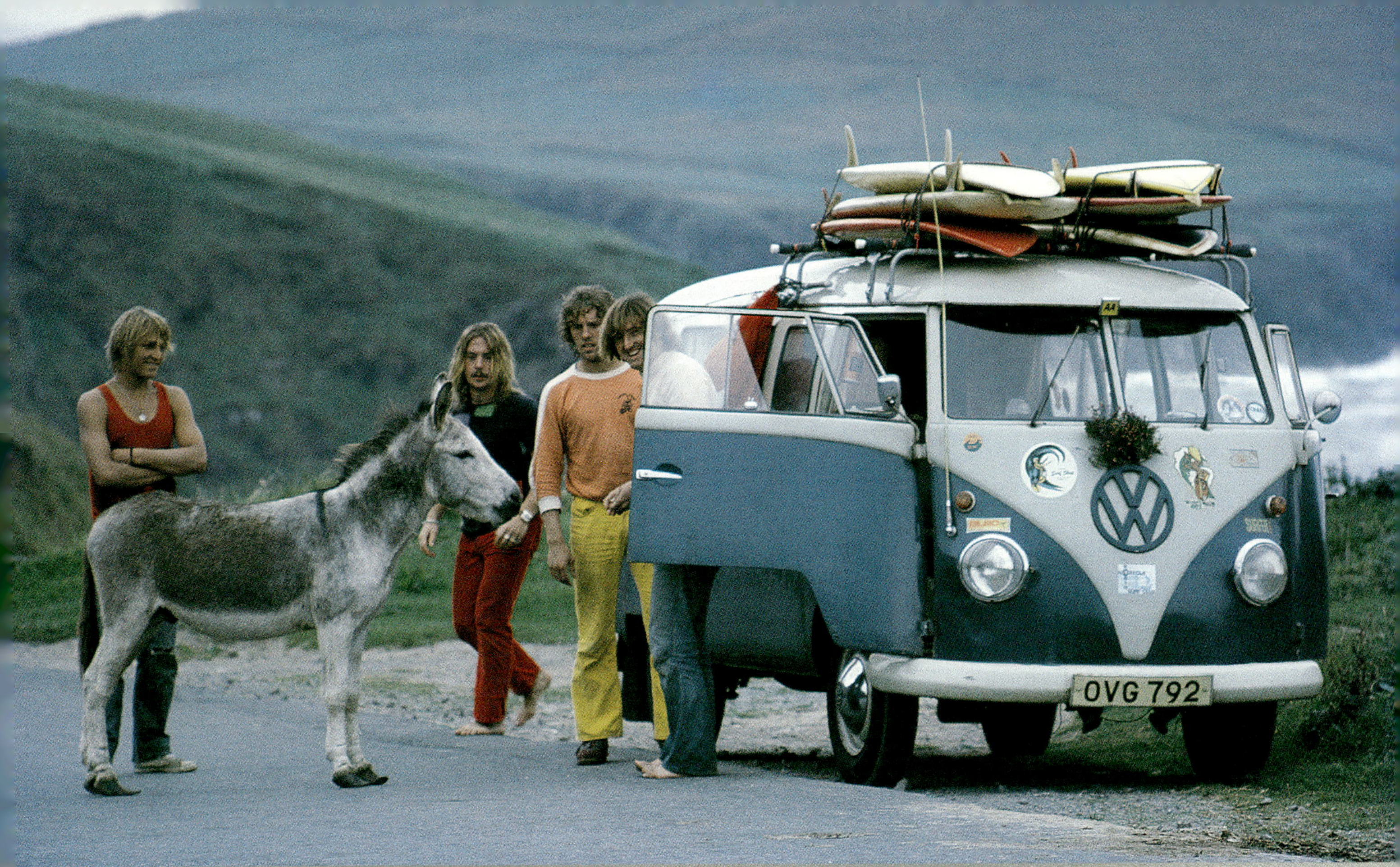
OVG 792

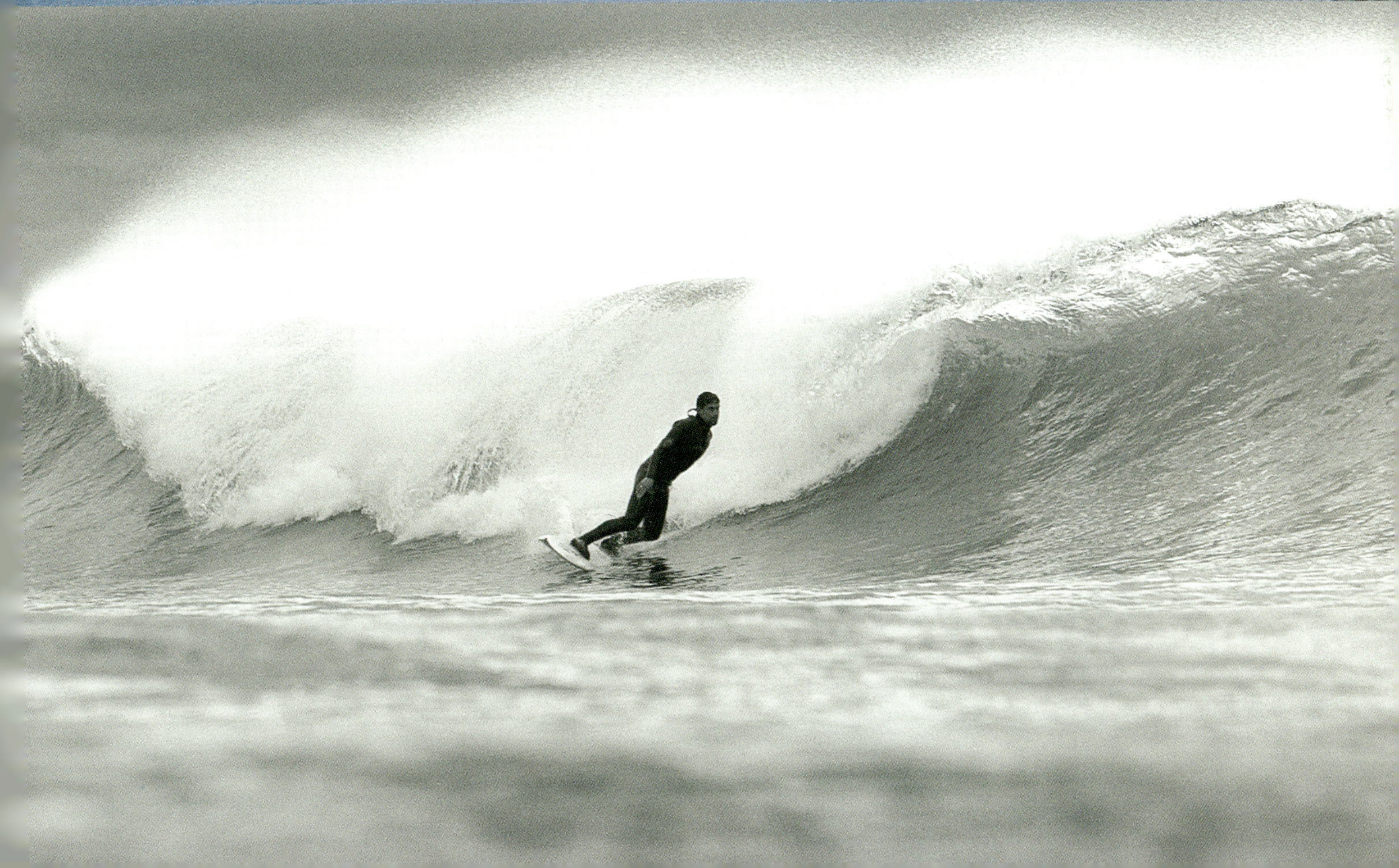

Morocco became a popular winter getaway for British surfers in the '70s. Jersey's Bobby Male hurtles down the line at Anchor Point, circa 1974. PHOTO: PETER LE BREUILLY.

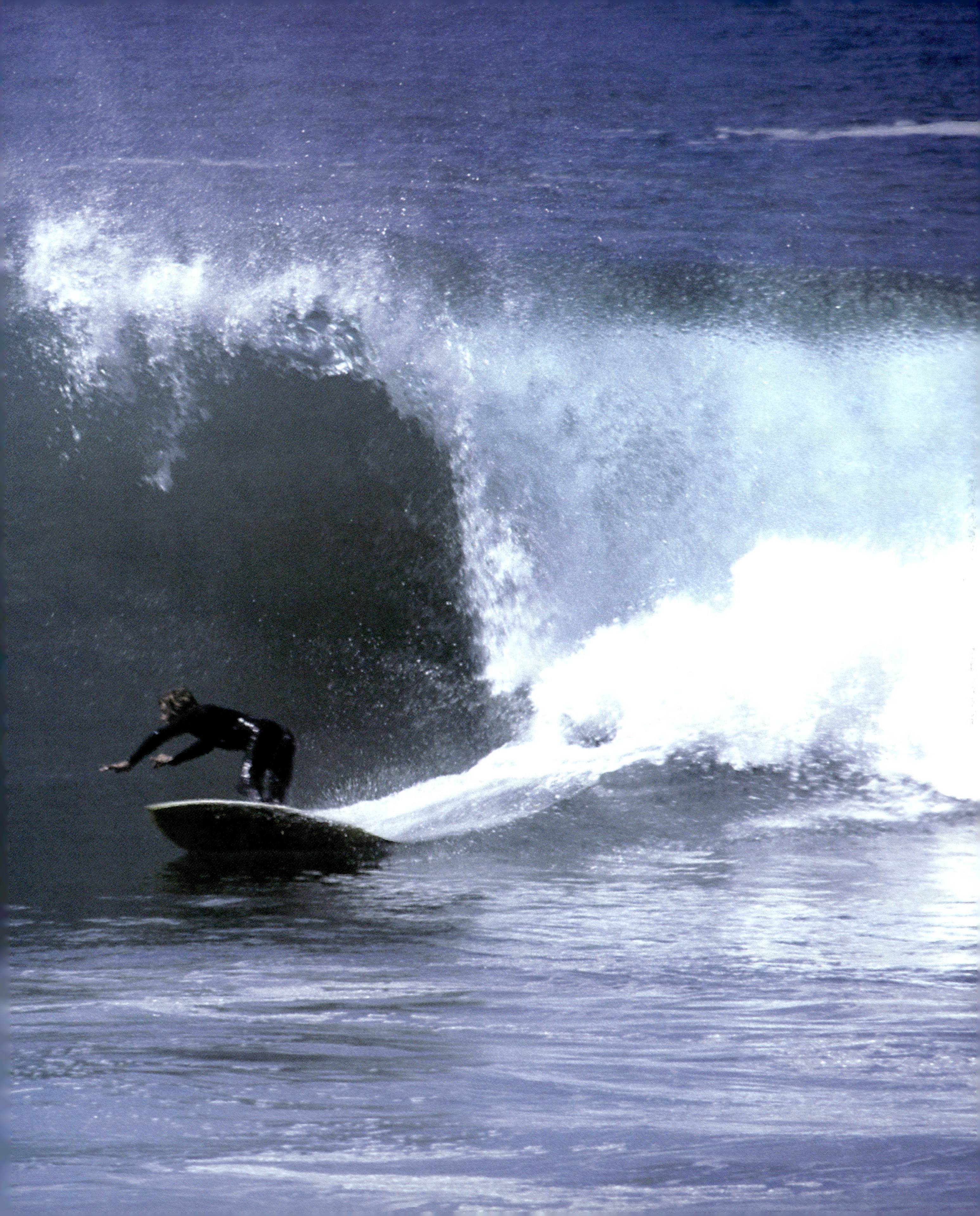

ROB WARD: UNDERGROUND EXPLORER

The story of British surfing would not be complete without reference to its underground surfers, those who passed up competition and media exposure for the chance to travel and search for perfect waves. These are the 'soul surfers' – guys like Rob Ward, who was a standout big-wave surfer and adventurer in the '70s, '80s and '90s.

Rob grew up on the Isle of Wight and became interested in surfing in the early '60s. Educated at Pangbourne Nautical College in Berkshire, he went on to become an officer in the Royal Navy. In 1964 he found himself aboard HMS Jaguar, a destroyer stationed off the coast of South Africa. When the ship docked near Cape Town, Rob took a day's leave and went to find a surf shop. "I bought a board which cost me £30, a month's wages. It was the most beautiful thing I'd ever seen."

During the next three years Rob surfed in South Africa and Central America as he travelled with the navy. After returning to Britain, he enrolled at the Royal Naval College in Dartmouth; but the lure of surfing was too strong and after a while he quit the course.

He and a friend bought a van and loaded it up with cut-price blanks from a defunct surf business in Newquay. Together they built a dozen boards in the Isle of Wight, then headed down to Guethary in France. There then followed nine months of bliss.

"Those early days surfing in France were some of the best days of my life," reckons Rob. "I grew my hair for the first time ever, and surfed every day it was possible. I camped in a tent in the Cenitz valley, then later stayed in a villa with Alan McBride from Newquay. I was just totally focused on riding big waves at Guethary."

Rob paid his way by building boards at a small workshop on the outskirts of Bayonne. As his surfing improved he entered a few competitions. He even won an international paddle race, beating the course record – set by 1965 World Champion Felipe Pomar – by five minutes.

However Rob soon realised that travel, not competition, was his calling. In subsequent years he travelled extensively in California, South Africa and Australia. He often chose relatively obscure big-wave destinations, such as Outer Kommetjie in Cape Town, Margaret River in Western Australia, and Cactus in South Australia. With no lifeguards and few other surfers around, some sessions were a true test of his nerve. "One time I remember going for a surf at a desert spot in South Australia. The waves were extraordinary, but no-one was surfing because a large shark had supposedly been sighted. I spent an hour alone in the lineup, filled with both fear and elation. When I came in, I actually fell on my knees and thanked God for my existence."

Rob had an innovative attitude towards surfboard design at this time. He had a long relationship with experimental shaper Tom Hoye of Precision Equipe in California who would ship Rob the latest, sometimes

below
Rob aboard his surf charter boat Orinoco Flo. PHOTO: ROB WARD COLLECTION.

quirky, designs to ride wherever he was in the world.

In the '80s Rob set up base in Cornwall and ran a surf shop in Newquay called Ocean Imports. During this period, a friend persuaded him to buy a yacht with him and make some trips to Morocco, smuggling hash. It seemed an easy way to make money...but inevitably Rob was caught, and the penalty was harsh. "Of the six-year prison sentence, I served four years. I had no excuses. I didn't feel sorry for myself. Being imprisoned was awful, but I was grateful for the opportunity to take an English course via the Open University."

Upon his release, Rob turned his hand to boat building. One of his projects was a 40-foot catamaran, Orinoco Flo. When it was finished he operated it as a surf charter boat in the Canaries, before setting off on his next adventure – a surfing circumnavigation of the world. This epic two-year voyage, financed by surfers who travelled on various legs of the trip, included a pioneering visit to Easter Island.

During the trip Rob met his second wife. They now live in Queensland, where Rob is still involved in boat building and where he still surfs with blistering form.

Rob Ward's surfing achievements have been inspirational and he would have been better known, but for his lack of interest in surf contests. "I'm 60 now, and looking back at the 40-odd years I've dedicated to surfing, I suppose I should harbour some regrets. I abandoned a good career in the navy...I slept in the back of a van for months in Mexico and California, and under the stairs of a villa in France...and I served a jail term as an indirect result of my barren economic circumstances. But actually, no, I don't have regrets. [American writer] Joseph Campbell once said, 'Fortunate is the one who finds his bliss.' It's an odd phrase but that's what surfing has been for me. And I feel fortunate indeed."

above
Travelling and charging solid waves have always been two of Rob Ward's biggest passions. Here's Rob in action at Jeffrey's Bay in South Africa in the mid '70s. PHOTO: UNKNOWN/ ROB WARD COLLECTION.

11 | Girls in the curl

JUMPING THE GENDER GAP

below
Sarah Newling, Tigger's sister, collects a trophy from BSA Chairman Reg Prytherch at the '69 British Championships at Watergate Bay.
PHOTO: DOUG WILSON.

Women have always surfed. In ancient Hawaii they shared the sport equally with men. When Duke Kahanamoku introduced stand-up surfing to Australia in 1915, local Isobel Latham rode tandem with Duke, and she became Australia's first surfer when she rode a few solo waves on his board.

Nearly 50 years later, when Australian Tanya Binning paddled out in a bikini at Great Western in Newquay in 1964, she raised a few eyebrows by surfing the three-foot summer waves better than many of the guys who were out.

Roger Mansfield recalls a similar double-take while in Australia with the British team for the 1970 World Championships. "We arrived at Bells Beach after a long drive from Sydney in our stationwagon. It was approaching dusk. It seemed like a long paddle out and we stopped short of the far point to ride the six-foot walls breaking in the middle section. The surf felt challenging – it had far more power than Manly, where we'd done most of our surfing since arriving. There weren't many other surfers out, just a handful further up the point. One was really good: reed-thin and swooping into waves with a beautiful, graceful style. I wondered who it could be, as I knew I was about to meet many of my international surf heroes, the men I idolised! In the fading light I was waiting to pick off my last ride, when the mystery surfer raced past, turning with speed and poise. It was a girl! I later found out it was Margo Godfrey [later Oberg] from the USA, who was destined to become the women's world champion four times. I never treated women in the waves with any double standard from that day on."

In truth, during the '60s and '70s a testosterone-flavoured atmosphere surrounded British surfing. It was effectively a male dominated pastime. The music of the era inadvertently reinforced this. In their famous song 'Surf City' Jan & Dean told us there were, "Two girls for every boy." The doctrine of the day was that girls were there to decorate the beach, while men rode the waves. Fashion also played its part. The bikini presented women in a new sexually enticing way, as seductresses. The bikini was in fact named after Bikini Atoll, the location where the hydrogen bomb was tested in the South Pacific. It suggested the swimwear's explosive potential. Women were certainly central to British beach culture, and their very image – riding bellyboards in resorts like Newquay and Woolacombe – had been used to sell the holiday dream since the 1930s.

It wasn't long before we had our own 'wahinis' (the Hawaiian term for 'women who surf'). By the mid '60s, Newquay girls Jill Costa, Annette Hughes, Maureen Burnett and Janice Pearce were keen surfers. Annette was petite and agile and caught the attention of Rod Sumpter, who was looking for a tandem surfing partner. He wanted to expand his profile as the nation's top surfer by showing his versatility. They became a skilled act, riding towards the beach on a single board, performing a sort of surfing ballet, sometimes in specially organised public displays at Watergate Bay. A number of years later they both competed at the 1968 World Championships in Puerto Rico in the Tandem event. They made the final and finished fourth. Rod's relationship with another Newquay girl, Simonne Renvoize, would also play an important role in the growth of British surf culture, notably surf films and magazines.

In the late '60s, the Bilbo factory in Newquay employed the first woman in the British surfboard industry. Rose Holmes, Bill Bailey's sister-in-law, became responsible for the company's revolutionary moulded board production. Aimed at the general public, this design was a cheaper starter surfboard for the novice. It was rapidly nicknamed 'the popout' by the surfing establishment and considered too crude and un-personalised for advanced surfers. In Newquay Rose became known as 'the Popout Queen'.

In the waves it was Cornish girl Gwynedd Haslock who became the first top female British surfer. The graceful naturalfooter broke down the gender barriers, which culminated in the BSA adding a Women's division to the British Championships in 1969. Gwynedd learned to surf in the mid-'60s. Her family

above
Cornish girl Gwynedd Haslock won five British Women's titles in the late '60s and early '70s. PHOTO: UNKNOWN/GWYNEDD HASLOCK COLLECTION.

above
Arlene Maltman, warming up for the 1982 World Championships in Australia. PHOTO: PETE BOUNDS.

lived in Truro but they spent warm summer days at their beach hut on Tolcarne in Newquay, where they went swimming and bellyboarding.

In 1966 Trevor Roberts, the Tolcarne lifeguard, promised to teach Gwynedd to surf if she could carry a 10-foot board down to the water unassisted. The athletic 21-year-old found it no problem. Roberts and his American colleague, Jack Lydgate, supported her efforts and raised her confidence as a lone surfer girl. With Bob Head and Rod Sumpter as further inspiration, Gwynedd progressed quickly, and became an early British surfing heroine. "In those early years I didn't see any other female surfers in the water, but the guys were all so helpful. They gave me advice and showed me respect," says Gwynedd. "Trevor Roberts was great and gave me lots of support."

Buying your first surfboard is a proud moment for any rider. Gwynedd's was a 9'0" foot Bilbo, which was short for the time because most men were riding 10-foot-plus boards. "It was just right for me – very functional because it was shorter than the guy's boards and narrow enough to fit under my arm. I liked it so much that I rode it for the next 20 years."

Late in the summer of '66 Gwynedd entered her first competition, the surfing event at the SLSA National Championships at Fistral Beach. She made the second round in an all-male contest. Gwynedd had made her point, and as more female surfers took up the sport, surf contests started to include a Women's division. Gwynedd was the first British Women's Champion in 1969. "It was great to have a contest just for women. In the early days there were only about six of us who would turn up to compete. Finding transport wasn't always easy, as not many women had their own cars. I think there were others who would have competed if they could get there. I remember when Linda Sharp appeared on the contest scene in the '70s. She travelled alone from Wales to Newquay by train, and then walked from the town centre with her surfboard all the way up the coast to Watergate Bay. With that sort of determination it's no wonder she did so well!"

Stylish goofyfooter Sarah Newling was the eldest of in the Newling girls (along with Rachel and Alison), and lived in Treyarnon Bay on the north coast of Cornwall. Sarah had started surfing in 1967, influenced by her elder brother Tigger, who by the late '60s was one of Britain's top surfers. The family home was frequently in the press or on TV, as the media latched onto them as Britain's archetypal surfing family. Sarah won the British Women's title in 1971; she would probably have gone on to win more, but after marrying Australian surfboard-builder Mickey McCohen the couple left Britain to continue their surfing lives Down Under.

Although Newquay girl Simonne Renvoize did not surf, she had a long affair with surfing and the ocean, and her networking skills brought many disparate talents together. Following her break-up with Rod Sumpter, she went out with and later married Paul Holmes. Together with Fuz Bleakley the three published Surf Insight magazine in the early '70s, and ran a company showing surf films, Aqua Gem Surf Flicks. Her greatest coup was to persuade Aussie legend George Greenough to let Aqua Gem show his films *Crystal Voyager* and *The Innermost Limits of Pure Fun* in Britain's capital. They took Greenough's brilliance to the Electric Cinema in Portobello Road in London, where they screened the films to packed audiences. Greenough himself had persuaded psychedelic rock band Pink Floyd to allow the use of their music for the in-the-tube sequences of *Innermost Limits*. It was a sensation. The groundbreaking cameraman had strapped a camera to his back and shot the first genuine in-the-tube footage, with Floyd's 'Echoes' providing the perfect backdrop. Simonne managed to get it all happening at the London epicentre of the swinging '60s revolution.

On the contest scene, Gwynedd Haslock stuck to her trusty nine-foot Bilbo and reigned supreme as national champion into the '70s, racking up five British titles. She usually competed with the likes of Jill Jennings from Somerset, Lynn Daniel from Devon and Judy Heyworth from St Agnes. By this time a younger crew of girls were getting into the sport, riding shorter and more manoeuvrable boards.

Linda Sharp became the new shortboard dynamo. She was a young swimming champion from Wales, and brought a new aggression and athleticism to surfing during the mid '70s. Linda went on to win 10 British titles, with a flair and power not previously seen in British women's surfing. This impressive performance, plus her success internationally, made her the prominent role model for British girls during a critical period of national growth in the sport. 'If she can do that, then so can I,' thought the likes of Eden Burberry, Shelly Matthews, Jill Moss and Arlene Maltman. Jill became British Champion in '78 and '80, and Arlene in '84.

The outstanding performer of the '80s, however, was Eden Burberry from Newquay. Eden was a keen swimmer and something of a tomboy. She was encouraged by Linda's confident stance as an internationally recognised surfer, and received some valuable coaching from her. But Eden spent most of her time hanging out with Newquay's top male surfers, and she always tried to push her surfing to their level. She went on to claim five British Women's titles, and she also won the European Championships in Portugal, the same year that Russell Winter won Juniors. It made the duo superstars in Newquay. Eden was eventually drawn to the more powerful, warmer waves in Lanzarote, where she still lives. Importantly, she set the standard for a new guard of European female professional surfers who followed in her footsteps.

below left
Linda Sharp mastered all kinds of surfboards during her long and impressive career. Here she is in 1969 at Port Eynan on The Gower on a 9'0" pintail.
PHOTO: MARK SHARP.

below right
Five-time British Women's champ Eden Burberry.
PHOTO: CHRIS POWER.

LINDA SHARP: WELSH WONDERWOMAN

Linda Sharp grew up in the shadow of the Port Talbot industrial complex in South Wales and her local break was one of the most polluted in the country. But the mucky water didn't deter her and she went on to dominate British women's surfing for the next two decades.

The Sharp family home on the Sandfield estate in Aberavon was close to the beach, but children were discouraged from swimming there due to the pollution from the nearby British Steel works and a petrochemical refinery. Instead, Linda learned to swim at the town's brand new 50-metre lido, and it quickly became her favourite pastime.

In 1968 Linda joined the Lifeguard Club in Aberavon and gained access to the club's collection of boards. Encouraged by her friends, she tried surfing and stood up first time. As she had no fear of the water she soon became totally committed to surfing. She sold her bicycle to buy her first surfboard; it cost her £13 from Lindsay Morgan's surf shop in Porthcawl.

Under the right conditions, the bowling peak off Aberavon's breakwater is undoubtedly one of Wales' best waves. Linda was the only girl who ventured out the back on solid days, trading waves with the 20 or 30 guys who made up the lively local crew at the time.

In 1971 Linda and two other girls lobbied the Welsh Surfing Federation to include a Women's division at the Welsh Championships. They agreed, and Linda won it. Having achieved instant success, Linda then took a three-year break from competition while she attended college in Kent, where she studied Physical Education. She surfed the local spots like Joss Bay but missed the power of her home coast. As soon as she completed the course she headed straight back to Wales and returned to surfing with a competitive zeal not previously witnessed in the women's ranks.

In 1975 Linda not only won the Welsh Women's title again, but she also defeated Cornwall's Gwynedd Haslock to become British Women's Champion.

In the same year she travelled to southwest France for the European Championships, armed with her trusty 7'4" Tiki single-fin. Linda saw foreign competitions as a much greater challenge than domestic events. "In truth, at the start, there were only a few good female surfers in home waters and the competition wasn't that demanding, so I was ambitious to compete abroad. I was always very competitive by nature and embraced the challenge." In perfect six-foot waves at Seignosse, she beat the best girls on the continent to scoop the European Women's title. It was the first time a British woman had 'done the triple'.

The following year, as the reigning European Champion, Linda was invited to the Hang Ten Women's International Pro at Malibu in California. There she witnessed some inspiring performances, especially from the eventual winner, stylish Hawaiian surfer Lynn Boyer. Linda also encountered a hard-headed professional attitude among the competitors. She watched, listened and learned.

At the 1980 World Championships in Biarritz, Linda was more focused than ever and styled all the way to the final, where she finished in fifth place. Not since Rod Sumpter's fifth place in 1966 in California had a British team member reached a World Championships final. But despite the possibility of turning professional, Linda kept her focus on teaching as a career.

With age came responsibilities, and Linda worked tirelessly as Secretary of the Welsh Surfing Federation through the '80s and much of the '90s. She coached junior surfers and played a huge role in the running of the WSF as well as serving on the Executive Committee of the BSA.

Over a 20-year competitive career her achievements were remarkable. She won the European Women's title twice, the British Women's title 10 times, and the Welsh Women's title a staggering 19 times.

In the late '90s Linda finally hung up her contest vest and reluctantly handed over the reins of the WSF. Today she still lives in her beloved Porthcawl with her husband Huw 'Herbie' John and daughter Angharad – a complete surfing family. Without Linda, British surfing would not be where it is today. She is the most successful and influential British female surfer of all time. "Linda's pure determination to win and her refusal to be intimidated in any sized surf was always amazing," says top Welsh shortboarder Mark Vaughan. "She is an inspiration to us all."

above
Single-fins, twins, thrusters...Linda always quickly adapted to best board design of the era.
PHOTO: LINDA SHARP COLLECTION

opposite
Linda in action at her home break of Aberavon in the early '80s. PHOTO: PETE BOUNDS.

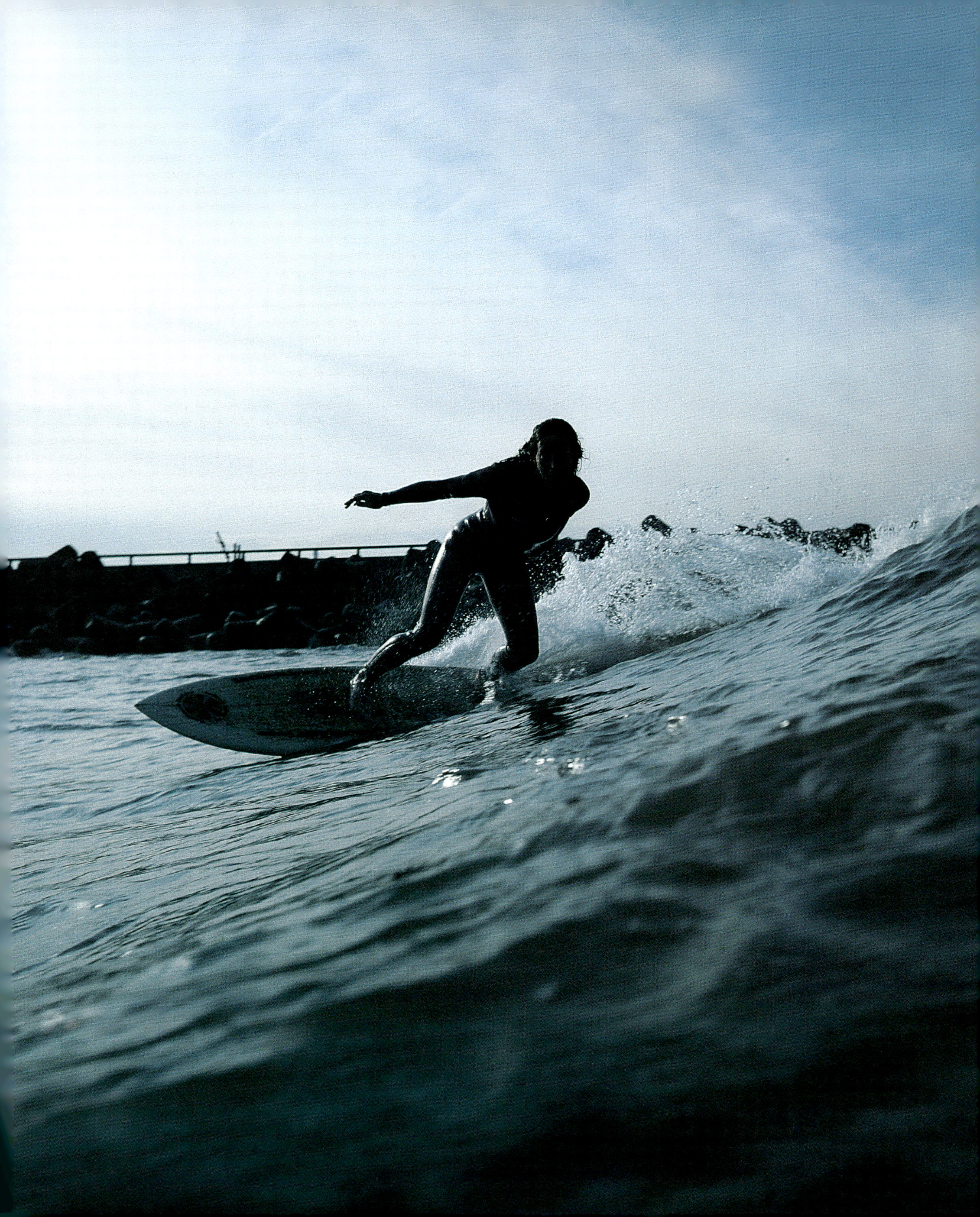

12 | Boards for Brits

THE SHAPER: FEELING THE FOAM

A snow of sanding dust, feet covered in foam shavings, the pungency of polyester resin — that precious moment when your first board was born. In the beginning the board had totemic significance. Size, shape and label could be used to identify your tribe. But getting your hands on one was not easy. The difficulty and expense involved in importing a surfboard from California or Australia, even if you knew who to contact, pushed many individuals to attempt to make their own…if they could get their hands on the raw materials. Some were crude, some were outright failures but others were fine waveriding vehicles capable of gliding across the face.

Before surfing was popularised, the skills of the board builder were with wood. The early Hawaiians carved alaia and olo boards from beautiful redwood trees. Likewise the 14-foot boards that Jimmy Dix and Pip Staffieri rode were wooden Tom Blake inspired 'Cigar Box' shapes. This 1929 design had square rails, a flat bottom and was hollow, making the boards considerably lighter (averaging 45 lbs) than the Hawaiian planks that went before them. This design lasted for an incredible 30 years.

Although still finless, another breakthrough in board design was the 'Hot Curl' redwood board, created in 1937 at Waikiki. These opened the door to riding more demanding waves and to trimming tighter in the pocket. Crucially, they allowed improvisation, as surfers could play with weight distribution. In a search for speed, innovative Hawaiian surfers like Rabbit Kekai moved to the front of the board, producing downward force to go faster. At Queen's Beach Rabbit would fade right, stall, swing left, move up to the nose and shoot the curl on a high line in a soul arch. Turning and using the nose was born. And since the board was all wood, if the design didn't work, the surfer/shaper could simply go ashore, alter the outline, and paddle back out to see if it was effective.

In the 1950s technology from the aerospace industry in California encouraged the use of fibreglass and polyester resins to make lighter, stronger surfboards. Bob Simmons, Joe Quigg and Matt Kivlin were the first to coat balsa wood in fibreglass and resin and add a fin. They created the ground breaking 'malibu board', named after its testing ground. The foam core arrived in 1956, further enhancing the performance. The new boards were lively and responsive. Weighing about 22 lbs and, with Dale Velzy's 'pig' shape, they allowed the hot dog style of surfing, centred on turning, walking, speed and control. Mix in Hollywood, and Californian beach culture skyrocketed. By the late '50s in America, "Hang ten" was the sport's favourite phrase, and the cobble point at Malibu was the crucible of noseriding, then the ultimate goal in surfing.

In Britain an embryonic garage surfboard industry had evolved by the mid '60s. Every board built was quickly bought by a new audience of aspiring British surfers, hungry to ride the waves. This production enabled surfing to grow from a small cult activity to a nationwide sport. The trio of Bill Bailey, Bob Head and Freddy Bickers in Newquay, Charles Williams in St Ives, Bob Groves in Bournemouth, and the Reece brothers in Wales all had loyal regional followings. They were the most important members of the early surfing tribe. Getting a surfboard involved face-to-face business with the artisan, who could supply a wealth of information on how and where to use it.

Hand-sculpted boards have always given surfing a unique edge in the world of sport. In the '60s a shaper's workplace was the second-most frequented point of social contact after the beach. And surfboard builders have primarily stuck with the same materials they began working with in the '60s, quite simply because they were the best available, easiest to shape and most suited to performance.

1937
Tom Blake
14'2" hollow wooden 'cigar box' surfboard
Builder:
Tom Blake (in Hawaii)

1965
Bilbo Surfboards
10'0" single fin
Shaper:
Bill Bailey

1966
Bilbo Surfboards
9'6" single fin
Shaper:
Bill Bailey

1968
'Bilbo Baggins'
8'0" vee-bottom single fin
Shaper:
unknown

1969
Bilbo Surfboards
7'7" single fin
Shaper:
Chris Jones

161 | THE SURFING TRIBE

BILBO SURFBOARDS: THE MOTHER OF INVENTION

The moment that Bilbo was created in February 1965 it dominated the British surfboard industry. The parent European Surfing Company was formed by Bill Bailey, Bob Head, Doug Wilson and Freddie Blight, and Bilbo surfboards quickly employed and trained a team of Newquay locals to work at the factory. Chris Jones, Ian 'Porky' Morcom, Andy Pickles, Brian Schofield and Alan McBride were taught to blow foam, to shape, to laminate, to sand and to make skegs. Then when Doug Wilson opened the Bilbo shop on the station forecourt in Newquay, it marked the first large-scale dedicated surf store in the country.

The factory at Pargolla Road grew to become arguably the finest surfboard factory in Europe. They churned out beautiful surfboards and sold them for £25 each. In 1967 Bilbo employed 40 people and produced around 70 boards per week in the high season. By then new shapers had joined the team, including Peter 'Mooney' McAllum and Paul Holmes. In 1968 Bilbo sent top team rider and competitor Dave Friar to open a shop in Mumbles, Swansea, to feed the hungry Welsh surf market. By 1970 an estimated 12,000 boards had been built at Bilbo, which not only fuelled the home market, but the earliest equipment needs of both France and Ireland.

Bilbo was about open communication and constant innovation and welcomed visiting surfers such as Keith Paull, Bob Cooper and many lesser-known surfers – who passed on their knowledge to the local workforce. When Mick Jackman joined the Bilbo shaping team his innovative designs were totally embraced. The squat and likeable Australian was a hot surfer, who already had experience as a Newquay lifeguard and surf shop owner. Mick pioneered woodblock tails and noses. Rod Sumpter also had a big role. Rod recalls: "When I first arrived I looked at the boards they were doing and showed them some of the things I'd learned while I'd been in California working at Hobie surfboards. I made the model with the Union Jack to go to the World's in 1966. It was such a success that we made loads of them. Bill Bailey's foam was so hard it was actually really easy to finish. But the problem was you had patches of different densities, so no matter how good a shaper you were, you'd always have a few lumps and bumps. But with the heavy fibreglass, the weight of a board was about 30 pounds, so they lasted a long time."

Ultra-talented Australian surfer Pete Russell was working in London when Bilbo formed. "I had a drab and depressing dishwashing job at a factory at Woodford, saving money after travelling around Europe. My salvation came in about March 1966 when an old surfing pal from Sydney sent me an article from The Australian Women's Weekly about surfing in Cornwall, featuring Bob Head of Bilbo. Looking for any escape from the dreary hole I was in, I got the number and rang the factory in Newquay. I drove down at Easter for an interview with Bill and got a job as sander. I lived with my girlfriend in a caravan at St Columb Minor and was quickly accepted into the small and friendly surfing group. Of course the cold water and massive tides were a bit of a shock, but the nightlife at the Sailors Arms, Pentire Hotel and Tall Trees made up for it. After falling out with my girlfriend I moved into the back of an old Bedford van parked in the grounds of the Bilbo factory on Pargolla Road where Dave Friar also lived in a caravan. It was certainly close to the job and to any news that the surf was happening. I spent that first season hanging out with John Conway, Trevor Roberts and a few other locals. At the factory Bill was like a father to all of us."

Chris 'CJ' Jones was the best young surfer in Newquay in the mid '60s, but aged 15 he made a career choice to set off for Romford in Kent to become

below
The original Bilbo Surfboards factory on Pargolla Road in Newquay, in 1965. The TV crew in the photo were filming a news piece about the company.
PHOTO: DOUG WILSON.

an apprentice engineer for Ford. Trouble was, every day he passed a huge billboard showing a surfer riding a wave, advertising Australian fruit. It only took five months of city life for CJ to abandon that career and return to Cornwall. Bill Bailey rewarded his frustrated ambition to build things with a job at Bilbo. Chris was mentored by Bill in the shaping bay, and by 1967 was creating eight boards a day. This is the limit of human shaping capacity and as demanding a situation as any production-shaper anywhere in the surfing world. As a top performer in the surf, surfers trusted CJ's opinion. This sort of attention helped to establish his reputation as the best known and one of the most respected shapers in the country, especially when he started producing his own innovative shorter boards.

There were very few exciting employment opportunities at the time in Cornwall, so for many British surfers, a job at the factory or the shop, or a place in the competition team, was a springboard to a career in surfing. Bilbo sold the earliest Gul wetsuits, as well as Big Gun surfwear and Bilbo skateboards. Many of the techniques pioneered at the factory were passed on to the general surfing community as it grew, enabling other similar manufacturing ventures to start up in different parts of the country. Put simply, Bilbo was the single most influential force in the development of the early British surfing industry.

The Bilbo shops followed in the mould of Southern Californian surf shops, becoming a magnet and hang out for the good, the bad and the ugly. "The Bilbo shop was a micro culture," says Fuz Bleakley, who worked there over four consecutive summers. "It provided a focal point for the Newquay scene. Cool cats like Newquay newcomers Colin 'The Chat' Paull, Martin Geary and Vince Ward would either hang out or work at the shop. There was always a big turnover of ideas and good music being played. We were the first place to play bands like The Grateful Dead, Jefferson Airplane and Love. The counterculture was happening right at the counter."

above
Aussie lifeguard turned shaper Bob Head in his workshop, 1964.
PHOTO: DOUG WILSON.

MATTERS OF SIZE: THE SHORTBOARD REVOLUTION

Culturally, the late '60s was a time of progress as society moulded a belief in personal freedom with an insatiable desire for change. The 'counter culture' was at its zenith and lifestyles were pushed into experimental places, minds often fuelled by psychedelic drugs or spiritual practices like yoga and meditation. It was a period when surfing styles and surfboard design changed radically. While minds expanded, boards contracted. It was a period of casting off the shackles, later labelled 'the Shortboard Revolution'.

In 1967 a dynamic new movement began in Australia called 'Chasing the curl'. It was an intense direction change from cruising on 10-foot logs that experimented with the power of the wave as a means of self-expression. George Greenough (widely considered to be the design guru of the shortboard era) inspired a handful of hot young Aussies, including Nat Young, to build nine- to eight-foot vee-bottom boards. Greenough's kneeboard hulls provided the blueprint, and he showcased on his knees what could be done standing up. The new boards were 2-1/2" thick and 22" wide with deep, flexy single fins. Their turning ability allowed both tight direction changes and carving arcs. 'Involvement surfing' was born in Australia: a progressive drive to ride the critical pocket area of the wave.

The first distinct design to emerge from this creative nucleus was Bob Mctavish's vee-bottom malibu. This was essentially a shorter malibu with a deep vee-shaped bottom, a wide tail and a narrow, flexible Greenough fin. In the winter of '67/68, Nat Young, Bob McTavish, George Greenough, Ted Spencer, Russell Hughes and Keith Paull showed up in Hawaii with these boards and an aggressive style of riding, quite different from the fluid 'rubbery' surfing personified by Hawaiians like Gerry Lopez and Reno Abellira. They inspired a surfboard size change literally overnight. Dick Brewer built Lopez an 8'6" as soon as he saw the Australian vee-bottoms, and Brewer's mini-gun, based on the hydrodynamic principles of the waterski, became the prime big-wave tool for a handful of elite Hawaiian surfers.

Paul Holmes (who would later become editor of Surfer magazine) was working at the Bilbo Surf Shop in Newquay in 1968. "We knew what the Aussies had been doing in Hawaii that winter with their eight-foot vee-bottoms thanks to Paul Witzig's new flick *The Hot Generation*, which Rod Sumpter and Simonne Renvoize were showing throughout Britain," says Paul. The inspiring footage of Bob McTavish and Nat Young at Honolua Bay in Maui made it clear that these boards were the future. "Everyone was a-buzz about the new concept, but nobody had any real idea what the actual designs might look like," says Paul.

Paul recalls the day the revolutionary new boards made their first appearance in Newquay. "Late one afternoon in mid June 1968, a camper van pulled up outside the shop with a bunch of the weirdest looking boards we'd ever seen on the roof. We knew at once this was it." It turned out to be Ant van de Heuvel and a group of South Africans, who were travelling through Europe, working as private lifeguards. "They assured us their boards were exact copies of what the Aussies were riding. Brian Schofield, the Bilbo factory manager, instantly took templates and noted key measurements and within a week prototypes based on these designs were coming out of the factory."

Around the same time the Australian Keith Paull was surfing throughout the British Isles on an 8'0" egg-shaped vee bottom, advocating yoga and blowing minds with his wave-riding ability. Having recently won the Australian national title and been on the landmark trip to Hawaii, he gave Britain a fresh parade of cutting-edge design and an explosive new style of surfing.

opposite top
1968 was a dramatic year in the history of surfboard design. Boards dropped radically in length, and surfers suddenly found themselves riding far more responsive shapes. Sam Walsh at Great Western. PHOTO: DOUG WILSON.

opposite bottom
Brian Schofield, Chris Jones and Dai Jones from Bilbo display some of their latest shapes, 1971. PHOTO: DOUG WILSON.

In board factories throughout the country there was a frenzy of foam mowing as shapers like Tim Heyland and Chris Jones hacked down blanks to create these new shorter boards. "Today the eight-footers don't look much different to longboards (because they were still quite wide)," says Jersey surfer and shaper Steve Harewood, "but at the time it was a major shift in our style of riding because you stopped walking the board to hang ten and rode more off the tail." The Aussies, inspired by Greenough, were already thinking that surfing could move from long turns to short arcs, but the big boards would not allow arcs, vertical turns and the use of a low centre of gravity. Once the boards got smaller, this became a reality. Vertical thinking then took over from horizontal thinking (cruising in trim) and boards and surfing followed. Rail-to-rail manoeuvres were now possible. The testing ground, however, had to be a decent wave face that would allow freedom of movement at the lip, in the pocket and under the curl.

On the wave the vee-bottoms turned harder, tracked higher up the face and most significantly allowed more manoeuvring nearer the pocket. It was a totally different experience in surfboard riding. On big fast walls you could lean with more conviction than ever before because of the long flexy fin. Then you could feel the board changing planing surfaces with a "klink" as you pushed off the bottom, followed by the "twang" from the flexy fin driving you up the face.

Paul Holmes managed to get one of the first Bilbo vee-bottoms. "It looked amazing. It was 7'10" and 23" wide, with an all-over orange tint, a two inch foam stringer (with a black coloured glue-up) and a classic clear volan Greenough-type fin. But it was the devil to ride. It proved to be too radical and hard to handle. But it was super exciting because it was obvious we had found a new approach to riding waves and we'd never go back to what we were doing before." The trouble was, for most surfers, these three- to six-inch deep vee bottom shapes didn't plane through the slow sections that plague our nation's beachbreaks.

Nevertheless the new ideas had a sweeping impact on European wave riding. "Surfing had a new energy and vigour," explains Fuz Bleakley, "People gave up surfing with the wave and began to surf against the face, riding more vertically. The speed was in the pocket and was gained through turns," a clear distinction from the longboard philosophy. The tube, not the nose ride, was now the ultimate.

Paul Witzig's influential 1969 film *Evolution* further documented Nat Young, Wayne Lynch, Ted Spencer and David Treloar in this new style. Wayne had unlimited natural talent and personified the 'Involvement era' taking surfing under, above, behind the curl and into the tube. Chris Jones recollects a trip to France in the autumn of '68 and seeing the movie being made. "The Aussies were tearing apart La Barre with some insane surfing. Although their boards were similar in the nose to our new eight-foot vees, already by then the widest point was forward and they were on slightly more gunny 7'6" and 7'4" models. Things were changing so quickly."

There was a breakthrough in thinking and surfers started looking for new possibilities in design and performance. Steve Harewood says, "Once people tried the Wayne Lynch type boards and discovered they could ride them, everybody thought, 'Wow, how short can we go?' It was an exciting time."

Prior to the 1970 World Championships

in Victoria, British surfing was influenced by what was going on in both California and Australia. Australia was the motherland of the revolutionary vee-bottoms and a more aggressive surfing style, but the west coast of the US was the base of a hip magazine culture with an obsession for gliding point breaks and drawing fluid lines. "We were surfing up and down the wave, but not too radically," recalls Chris Jones, by this time an innovative shortboard builder, "It was more the cruisey Californian approach. When I travelled to Australia in 1970 with Roger Mansfield and Tigger Newling, two of the youngest competitors at the event, we were wide open to new influences."

The British crew arrived in Torquay with soft-railed 6'6"s, but hard rails (or so-called down rails) were the latest development, giving boards more speed and drive, particularly effective in quality waves. So they got to work shaping themselves new boards at the Rip Curl factory. Chris Jones had noticed that the Aussies seemed to be one step ahead of the Americans. "The Yanks were still riding these Brewer inspired mini-guns between 6'6" and 7'0" with the wide point forward, while the Aussies were on really short boards with a rounded nose and tail and the wide point further back." The Brits took their lead from the Aussies and completely ignored what the Californians were riding. What came from Australia was an animal arrogance; a slash and tear approach that had not existed in surfing before.

Fresh home from Australia, Roger Mansfield won the British Championships in 1970 riding a totally new generation low-flotation shortboard. The single-fin Ellipse (6'3"x 20"x 2-1/2") had been built by Chris Jones as an adaptation for British waves using the best Australian design features.

In a fanatical pursuit to discover how short you could go, the experimentation in board size became ridiculous. Some boards dropped to 5'6" or less; but by compensating for the loss of length by putting floatation in the board, it was like riding a cork.

For the majority of surfers the really short boards were a major problem. After a period through the mid '60s when surfboards were produced for the mass market, design was once again targeted at the peak performers. Only the very best could successfully ride

1975
Fluid Juice
6'7" single fin
Shaper:
Adrian Phillips

1977
Ocean Magic Surfboards
6'10" winged single fin
Shaper:
'Mooney' McAllum

1980
Ocean Magic Surfboards
6'0" twin fin
Shaper:
Nigel Semmens

1987
Wave Graffitti Surfboards
6'0" thruster
Shaper:
Craig Hughes

2007
JP Surfboards
6'2" thruster
Shaper:
John Purton

167 | THE SURFING TRIBE

above
Twin fin afficianado Steve Daniel, 1980. PHOTO: ALEX WILLIAMS.

below
Vitamin Sea shaper Tad Ciastula (left) with team rider Jed Stone. The label was regarded as one of the best in the early '80s. PHOTO: GEOFF TYDEMAN.

the latest shapes. "By taking equipment to extremes, average surfers saw what was possible, and this really spurred us on to get in the water more," says Fuz Bleakley. "Some said the fun went from surfing, but what really went was the comfort factor. Surfing was now more of a challenge, and even average surfers wanted an experimental quiver rather than the trusted log."

In the early '70s shapers began to extend the length of boards

and refine shapes in a quest to recapture the glide. Chris Jones had been inspired by the whole Australian experience and became a highly prized shaper, not just copying, but also adapting and experimenting. In late 1970 CJ developed his 'Mini-disc' model. This was very original, not like anything they had seen in Australia. It had a rounded concave nose and the rest of the bottom was vee, with a big round tail. "I called it a platypus nose and it just flew," says CJ, smiling at the memory of a golden moment.

Between 1967 and 1970 board lengths dropped from nine-foot to six-foot, revolutionising what competent surfers were capable of doing on the wave face. The flip side was that the industry experienced a slump in demand from newcomers. Other unexpected factors caused the surfboard industry to change shape. A serious fire destroyed part of the Bilbo factory in September 1970 and with it the supremacy of the European Surfing Company. Bob Head and Bill Bailey had both devoted themselves tirelessly to Bilbo through the prime years of '60s surfing. Bob headed back home to Australia to warmer weather in '68 when shortboards boards took over. Bill also moved on. He was always a creative and technical thinker, but he was opposed to the shortboard. He felt such refined equipment no longer gave access to waves for the masses. It was a fair point. Bilbo, however,

168 | THE SURFING TRIBE

continued on a smaller scale for a couple more years with Chris Jones, Brian Schofield (father of TV presenter Phillip Schofield), Paul Holmes and Freddie Blight at the helm.

The decline of large-scale surfboard production was also fuelled by a social reaction against it. Everyone wanted the stamp of individualism that had been lost by board factories churning out basic models. The small-scale surfboard artisan thrived. There were numerous new smaller surfboard builders scattered in and around the Cornish community, such as John Conway of Conway Surfboards and Martin Geary of Outer Limits in Newquay. Regularfooter Martin Geary was a revered power surfer who also shaped incredible surfboards. He represented the spirit of the moment. "Surfboard building is a craft, not an industry," said Martin in a 1972 interview with Surf Insight. "It's hard to find the right people to make boards. Quality depends on the individual and if you've got a company who employ more than two or three people then the quality has to be carefully controlled. One man doing all the work can maintain the quality."

John Conway and Martin Geary were the first to really turn surfboards into art forms. Fuz Bleakley helped them both design radical graphics, experimenting with extreme colour combinations and fine pin lines. They worked perfectly for the new shapes, aesthetically drawing out the contours of the boards. It was all about refined equipment for pushing the boundaries of a new type of performance surfing.

In 1972 the World Championships were held in San Diego,

and the focus of British shapers shifted back to California. Pete Jones remembers being in the British team with Graham Nile, Gordon Burgis, Charles Williams, Chris Jones and Steve Harewood, and driving down to San Diego in a borrowed Cadillac. "We were all riding single fins between 5'11" and 6'3". The boards were very camel-decked and thick under your chest, thinning out towards the nose and tail, but they were loose and responsive," explains PJ.

Californian Jimmy Blears won the World Championships, popularising his fish design (5'10"x 21"x 3"). It had a short, wide planshape with an innovative outline, a swallow tail and twin keel fins, and it was best suited to small waves. Britain had plenty of those. But at first the fins were placed parallel to the stringer on each rail edge alongside a big wide tail. PJ absolutely hated twin fins, "I had one for a few months then dumped it to go back on the single fins." Tiki's Tim Heyland also shared these sentiments. "We even advertised that the fish was 'not something to get hooked on.' The early fish encouraged a jerky style of surfing far different from the flowing style achieved on longer, narrower boards. It was certainly not the board for the average British surfer to further his or her surfing ability."

It wasn't until the second era of twin fins, when brilliant Aussie regularfooter Mark Richards combined them with a swallow tail and altered their positioning and size that the twinny became a success. MR's twin-fin (6'2"x 20-1/2"x 2-3/4") shot into the surfing world in 1977. His radical and effective re-make of the twin-fin idea produced fast, swooping manoeuvres out on the face, punctuated by radical turns in the pocket. MR won four consecutive World Titles between 1979 and 1982. The Brits followed suit and found a whole new freedom for a kind of disco surfing, dancing in all directions, on our small- to medium-sized wave-faces.

The next board design revolution came again from Australia — Simon Anderson's Thruster three-finned surfboard (6'1"x 20"x 2-3/4"). It delivered speed off the bottom while maintaining speed off the top, thus fixing the problem of twin fins that tended to spin out if you pushed them too hard. In a stunning competition debut Anderson won in huge surf at the 1981 Bells Beach Easter Pro. Then he backed it up with another win at the Surfabout in Sydney, and concluded the year with a heroic victory at the Pipeline Masters in Hawaii.

For a while British shapers experimented radically with all the new board design options. They combined different numbers of fins and wings with varying tail and bottom shapes. A rider might have had a single fin, twin fin, thruster, quad and five fin board in the space of a few years. But eventually the majority concluded that the tri fin was the answer to high-performance surfing. This design set the standard for the '80s, '90s and beyond. The modern surfboard had arrived.

"Good boards became the norm thanks to Simon Anderson's thruster design," says Tigger Newling. "Three fins really worked. The thruster may have been as important a technical step forward as the shortboard. I really like the way a thruster reacts as the wave really hollows out and you're hanging in there on a little bit of rail and maybe just the inside fin. It doesn't spin out and delivers a huge speed boost when you need it most." Even a young Russell Winter recalls his '80s upgrade from a twin fin to a thruster: "It was like switching from a Skoda to a Porsche."

below
Today, surf shops offer boards of every style and size. PHOTO: MIKE SEARLE.

THE LONGBOARD RENAISSANCE: STEPPING FORWARD

above
Sennen longboard maestro Sam Bleakley, seen here at Porthleven.
PHOTO: ALEX WILLIAMS.

The total domination of the shortboard in the '70s meant the number of people starting to surf in Britain slumped. Novices struggled to catch waves and stand up on the wobbly, low flotation boards. Surfing had become quite an elite pastime, and a rider was ridiculed as a throwback for paddling out on a bigger surfboard. Although longboards had begun returning to the lineup by the end of the '70s in Australia and America, it was not until the early '80s that Britain followed suit.

In 1982 Mike Smith, a skilful young Brighton shortboarder, went to Australia and hung out with a posse of longboarders who had taken possession of the territory at Alexandra Heads in Queensland. Mike returned home in 1983 with an 8'0" board with a rounded nose and wide outline which had more in common with a short malibu than a long shortboard. Mike was living in Newquay and in mediocre surf conditions he often became the man to watch, the one catching most waves, riding further and dancing on his surfboard rather than standing in one spot, hopping and flapping. More importantly, he was clearly the one having the most fun. Mike had discovered an attitude towards surfing that embodied a more soulful approach. It was an instant reminder of the less competitive philosophy of the '60s. He convinced his friend Roger Mansfield, who had been riding shortboards exclusively since the end of the '60s, to get one for his quiver.

In 1984 Roger Mansfield and Mike Smith hosted a contest called 'Malibu Madness' at Watergate Bay in Newquay. Shortly after the hyper-competitive vibe of the ASP World Tour event left town, Malibu Madness was the antithesis. It drew together some of the most respected first generation surfers from the country including Rod Sumpter, Chris Jones, Alan McBride, Ian 'Porky' Morcom, as well as Pete 'Chops' Lascelles,

Keith Beddoe and Tim Mellors. It was to become a big influential talent pool of shortboarders who rode eight-footers. Malibu Madness grew in popularity every year and by the late '80s the 'Longboard Renaissance' was a recognised feature of surfing life in Britain.

The modern longboard was lighter, with a more refined use of rocker and often used a thruster or two-plus-one fin setup (normally one seven-inch centre fin and two small side fins). More generally, members of the surfing tribe were validating alternative boards. The experimentation also enabled a wide variety of surfboard designs to be tested, varying between 7'0" to 8'6". These boards, christened 'mini-mals', were well suited to British conditions and perfect for the beginner. The mini-mal represents one area of surfboard development in which British manufacture led the world, rather than followed.

Throughout the late '80s the old guard still clung to the longboard throne. Top '70s and '80s shortboarder Nigel Woodcock won the new BSA British Longboard Championships in 1987. The following year Rod Sumpter made a successful competition comeback, winning in perfect conditions at Thurso in Scotland, and represented Britain in this new division at the World Championships in Japan in 1990. But the new stars were Jerseyman Noel Creavy and flamboyant Welshman Chris 'Guts' Griffiths. Naturalfooter Noel was a pure stylist, surfing on the nose, drop-knee turning and radiating the type of fluid moves that defined the best malibu surfers of the '60s. Guts was a revered powerhouse, pulling nine-foot boards into waves the '60s generation would have not believed possible. Guts and Noel as well as Jock Paterson, Keith Beddoe and Tim Mellors led a new longboard charge.

Riding the nose is what sets longboarding apart from other forms of surfing.
For longboarders, second only to tube riding is hanging ten. It is the defining dance, the finest statement of balance. In the midst of frantic activity it is the quiet spot, where time and space seem to collapse into a moment's calm.

Functionally, noseriding is possible because the fin creates drag and the tail of the board is being pressed down by the breaking curl, acting as a counterweight, enabling the body weight to be pushed up. At the same time, water gathering underneath the board can cushion the nose. But to hang ten the board must literally be sucked into the wave. Every curve throughout the board from the rail shape to the rocker and bottom shape affects the flow of water in this suction process. Many of the best British surfers and shapers now had new and refreshing directions to explore in the shaping bay and on the wave face.

Longboarding, however, was still considered the realm of the old timers. It took Californian goofyfooter Joel Tudor to change that. Through the '80s young Joel Tudor had been socialised into a family of '60s surf titans at Californian longboard club meets. By the age of 11 in 1987 he was rubbing shoulders with the likes of Dale Velzy, David Nuuhiwa and Mickey Dora. Mentored both by Nat Young and his shaper Donald Takayama, Joel's surfing was honed by the legends. "It's rare that a kid listens to the elders," says Joel, "but for me they were still doing it. They had passion."

The elegant art of noseriding was a secret known only to a few in the '60s. American David Nuuhiwa had mastered the Zen paradox of noseriding — apply weight, remain weightless. His measured walking matched his poise on the nose, never hesitating, always confident, linking visualisation with body movement to read the wave. Joel studied Nuuhiwa and had the talent and bravado to reformulate the historical references into a unique style.

When Joel was caught on celluloid curling ten toes over the nose the longboard rebirth bomb was ignited. Surfing's retro revival may have been in the works already, but Joel certainly made it a hell of a lot more cool.

With modern lightweight shapes and radical turns advocated by Guts, combined with the traditional longboard aesthetic that radiated from Noel, plus a contest structure organised by Robert 'Minnow' Green, a whole new generation of youthful longboarders led by Lee Ryan, Nick Carter, Richard Balding and Will Eastham, plus full-time professionals Sam Bleakley, Ben Skinner and Elliot Dudley, would soon emerge and flourish in the small, but consistent waves in Britain.

above
By the late '80s the longboard renaissance was in full swing in Britain, and mal riders like Lee Ryan, Tim Mellors, 'Minnow' Green and Keith Beddoe were competing on a regular basis.
PHOTO: CHRIS POWER.

13 | top gear

SURFWEAR: IMAGE IS EVERYTHING

The early '60s was an exciting time for youth culture. As surfing was taking off in California, a new style of music emerged from the West Coast – the reverberating 'surf guitar' sound of bands like Dick Dale & The Deltones. Not long after, vocal harmony groups like The Beach Boys and Jan & Dean became hugely popular around the world. They communicated lyrically what they felt about sunny Southern California youth culture. Their statement was simple and relevant to the time: cars, waves and girls were happening. It all promised fun, fun, fun, and young people lapped it up. Post-war austerity was over and a more hedonistic age beckoned.

When British surfers started reading Surfer magazine, listening to The Beach Boys, and meeting visiting surfers from America or Australia, they realised it was cool to look the part on land as well as in the water. Young surfers went to great lengths to stand out and create an identity. Charles Williams recalls the impact American surfer Dave Rochlen had when he visited St Ives in 1962. "Rochlen showed us how to perceive ourselves as surfers. It was a great insight for us. We were something totally different. We were a clique. And our scene was happening."

Young people across the country were inspired to try surfing when *The Endless Summer* went on general release in cinemas in 1964. Bruce Brown's classic film documented Mike Hynson and Robert August on a global quest for the perfect wave. It reached out to ordinary young guys and generated a positive image that reverberates to this day. The surfer became a symbol of health, adventure and youth.

Away from the coast, a bold and brash fashion industry had sprung up in swinging '60s Britain. It was built on an attitude of 'anything goes' and reflected the shifting politics of the day. The fashion revolution was youth-driven and began on the streets. The Baby Boomers were coming of age. Mary Quant edged the mini-skirt into the mainstream and encouraged women to expose as much leg as possible. Boutique shops were hip and young people felt more comfortable shopping in them than in huge department stores.

For British surfers, however, California not London was the fashion capital of the world. From reading Surfer magazine and watching the occasional surf film, young surfers around the country saw the styles worn by the top surfers in California. Shops and manufacturers picked up on this demand and came up with the goods. In Newquay, Maui Surf Shop led the way, selling floral boardshorts handmade at home by Bob Westlake and his wife Annie. The success of this line inspired Bob to produce a wider range of clothes, and he went on to set up Alder Sportswear, the most successful British surfwear brand of the '70s and '80s.

Meanwhile, the European Surfing Company's label Big Gun made shorts, jackets and t-shirts. Again, these were all heavily influenced by Californian styles.

In 1966, top women's fashion magazine Petticoat organised a photoshoot at Porth Beach in Newquay, and recruited four Bilbo team riders to provide the brawn. The guys were kitted out in Hang Ten outfits, while the girls modelled mini-skirts and bikinis from the top London designers of the day. It was a classic fusion of Californian influence and London fashion.

Another hugely successful American brand of the era was Levi jeans. For surfers in the '70s, the ultimate outfit was a pair of Levi's and an American t-shirt with a bold print on the back. Levi's was just one brand among many, yet they were perceived as original, authentic and carrying the kudos of hard-riding cowboys from tumbleweed towns in the American West. Hollywood actors and rock stars wore them. You felt like you had some sort of membership, some spiritual affinity, with this romanticised Wild West ethos just by wearing them. You couldn't find a bigger contrast between the crashing waves of the ocean and the dusty Wild

below
Newquay surfers Dave Friar and Alan McBride didn't mind mingling with some top London models for a fashion mag photoshoot at Porth in 1966.
PHOTO: DOUG WILSON.

West. Yet surfing is just as marketable. Surfing sells products, but products also sell surfing. Many who started surfing in the '60s were certainly inspired to get into the sport because of the cool look of the scene. Critics of these dedicated followers of fashion probably don't appreciate how strongly the youth culture of the mid '60s set itself apart from the previous generation and its 'square' peers by wearing the tribal regalia of surf clothes. How cool was it to wear a colourful printed t-shirt and a pair of boardshorts in an era still suffering from the post-war buttoned-up mentality?

In commercial terms, it wasn't until the early '80s that surfwear manufacturing really took off. The rise of professional surfing sparked a global boom for the industry. Surfwear manufacturers promoted themselves by sponsoring the best pro riders, and ordinary surfers got the chance to wear the same boardshorts or shirts as their heroes. The surfing look was cool, and the garments were practical and functional. Surfwear became a multi-million dollar sector of the industry with brands like Quiksilver, Billabong, Rip Curl and O'Neill leading the way. As surfing boomed in the '80s and early '90s, those international labels jostled for a share of the British market with home-grown companies like Alder, Gul and Salt Rock. In the mid '90s, British brand Animal stepped into the arena. Based in Bournemouth, the company found its feet producing watch straps and sports watches, before expanding into the action sports clothing sector where it subsequently enjoyed phenomenal success.

Today, global surfwear companies exert considerable control over the public perception of surfing through sponsorship and marketing campaigns. Back in the '60s it was usually the nearest surfboard builder or a friendly local surf hero who influenced the younger generation; today it's the marketing departments of international surf companies.

In less than half a century, the surfer has evolved from a creature of social obscurity into a universal icon. Today, thousands of everyday folk who live miles from the ocean wear surf clothing, and some surfers question how meaningful it is to buy into a tribal identity that is so inclusive. But you can only claim the identity by actually doing it, by riding waves. Then it doesn't really matter what you wear.

above
Big hair, moustaches and tight shorts were all the rage in the late '70s!
PHOTO: ALEX WILLIAMS.

WETSUITS AND LEASHES: KEEPING WARM AND HANGING ON

In the early '60s most British surfers just wore shorts (and perhaps a t-shirt) when they went surfing. During the cool spring and autumn months, the most dedicated wave-riders paddled out wearing woollen jumpers in an effort to keep warm. Jumper manufacturers Woolmark even agreed to sponsor a couple of surf contests in the early '60s, presumably thinking that surfing might provide a new market for their products. However, surfers soon realised that neoprene, rather than wool, was the material they needed to use to insulate themselves from the chilly Atlantic water.

Around 1963, surfers in the South West and the Channel Islands took a lead from the diving fraternity and started making their own wetsuits. They bought dive-suit patterns, sheets of neoprene, contact adhesive and rubber tape, then got down to work. Typically the end product was a crude two-piece wetsuit, with a 'beavertail' on the jacket. These home-made wetsuits kept surfers warm but they were stiff and often chafed the skin around the neck and armpits. As the neoprene had no nylon lining, they were always a challenge to put on. Cornish surfer Tigger Newling still remembers an amusing incident with his first home-made suit in the early '60s. "My suit was really thick and stiff, so I had to use about half a can of Old Spice talcum powder to get it on. I surfed Constantine Point on my own for an hour or two and I came in pretty tired. The sun was hot and I was baking in my wetsuit. As I walked up the beach I decided I needed to get out of my wetsuit fast, before I melted, so I pulled the jacket over my head...and got stuck. Ten minutes later I was still thrashing around on the beach with my head trapped in the hood and my arms bound together. I was panicking and about to slip into an Old Spice-induced coma! But then, luckily, a fisherman came to my rescue and freed me from my rubber tomb."

In 1964, Londoner Dennis Cross came down to Cornwall to spend the summer season working at a hotel in Newquay. Dennis had done a bit of scuba diving and was keen to try surfing. He noticed that many of the surfers were keeping warm by wearing wetsuits; he knew how diving suits were made, so he bought some neoprene and made himself a surfing wetsuit. Friends at the beach asked if he could make wetsuits for them, so he made a few more. Word spread, and before long Doug Wilson got in touch to ask Dennis if he could supply wetsuits to the Bilbo shops in town. Dennis agreed and was soon making one a week from a lock-up garage behind the hotel where he worked. As time went on, he modified the cut of his wetsuits and sourced softer neoprene to make them more comfortable for surfing.

By 1967, Dennis was making enough wetsuits to think about starting a business. Inspired by Californian wetsuit company O'Neill, he set up a small factory at Bodmin and launched Gul Wetsuits. The company had a staff of three, and Dennis bought an industrial zigzag stitching machine to stitch the seams of the suits (previously the seams had just been glued and taped).

In the years that followed, Gul expanded to become a large international company, making wetsuits for a wide range of watersports. Dennis and his team invested heavily in machines and materials to keep their suits as good as any imported from abroad. Significantly, the company also sponsored many of Britain's top surfers, as well as surfing events.

Following Gul's lead, many more British companies started manufacturing wetsuits, among them Tiki, Second Skin, Circle One, Ra, Typhoon and C-Dog, and more recently Snugg, Alder, Sola, No Limits and C-Skins. As wetsuits have become warmer, lighter and more flexible over the years, surfers have been able to raise their performance levels and ride waves right through the cold winter months.

In the '60s, a wipeout usually meant a long swim back to the beach to retrieve your board. If you were surfing a reef or point break, there was a strong chance your board would be washed in and dinged on the rocks.

The idea of wearing an ankle-leash starting to germinate in the mid '60s. While on a trip to Morocco, St Ives surfer Charles Williams rode various sand-

opposite
Established in 1967, Gul made the first British wetsuits designed specifically for surfers.
PHOTO: MIKE SEARLE.

below
Gul founder Dennis Cross does a bit of product testing.
PHOTO: COURTESY GUL.

bottom breaks in Taghazoute village, such as Hash Point and Panorama's. But he knew there was a much better wave just up the road. "Each day I would walk up to Anchor Point and watch the sets rifle along the sandstone slabs. Mesmerised by the waves, I wondered how I could ride these gems without getting my board smashed on the reef. So I had the idea to get some strong cord, drill a hole in the fin of my board, and fasten the cord to my ankle."

There were many similar one-off examples of surfers using rudimentary leashes in the '60s, but nobody adopted the idea more generally. Many surfers thought the idea was inherently dangerous; a big, heavy malibu board could drag its rider a long way, and no-one wanted to get tangled up by a nylon cord after a bad wipeout. But others had an inkling that using a leash was the way forward. In Bude in the mid '60s, Pete Vickery started using a length of washing line to secure himself to his board. And across The Channel, Biarritz surfer George Hennebutte designed a cord with a Velcro strap, which he called 'le chevillere'.

In Cornwall, a visiting American surfer called Gary Moreno came up with a novel way of attaching board to body in the early '70s. The central component of his leash design was a cord made of stretchy surgical tubing; one end strapped onto your wrist, and the other to a suction cup on the nose of the board. Gary made and sold a considerable number of these locally on a cottage industry basis. Many surfers tried them, but not surprisingly they never really caught on.

Eventually, surfers realised that the best solution to the problem was a nylon cord attached from the ankle to the base of the fin. This was the archetypal leg-rope. It was simple and it worked, but it was heavy on the joints because of the tension in the cord.

In 1973, brainy Isle of Wight surfer Derek Thomson came up with an innovative and vastly-improved leash design. His cord comprised a length of stretchy rubber tubing with a thin nylon cord inside it to provide strength. The leash attached to the deck of the surfboard at the tail, and to the surfer's rear ankle with a functional and soft Velcro strap. The design took off, and Derek named his brand Cosmic Leashes. To meet the demand, he set up a small production line at an industrial site in Penzance. The brand dominated the UK market well into the '80s.

Over the years the leash became universally adopted. Ultimately urethane leashes superseded the original rubber-and-nylon-cord handmade versions. Today almost everyone uses a leash, and considering the crowded lineups we're all grateful for that.

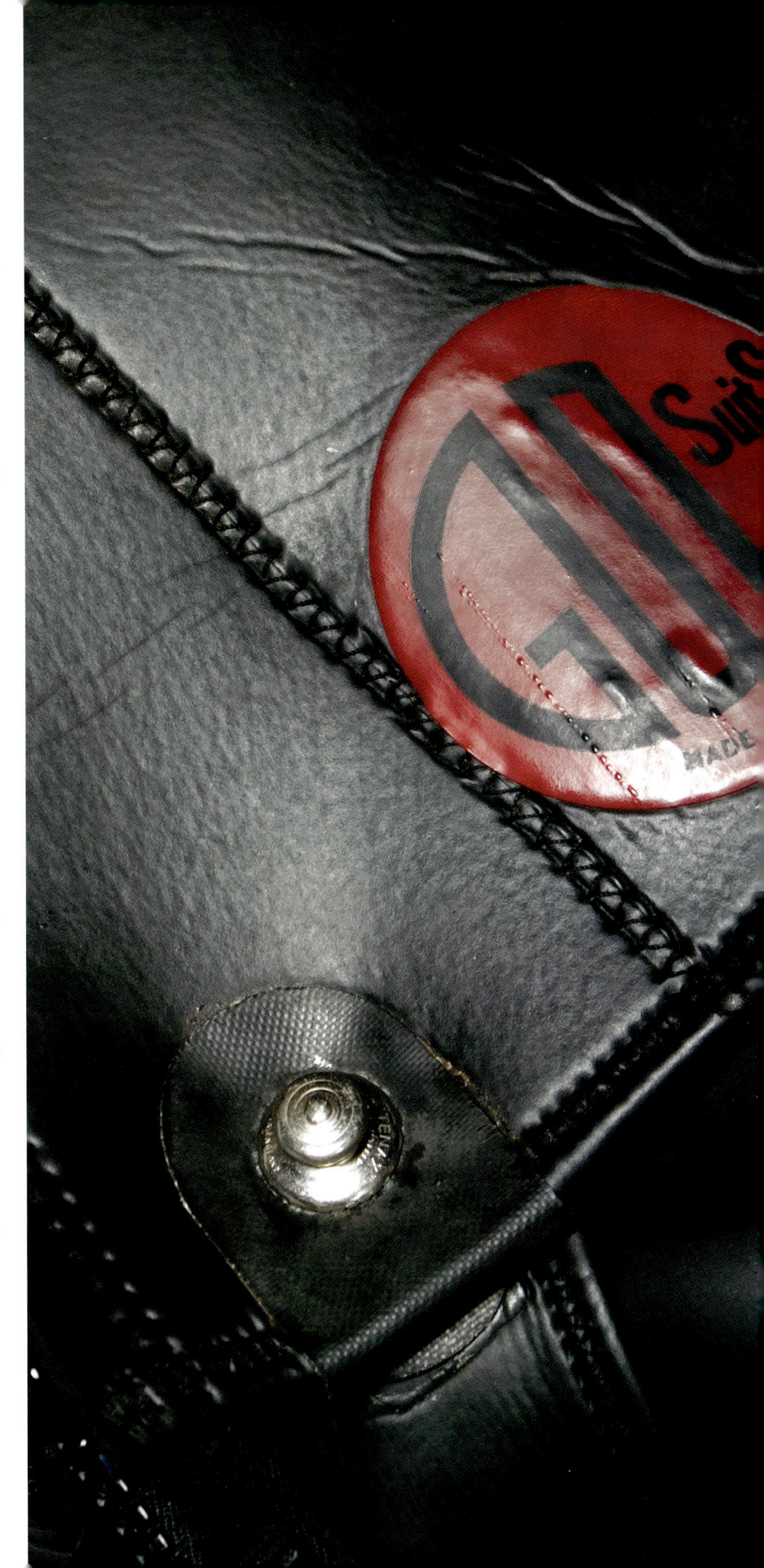

SKATEBOARDING: THE STREET CHILD OF SURFING

As surfing's popularity grew and radiated from Southern California in the early '60s, so did 'sidewalk surfing.' It boomed in the USA, where 50 million skateboards were sold by 1965. In Britain young surfers spotted photos of skateboarders in the pages of Surfer magazine. It looked fun, so they tried making their own boards using rollerskate wheels, screwed onto short planks. Nailing wheels to a board to fly down a concrete slope without direct steering or braking was a big adrenalin rush. The potential for speed was greater than surfing, but the tricks were all surf inspired – soul arches, cross steps, on the nose and riding the curb.

Prompted by requests for authentic skateboards from the groms, the European Surfing Company decided to try stocking them in their Bilbo shops. Thus the British skateboarding industry was born in Newquay in 1966. The company imported clay wheels and engineered trucks from California, to which they added their own wooden laminated decks. Young Newquay surfers like Roger Mansfield and Chris Jones were soon skating the town's streets and the craze quickly spread to other surfing communities.

In the mid '70s skateboarders replaced their clunky old clay wheels with ultra smooth polyurethane wheels and skateboarding shifted up several gears. A progressive new skating style evolved in California, inspired by the radical low-carving Hawaiian surfer Larry 'Rubberman' Bertlemann, with the emphasis on riding pools and half-pipes. A skateboarding craze took off around the world and quickly spread through the urban communities of Britain.

South Coast youngsters Jock Paterson, Brian and Steven Kelner, Tim Duncerlay and Mark Barker were at the core of the skating scene in Brighton. "A whole gang formed at West Pier and we had a park underneath the arches called 'the Cage'. It was fully like the Dogtown sessions in Craig Stecyk's movie *Dogtown and the Z Boys*," says Jock, who went on to become a skateboard phenomenon in the late '70s. Jock and Steve Kelner dominated the '77 British Skateboarding Championships in Newquay. "The Brighton Boyz cleaned up!" says Jock. After the contest, in a whirlwind of excitement, adrenalin-pumped Jock and Steve hurtled down nearby Rejerrah Hill at breakneck speed. Their team manager had the stop clock at the ready and they broke the national skateboard speed record.

Jock would eventually swap his skateboard for a longboard and become one of the South Coast's best competitive surfers.

Newquay boy Jed Stone was another who excelled on the skate scene in the late '70s. Small, agile and up for the challenge, Jed was one of the best on a surfboard as well as a skateboard. He competed nationwide and held both the British high and long jump records, and he also had his own skateboard model. "The real kick for me was skating the bowl at Watergate. I loved it. But then I broke my ankle at a West Country Skateboards demo in Bristol. That was it. I gave up skating and put all my energy into surfing."

Up in the North East, Nigel Veitch was another top competitive skateboarder who subsequently crossed over to become a professional surfer.

A new form of street trickery began when Rodney Mullen from Florida perfected the flat-ground ollie. In the early '80s, Californian surfers John Glomb and Kevin Reed took this red-hot skateboard manoeuvre into the water. The outcome was the aerial. Another Californian called Davey Smith boosted performance further and soon airs were at the cutting edge of high performance surfing. Professionals like British-born Martin Potter and Californian Christian Fletcher launched their careers by perfecting their surfing aerial repertoires.

In Britain, Carwyn Williams became the top aerialist of the mid '80s. The Welsh prodigy learned to boost airs at his local skate ramp and was soon busting out of the waves at Langland Bay with a clean and crisp style. Since then, aerials have become an essential part of the repertoire of every modern pro surfer.

opposite
Newquay's Jed Stone was one of the top skaters in the country in the late '70s. PHOTO: ALEX WILLIAMS

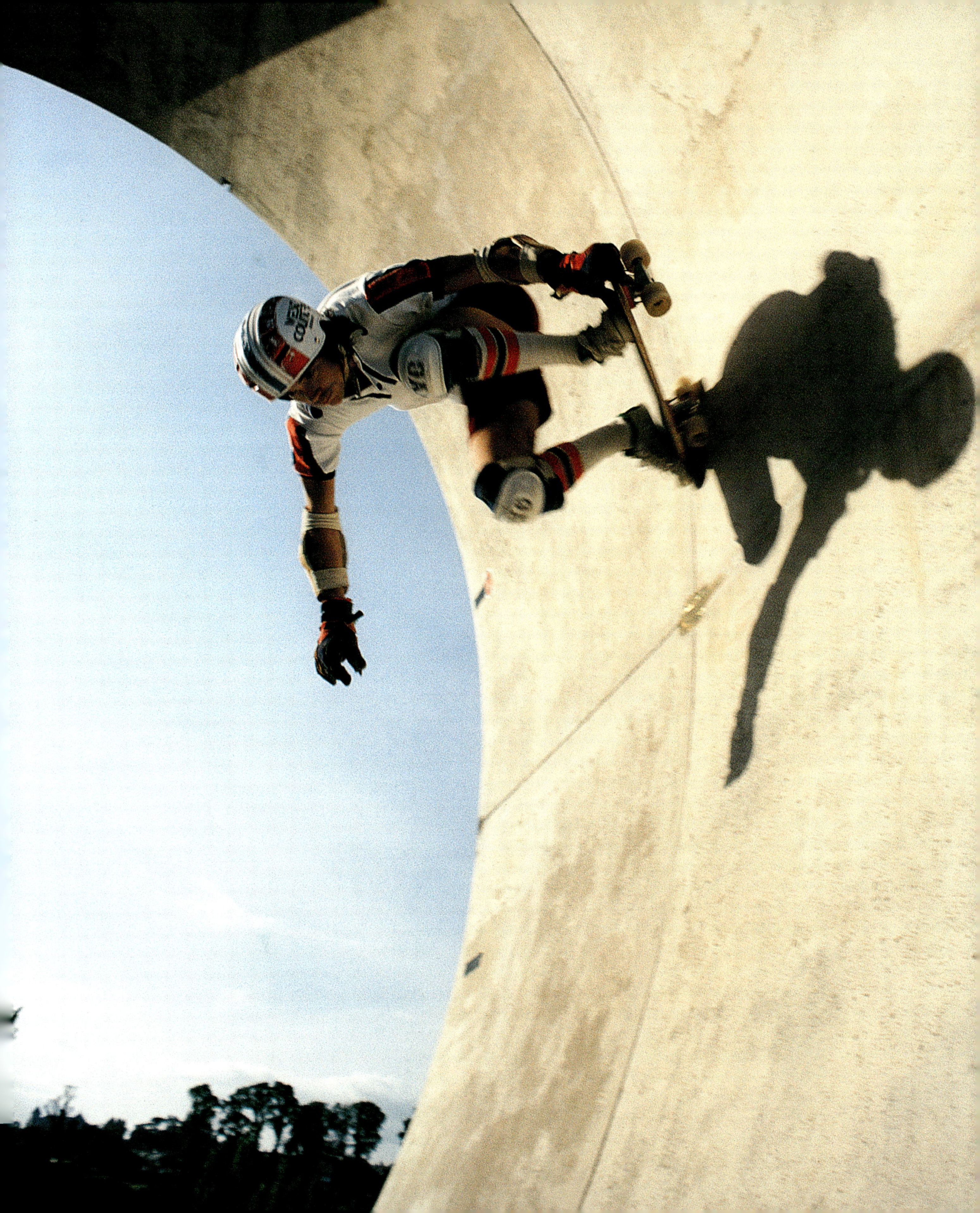

14 | communication skills

CELLULOID SLIDING

below
John Adams from Three S Films at work in the late '70s. PHOTO GEOFF TYDEMAN.

A village hall full of hooting surfers, ecstatic in the flickering light of a 16mm projector showing heroes sliding across huge foreign green wave faces: surf film shows were the peak social gathering for '60s and '70s surfers. In Britain, Rod Sumpter pioneered this industry. Not long after arriving in Cornwall in 1966, Rod met and fell in love with Newquay girl Simonne Renvoize (whose father, Jimmy, owned a photographic shop). They decided to start filming throughout Britain and Europe, editing the footage into *Come Surf With Me* (1967). Marketing the film to the tourists at the beach and in the pubs with fliers and posters, they packed out church halls rented cheaply throughout Cornwall and Devon.

"The atmosphere at the film showings was fantastic," says Rod. To begin with, most of the people who came to see the films were ordinary holidaymakers, and they were mesmerised.

"We filmed all the early stuff on a 16mm Bolex," continues Rod. "Cine cameras were clockwork. You'd wind them up and then you had 35 seconds to do the shot at 24 frames a second, normal speed. Or you could shoot in slow motion at 64 frames a second, but that gave you even less time." Simonne was talented behind the lens, filming most of the footage of Rod surfing and she also had an eye to market things in a uniquely British way.

"When I first tried doing water shots at La Barre in France for *Come Surf With Me* I didn't have a housing, so I just put the camera in a plastic bag and paddled out on my board," says Rod. "I sat on the side of the peak taking pictures, and just hoped the camera wouldn't get wet. But even if it did get a little bit wet, you could dry it off and carry on the next day. Those cameras were very robust. They never broke down."

St Ives surfer Charles Williams recalls the exhilaration of seeing perfect foreign waves on the big screen. "It was amazing to see water shots of big beautiful La Barre. It looked so idyllic, we just all wanted to get travelling." The influence was profound. Not only was Sumpter pointing the camera at British shores, which was a great boost to British surfers' self-esteem, but he was also driving around the country showing the surf films at all these different places and surfing there. "Over the next couple of years as more people took up surfing, the audience changed," Rod explains. "They wanted to see performance surfing rather than a tourist type of film. By the time we made a few films, we were showing it to a crew who knew a lot about surfing."

Rod created seven films between 1967 and 1979, logging his incredibly widespread travels, the growing national scene and the shortboard revolution. The early movies, including *With Surfing in Mind* (1968) and *Freeform* (1970) were in the happy-go-lucky vein of sun-drenched Californian Bruce Brown flicks. But *Oceans* (1971) and *Reflections* (1973) were regarded as pretty far-out with religious imagery and a psychedelic feel, much in the flavour of John Severson's *Pacific Vibrations* (1970). Many people thought Rod had undergone a religious conversion. Certainly they were highly personal and much under-rated films. Rod was very influenced by outgoing Australian filmmaker Paul Witzig: "He always came up with new techniques which gave his films a very different look. He'd use a 1,000mm lens on a 16mm camera to shoot into the waves, instead of 'front-on', so you were looking right into the barrel. That was unheard of at the time, and it was quite amazing."

White Waves (1979) and *Hawaiian Surfari* (1979) became B-movies on the conventional British cinema circuit. Rod's footage of young tube-riding specialist Rory 'The Dog' Russell at Pipeline appeared as a sequence in Alan Rich's epic *Salt Water Wine* (1973). It was also used in a celebrated Old Spice advert, which is still shown on television backwaters around the globe today. Rod maintained his link with TV and his excellent technical talent served him well in a successful career as a freelance cameraman, primarily for the BBC, throughout the 1980s.

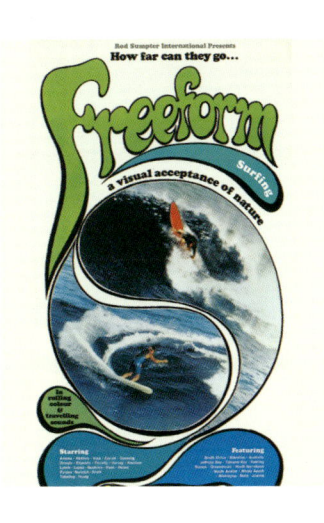

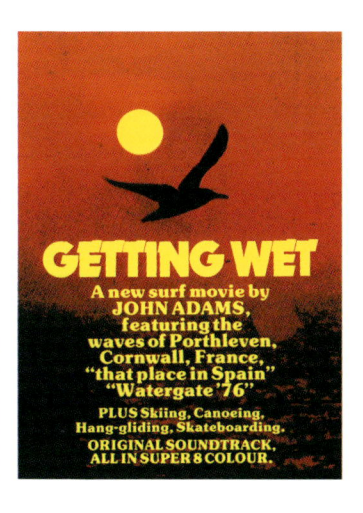

The influence of surf films on the British scene
cannot be understated. Paul Witzig's *Evolution* (1969) defined the opening phase of the shortboard revolution, capturing the spirit of the times and showcasing the 17-year-old sensation from Victoria, Wayne Lynch, as the first surfer to really bank off the crest and hit the lip. In the same year, barefoot genius George Greenough took the viewer deeply and hypnotically inside the tube with groundbreaking water photography throughout *The Innermost Limits of Pure Fun* (1969). Through Rod's contacts with filmmakers, the trio of Simonne, Paul Holmes and Fuz Bleakley showed the latest surf films throughout Britain through Aquagem Surf Flicks. These included early '70s Hal Jepsen classics *Sea For Yourself* and *Cosmic Children*. Alan Rich's *Saltwater Wine* was another hit. The impact of these films helped to educate British surfers in an era when cheap travel just wasn't available. "You wouldn't believe the level of stoke at these showings," comments Fuz. "People would hoot, gasp and applaud at every move. On Saturday night they would be watching Rory Russell at 12-foot Pipeline, and they'd be so fired up they'd rush out to surf two foot slop at their local beach the next day…and have a brilliant session!"

In 1969 Penzance surfer John Adams and Australian Dave 'Stickman' O'Donnell also started showing surf films. While Johns' venue, The Winter Gardens, was headlining the best contemporary music — including The Who and Fleetwood Mac — surf film showings became the social pinnacle of surf culture. Inspired by the films he was showing, John soon developed a passion for making his own films. In 1975 he made *Tubular Swells* featuring Sennen legends Colin Wilson and Harvey Hoare. *Taking Off* (1981) was a classic, following the groundbreaking launch of Nigel Semmens, Steve Daniel and Ted Deerhurst's pro careers. John formed a film company, Three S Films, and made seven films up to 1992, and became the primary distributor of international surfing films in Britain.

Tigger Newling was another Cornish surfer who followed in Rod's footsteps and developed an interest in filmmaking. "The first camera I operated was Rod's 16mm Bolex, wrapped in a plastic bag, to get watershots of him at Guethary in '68," says Tigger. Over a decade later, while studying Anthropology at the University of Sydney, Tigger began shooting culture-based documentaries, culminating in his first full length film, *Thriller in Manila*. Soon afterwards Tigger formed his own business, Screenland Film and Video Production. Not surprisingly, Tigger's forte is water footage, and he has worked extensively with close friend Tom Carroll cutting together mind-blowing surf footage.

Sadly, the touring surf film has had its heyday. Three S Films put on national tours of *Surfers: The Movie* and *Rolling Thunder* in 1990, but they were a last gasp in Britain. The neon generation of surfers had turned their backs on rollicking nights of debauchery at surf flicks because they could buy a video and stay at home.

A few years later Cornwall got a big bite of the British film industry when Carl Prechezer filmed *Blue Juice*, a clichéd surf story set in Cornwall. Most of the film was shot in Mousehole, Gwithian and St Ives, and at some level or other pretty much every Penwith surfer got involved. The main crowd puller, however, was the smouldering Welsh actress Catherine Zeta-Jones.

WRITING STYLE

For the devoted surfer in the '60s, the leading purveyor of news and inspiration was the American magazine, Surfer. When it started in 1960 as a black-and-white booklet with a duotone cover, it was effectively a brochure to help promote surf movies made by John Severson. But it quickly took on a life of its own and filled a niche for wave hungry surfers. Air-freighted from California and delivered through the postbox, it was the Bible of surfing.

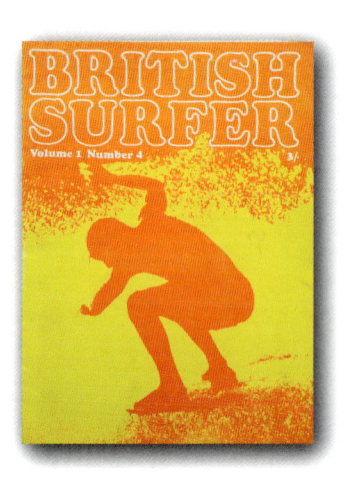

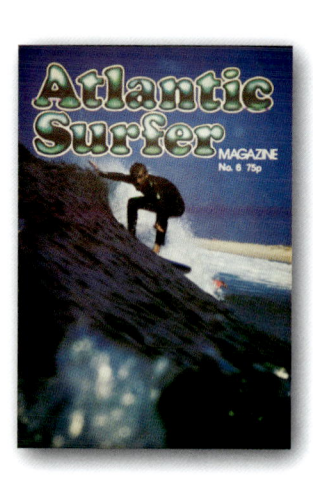

Cartoonist Rick Griffin was elevated to legendary status through 'Murph the Surf', and the pages of Surfer glowed with travel ideas. To the innocent early British surfer, the magazine provided answers about everything — waves, boards, style and attitude. Doug Wilson was the first to import the early volumes of Surfer into Britain, selling it from his surf shop in Newquay, and every issue was read from cover to cover and passed on to friends.

In 1969 Rod Sumpter diversified from filmmaking to figurehead the UK's original surf magazine, British Surfer, which was printed in Bristol and became a forum for some good old patriotism: "For too long we have followed the Americans and Australians through their fads and phases," wrote Rod in the opening feature. "It's time to make our own future. If we exchange ideas, travel and become totally aware of what is happening we can produce a world champion." However British Surfer tended to be short on content and only lasted a few issues.

Paul Holmes, Fuz Bleakley and Simonne Renvoize started Britain's second and more influential magazine, Surf Insight in 1970. Like Tracks in Australia, it was in newspaper format and was cutting edge – the counterculture alternative to the persona of Surfer and International Surfing — focusing more on the holistic surfing lifestyle, from contemporary environmental issues to deep probing interviews with all the top Brits. Styled on Rolling Stone, it had photos, Rick Griffin-esque cartoons drawn by Fuz, and well-written articles ranging from cosmic to hilarious. Surf Insight took surf journalism forward because it was written by surfers for surfers and wasn't afraid to confront political and social issues; it even had an environmental page that fought for keeping beaches open to surf.

Surf Insight offered a springboard to Paul Holmes, who went on to became an iconic figure in the world of surf journalism. He worked as editor of the prestigious Australian surfing newspaper Tracks in the late '70s, before moving to California to work as editor of Surfer magazine, producing the world's number one title between 1981 and 1989, during the cash-rich neon-lit surf boom. Later he published the groundbreaking Beach Culture magazine with top graphic designer David Carson, and more recently wrote a book, *Dale Velzy Is Hawk*, the first major work on the late iconic Californian surf hero.

Britain has experimented with tens of surf magazines since the originals.

In 1978 Greg Haythorpe moved from Australia to Newquay to start Atlantic Surfer, grafting his experience from the skateboard magazine boom into surfing. Greg edited a few issues but ran into personal difficulties, resulting in John Conway taking over in 1980. Ultimately the magazine folded, but John's interest in surf publishing did not sink with

Another innovative but short-lived title that appeared in the '80s was Welsh-based Edge magazine. A crossover magazine featuring half surfing and half skateboarding, it featured photos and articles by Phil Holden, Paul Gill and Chris Power amongst others. It folded in 1987 due to financial difficulties.

In 1994 Chris Power, who had been publishing the BSA's newspaper Groundswell, joined forces with bodyboarding magazine ThreeSixty publishers Mike and Louise Searle to launch CARVE. They were soon joined by Aggie surfer Steve England. With its blend of contemporary design, top quality photography, humour and an adventurous choice of trips such as Chile, Galapagos, Norway and El Salvador, CARVE overtook Wavelength as the pre-eminent British surf magazine within a few years. More recently, CARVE has continued to innovate, with groundbreaking discoveries in Ireland courtesy of standout

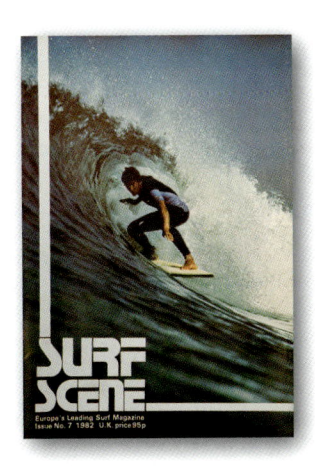

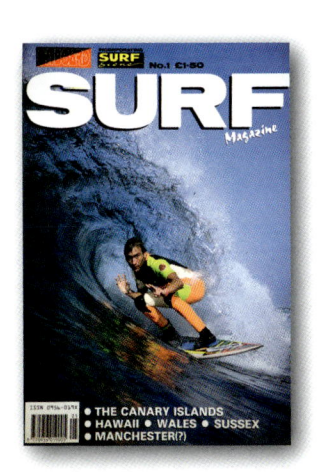

it. In the summer of 1981 he launched Wavelength as a large-format glossy magazine and the title thrived throughout the '80s and into the '90s. John supplied much of the photography himself and went on numerous trips to France and the Canaries. Based in Newquay, he tended to put the emphasis on Newquay surfers including Grishka Roberts, Spencer Hargraves, the Owen twins and Nigel Semmens, much to the frustration of surfers outside of the UK's 'Surf City'. A brash, lovable rogue who drove a Porsche, John Conway died in 2003 from cancer and Wavelength was subsequently bought by newspaper group Cornwall & Devon Media. Recently the title has improved greatly with editor Tim Nunn at the helm.

photographer Mickey Smith.

1995 saw the launch of The Surfer's Path edited by Alex Dick-Read. Initially focussed on British stories and travel, it slowly morphed into an international travel magazine with strong environmental credentials. It was the first surf magazine to be printed on recycled paper using vegetable-based ink.

Contemporary British surf magazines raise the profiles of British heroes, spread news, inspire and aid a solid national surf industry. They also boost a sense of sporting identity, frequently reminding us how good British waves and surfers are. Today a host of full time photographers are supported by the British magazines, which remain an integral part of British surfing, commercially and culturally.

15 | living for surfing and surfing for a living

GETTING PAID TO SURF? YOU MUST BE JOKING!

Competition is central to every sport. It's a way to push boundaries, make progress and gain prestige. In Britain, the early competitions became the tribal meeting occasions of the clan members. They were less about winning and more about entering, and often simply provided an excuse for a party. It was a chance to exchange stories and spread knowledge.

In the '60s it took highly innovative individuals like Rod Sumpter to make a living from surfing. "It was a big event when Rod arrived in Newquay," says Doug Wilson. "He was the best surfer we had ever seen. Because of his sporting reputation, local surfers put him on a pedestal. He came to our Bilbo factory and put forward lots of ideas about board shapes and the latest techniques from the States and from Australia. He was a major contributor to board improvement in Britain. In return we'd give him boards, promote him, and pay him to shape signature models." This partnership helped both the surfer and the company. It also resulted in one of the most memorable images in the sport. When Rod joined the British team for the World Championships in '66, the sprayjob on his board was a huge Union Jack covering the deck of his board. It became his trademark. At Ocean Beach, San Diego, Rod finished fifth in the final behind surfing titans Nat Young, David Nuuhiwa, Corky Carroll and Jock Sutherland. "Even though we all knew he'd learnt to surf in Australia, we were flushed with national pride," says Paul Holmes. "It was like, 'Hey, we're not some no-good little backwater'. There was obviously going to be a future for British surfing, so the fact that Rod embraced it all was really inspirational."

Rod raised British surfing performance levels by example, setting a standard that would take years to emulate. When surfboards mutated from 11-foot logs to six-foot pocket-rockets in the late '60s, surfing moved into a whole new era of vertical expression and the best riders gathered to show off their latest moves.

But for some, surf contests became a real turnoff. A new generation of soul surfers appeared who despised anything associated with 'rules' or 'organisation'. By 1972 the soul surfing era was in its prime. Many British surfers chose to enjoy their surfing in a more private way, kicking back and travelling to tropical retreats like Sri Lanka and the Caribbean.

By 1974 however, competitive surfing was back in fashion Down Under. The 'Bronzed Aussies' (Ian Cairns, Pete Townend and Mark Warren) put professionalism back into surfing, with sponsorship deals, dedication to the growing contest circuit, and high-profile exposure in magazines. Commercialism was suddenly in vogue.

Here in Britain, after Rodney Sumpter's early example, Ted

Deerhurst became the next pro surfer, and the first European surfer to join the new IPS (International Pro Surfers) circuit in 1978. English-born Ted was the son of the 11th Earl of Coventry, but learned to surf in California. His example is inspiring, but at the time his impact on the British stage was minimal. His best domestic result was a fifth place finish in the Juniors at the 1973 English Championships at Sennen. But Ted was ultra ambitious. He qualified for the British Team bound for the World Championships in South Africa in 1978, and then set his sights on the IPS tour. Articulate and likeable, Ted engineered what Australia's Surfing Life magazine called 'a strangely beautiful surfing career.' He was proud of his British heritage and incorporated it in his surfing identity as he travelled to compete at IPS contests, claiming, "I've decided to put my money where my mouth is."

Ted's aristocratic background, and the fact that he was the only touring European pro, made him a novelty and popular figure. He made frequent visits to Hawaii, building his ability to surf in heavy conditions. In 12-foot waves at the Jose Cuervo Classic at Sunset Beach, Ted reached the semi-finals by knocking out Cheyne Horan and Shaun's brother Mike Tomson. Returning to the UK he commented, "British guys need more exposure to powerful surf if they are to make the international grade." It was true.

Ted loved the warm weather and consistent waves in Australia, and he emigrated there in 1979. While living Down Under he started his own surfboard label Excalibur. In 1982 Deerhurst featured on the cover of Surfer magazine as 'Aristocratic Lord Ted', posing with five custom surfboards and two hunting hounds on the lawn of the family manor house outside Coventry. The same year he featured in Dick Hoole and Jack McCoy's film *Storm Riders*. Later, in 1991, he appeared in *Rolling Thunder* by Scott Dittrich. Although he never made a final in his career, Ted competed as a pro, with occasional top 16 finishes, until 1987. Despite proclaiming, "I'm just a playboy on the circuit," he was loved by many, and worked hard to maintain his profile. He was also devoted to deprived children, taking them surfing and organising charity contests.

Ted moved to Hawaii in the '90s where he became a solid performer in big waves like Sunset and

opposite
Surf contests attracted mainstream sponsors right from the mid '60s. Rod Sumpter in action at the Gold Leaf Great Britain & International Championships at Fistral Beach in 1967.
PHOTO: DOUG WILSON.

Waimea. But his life was cut short in October 1997. He was found dead in a hotel room in Honolulu; the cause of death was given as heart failure. Pete Jones says he'll always remember Ted as a good big-wave surfer. "I remember surfing with him at Sunset in 1976 in a really big swell. Ted had no fear and was charging, taking off behind the peak and not being intimidated by the pack. In fact, he was friendly with all of the famous guys in the lineup. He gained a lot of respect for his big-wave surfing on the North Shore, and he totally dedicated himself to the sport he loved."

Nigel Semmens and Steve Daniel upped the ante

when they pioneered European professional surfing in the late '70s and early '80s. Not only did they dominate at home, they achieved good results competing at events in South Africa, Hawaii and Australia on the World Tour.

The moment Nigel got a taste for contest success he was driven to get to the top and to stay there. "I remember the start of my career, when I was surfing in the Juniors at the English Championships at Sennen in 1973. I got into the final and finished third, and that was a true buzz. It was such a proud moment. I was more nervous getting up onto the podium than I was in the actual competition. I really knew I wanted to keep competing after that." Nigel won the British Junior Championships a few weeks later.

Nigel realised that frequent access to quality waves at home and abroad could help take him to the top. But it was the pure act of surfing that was always the real kick. "I was 16 on my first Morocco trip in 1975. I can clearly remember this classic three hour session in beautiful surf at Anchor Point. I came in at the cove where you land. The little rocks there were really hot where you climbed up. I walked back along the point, just watching a set peel and my friends riding towards me on clean, green waves. 'Life can't get much better than this,' I thought. 'I've just had some of the best waves of my life, and all I'm thinking about is when I'm going to get back in the water again!' That for me was a state of absolute perfection."

Nigel had a straightforward approach to competition "From the age of 18 my personal focus was to be the best in the water at every beach I went to. Although the prizemoney and sponsorship increased, the reality of being a pro was that you were more or less on your own. You were finding your own way, with no managers or trainers for guidance like other sports. Ideally a totally organised approach was needed, with a coach and manager and physiotherapist. But it just wasn't available back then."

Despite winning four consecutive English titles and the British title (in 1979), Nigel became disillusioned with the BSA. "I didn't feel that the BSA contests were being run properly. Competition was being forcibly contained at an amateur level. I believed there had to be something beyond the English and British titles. I needed to gear up another level. I wasn't a hippy surfer, but committed to being a pure sportsman on a professional basis, like a footballer."

When 18-year-old Nigel went to Hawaii with Steve Daniel for the Smirnoff Pro-am at Sunset in 1977, he put on a fearless and memorable performance in his heat with Gerry Lopez and Barry Kanaiaupuni. Despite this taste of international acclaim, Nigel realised that he couldn't rely on contest earnings or sponsorship money to live and travel. Fresh back from Hawaii, Nigel's friend and mentor Graham Nile introduced him to Peter 'Mooney' McAllum, a Kiwi shaper who had worked at Bilbo in Newquay before starting his own board building business, Ocean Magic. His business partner Graham sold the boards through his shop in St Austell. With an opportunity to get involved in a surf company, Nigel joined Mooney as an apprentice shaper. It was a wise move.

Over the next eight years Nigel became one of the most famous surfers in Europe. He also become a partner in Ocean Magic when the business shifted to Trevemper on the outskirts of Newquay in 1979. "Once I'd got my teeth into competition surfing, my major goal was to become European Champion. I achieved that title at Thurso in Scotland in 1981 in true quality waves. To beat guys like Pete Jones, Paul Russell and Pete Lascelles, in perfect six foot conditions, that really was a crowning achievement for me."

Despite all his achievements at amateur level, it was Nigel's success in the burgeoning era of professional surfing that set him apart. Competing in Australia on the IPS World Tour in 1981, Nigel had an excellent result at the Stubbies Surf Classic in Burleigh Heads. Mark 'Wounded Gull' Richards swooped to first place, but Nigel gained a lot of respect from the other Tour surfers. Back home, Nigel won the first British pro-am event, the Newquay Surf Classic at Fistral in 1981. First prize was £800. He backed it up the following year by successfully defending his title. With Steve Daniel, Nigel continued to compete at occasional events in South Africa, Hawaii and Australia on the IPS World Tour in '82 and the new ASP Tour in '83.

opposite
Ted Deerhurst flew the flag for Britain at international contests in the late '70s and '80s.
PHOTO: STEVE DANIEL.

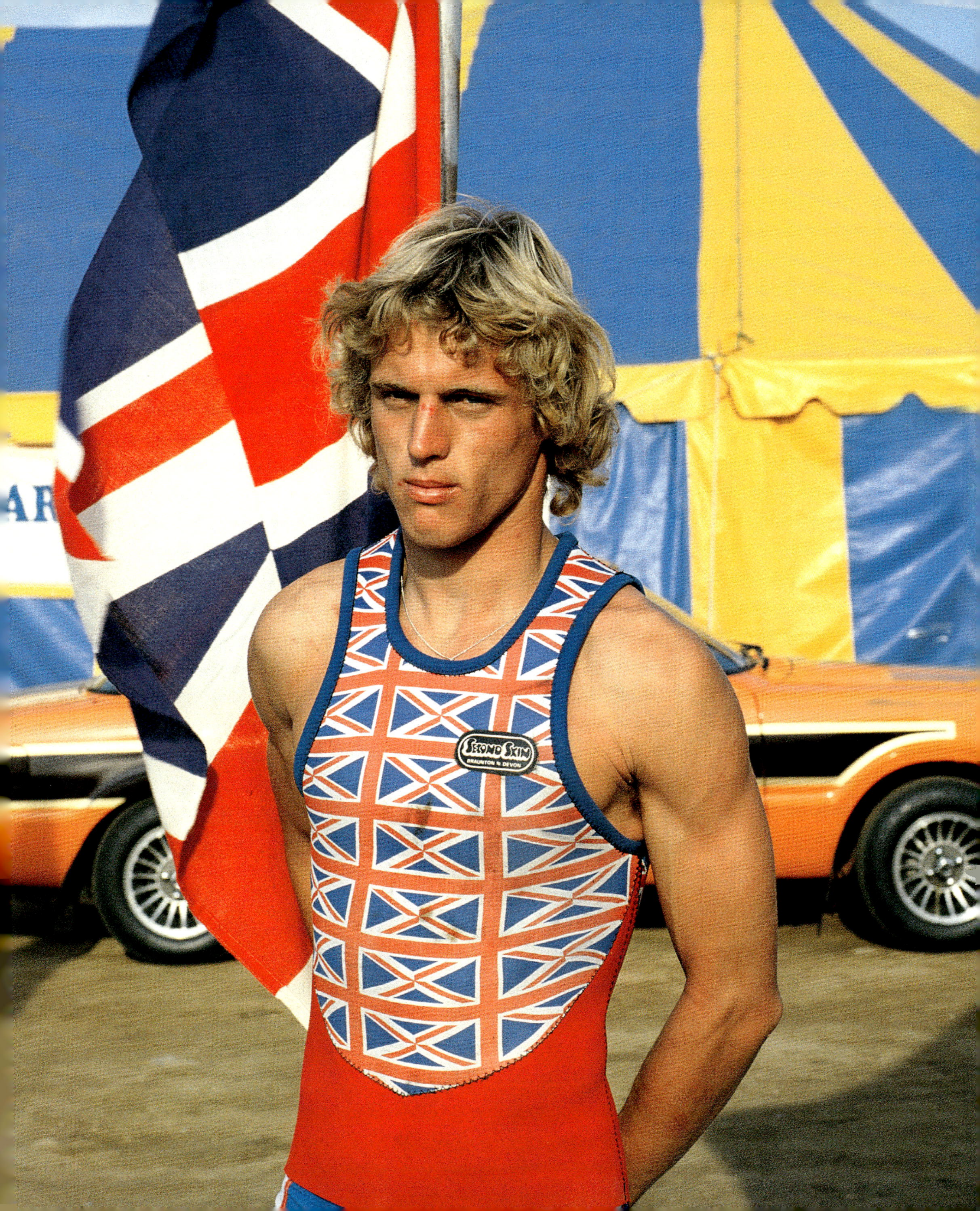
SECOND SKIN
BRAUNTON N. DEVON

above
Brits Steve Daniel and Nigel Semmens (far left) join the all-star cast of ASP pro's at the 1983 Foster's Pro at Fistral Beach, Newquay. Among the famous faces are no fewer than five past and future world champions.
PHOTO: ALEX WILLIAMS.

Thanks to Nigel's contest prowess and his shaping ability, Ocean Magic's board sales flourished. "Surfing to me was always a complete lifestyle," says Nigel, "and shaping was a way I could continue to make a living from surfing." Nigel later became the sole proprietor of Ocean Magic and moved its headquarters to Pargolla Road in Newquay in 1985. It was close to where Bilbo pioneered the European surf industry two decades earlier. Nigel Semmens also was a pioneer, charting totally new territory in British professional surfing. As the commercial benefits of surfing continued to grow, others would follow in his footsteps.

By the early '80s, first generation Newquay surfer John Conway was at the helm of a brand new British surf magazine, Wavelength. From this platform he took the initiative and engineered British surfing's entry into the professional era. John co-ordinated the Gul/Alder Pro-am at Fistral Beach, Newquay in 1981. With £6,000 prizemoney it was Britain's first pro-am surfing contest and linked up with the IPS tour. Surfers such as Shaun Tomson visited Britain for the first time ever to compete. Early on, the conditions were excellent, but the swell died for the finals and the prize for first place was split between Wayne 'Rabbit' Bartholomew and Cheyne Horan. The arrival of some of the world's best surfers on British shores resulted in massive media attention, and amplified the public's awareness and excitement about surfing. Later that year Ian Cairns' Association of Surfing Professionals (ASP) replaced the IPS.

The first ASP World Tour in 1983 comprised 16 contests in 10 countries. It grew to an exhausting travel schedule of 25 events in 12 countries in the next year. But now there was a new generation of surfers earning a living solely from prizemoney winnings and

The ASP event at Fistral continued with various new sponsors through the mid to late '80s, including Hot Tuna and Alder. Tom Curren won in '85 and '86, Martin Potter won in '84 and again in '87, Damien Hardman in '88, and Barton Lynch in '89. Like bees to honey, the pro's were drawn to the cash and points on offer at Fistral Beach. The contest also gave locals a chance to see top pro's in action, and to mix with them in free surfs.

In the early '90s there were two major changes to the structure of the ASP tour,

which had a major impact on the Newquay event. Beginning in 1992, a new two-tier tour was introduced with an elite WCT (World Championship Tour) with the world's top 48 male and 18 female surfers, and a WQS (World Qualifying Series) tour where surfers would compete and try to qualify for a spot on the WCT the following season. Now the ASP organisers could be more selective about where they staged the WCT events. Instead of locations being chosen for their commercial value they were picked for their surf. The ASP also had a major satellite TV sponsor, which meant the number of people attracted to watch at the beach became less important. "Unfortunately Newquay was not on the WCT list," says Dave Reed. "We were a good quality location in commercial terms, supported by good public access, but not so good for surf. It meant Newquay would have to just host a WQS." The pinnacle of professional competitive surfing in Europe now shifted to be the higher quality waves of Hossegor in France.

Newquay continued to deliver a well organised WQS event at Fistral, sponsored over the years by Hot Tuna, Virgin Cola, Headworx, and Rip Curl. In 2002 Newquay local Russell Winter became the first British (or European) surfer to win the ASP contest in Newquay. At the time Russell was Europe's only WCT surfer, and his first ever WQS win marked a long-awaited triumph for a born-and-bred British surfer in the ASP arena.

sponsorships deals. British waves did not compare in quality to those of Hawaii or Australia, but the ethos of the ASP was to transform their events into huge beach carnivals like the OP Pro at Huntington in California.

In 1983 the Fosters Surfmasters event was held at Fistral, the first ASP World Tour contest to take place in Britain. Pint-sized Australian Tom Carroll took the £15,000 first prize en route to his first world title. Five years later Tom would sign the first million dollar surf sponsorship deal with Quiksilver.

Dave Reed, a talented local surfer, was given the opportunity to judge at the Surfmasters in 1983. He did so again the following year and achieved the highest rating on consistency at the event. Dave was consequently invited to become a full-time ASP judge. He stayed with the expanding ASP for over a decade, making him British surfing's main man inside the structure of global professional surfing, an unsung hero.

above
The phenomenal Tom Curren, on his way to victory at the 1986 Foster's Pro.
PHOTO: ALEX WILLIAMS.

below
British-born Martin Potter had the crowd behind him when he won the Hot Tuna Surfmasters at Fistral in '87.
PHOTO: CHRIS POWER.

THE SURFING TRIBE

BRITS ON THE GLOBAL SCENE

Cornish charger Spencer Hargraves wails through the inside section at Sunset Beach during the 2000 Rip Curl Pro WQS event.
PHOTO: JOHN BILDERBACK.

Despite the efforts of the early professionals, pro surfing in Britain didn't really take off until the mid '90s. From this point on, a handful of top British performers could realistically expect some sort of career from surfing through sponsorship wages. Today, surfers like Russell Winter epitomise the recognition that Brits really can surf. The rise of professional surfing in Britain carries our story up to the present day.

By the early '80s surf companies were big business in Europe. An offshoot of the ASP was a new continental pro tour, the EPSA, which started in 1984 and was sponsored by Quiksilver Europe. The thriving contest framework gave aspiring British surfers a chance to earn a real living in the waves. Welshman Carwyn Williams proved it could be done, finishing runner-up on the inaugural EPSA tour, and winning it the following year. While Carwyn was focusing on global ambitions, fellow Quiksilver team rider Grishka Roberts from Cornwall was acutely aware of his greater value to companies in Britain and Europe, where the surf industry was booming, and he was known and recognised.

"France was where most of the contests where held," says Grishka. "So it meant you were living in Europe trying to survive on whatever contest money you won. The more events there were, the more you could make." Despite his contest focus, Grishka also knew that media exposure was the name of the game with professional surfing, and this didn't necessarily need to come from winning contests. Grishka, dark-haired and photogenic, formed a strong link with John Conway at Wavelength Magazine. He set the example that a good working relationship with a photographer was crucial to any aspiring pro. John photographed Grishka repeatedly on European free-surfing trips, cashing in on his looks and talent and thus helping to drive the magazine forward, as well as Grishka's career.

While Grishka was flying the flag for Britain

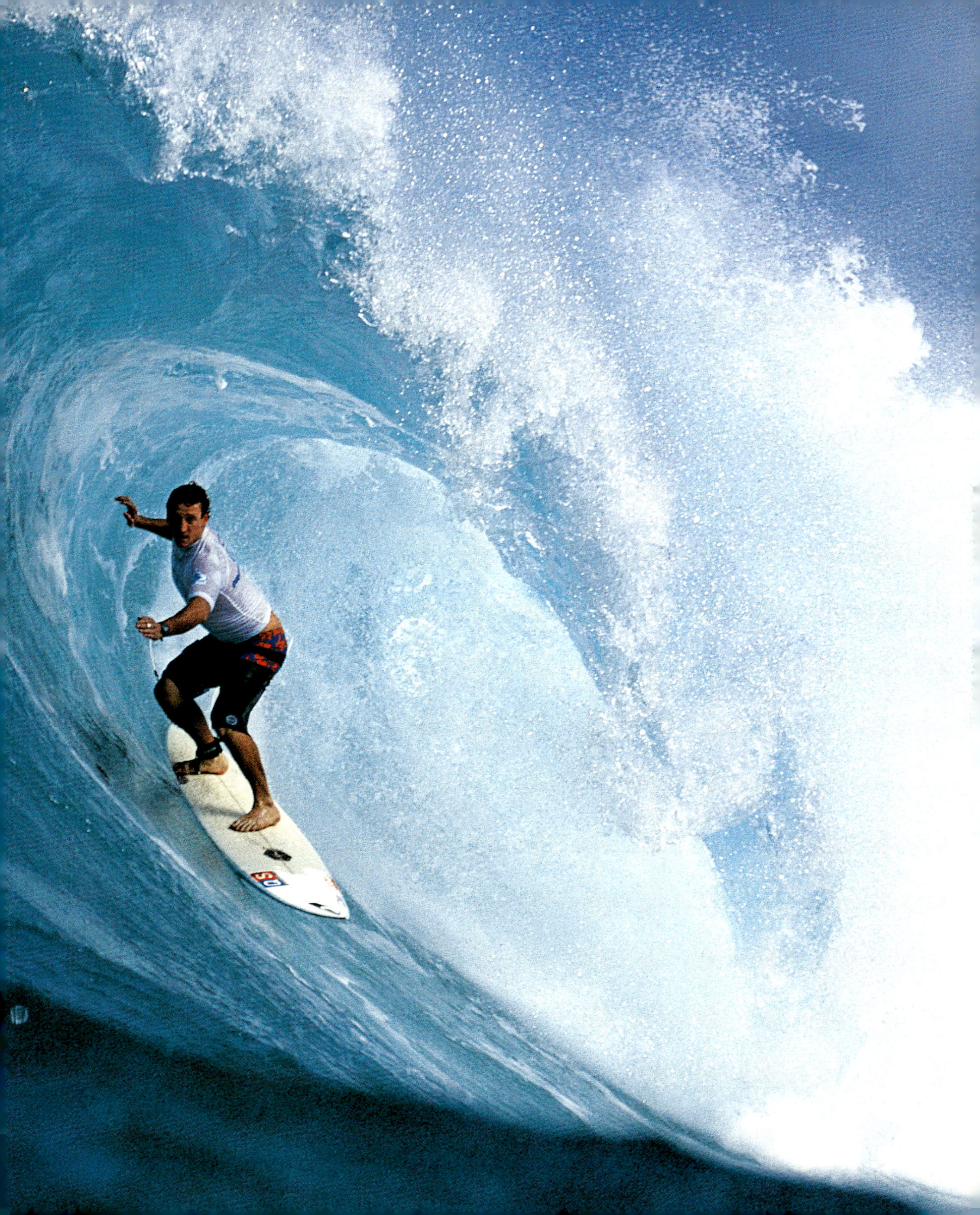

above
Newquay pro Grishka Roberts made a name for himself as a top competitor and free-surfer in the late '80s and '90s.
PHOTO: CHRIS POWER.

during the '80s, English born Martin 'Pottz' Potter was competing on the World Tour. Pottz was born in 1965 in Blyth in the North East, but his family moved to Durban in South Africa when he was two. Aged 10 he learned to surf in Durban's powerful waves, where he was spotted as a young talent. Pottz's impact on surfing was huge. A photo of one of his explosive aerials was used as a Surfing magazine covershot in 1984, and it inspired a new generation. Pottz constantly and flamboyantly pushed the limits of high-performance surfing with deep carves, never-ending floaters and never-attempted aerials. In 1989 he was crowned World Champion, earning a record £200,000 in prizemoney that year.

By 1990 a fair-haired flashy naturalfooter from Newquay, Spencer Hargraves, turned pro with 100 percent sponsorship from Quiksilver. It was a better package than the subsistence level Grishka was earning to compete and travel, and marked another rise in the profile of British professional surfing. At 17 Spencer already had five British trophies and the EPSA crown under his belt. 'Hurricane Hargraves' went on to have an exceptional career, maintaining his ties with Europe and becoming a name in Australia and the real proving ground for every competitive surfer – Hawaii. A barrel at the 2000 Rip Curl WQS competition was legendary. With the clock ticking down Spencer needed a solid score to get through the heat. Sunset was maxing-out at 10-to 12-feet. Spencer waited patiently until a west peak bomb feathered outside. He clawed in, set up with some turns and lined a huge tube through the inside bowl. The photographers in the channel began hooting wildly as the barrel stayed wide open instead of pinching shut as it often does. He kicked out in the channel, the beach erupted, and the judges scored a 9.8. It was a phenomenal achievement for a Brit to make such an impact in Hawaii.

In the '90s a new wave of British professionals rose to the fore. Gabe Davies, Sam Lamiroy, Lee Bartlett, Robyn Davies and Alan Stokes grew up in the so-called 'New school' era of lightfooted surfers, all heavily inspired by surfers like Kelly Slater and Rob Machado who showed the way forward in videos such as Taylor Steele's *Momentum*. "The thing you have to realise is that those guys are just flesh and blood,"

Lee Bartlett observed in a CARVE Magazine interview. "They're no different to you, they've just worked at it. By watching videos you can see what's happening and imagine how you'd do what those guys are doing." Lee won an unprecedented string of four British titles between '95 and '98.

O'Neill team rider Sam Lamiroy has been one of Britain's most successful pro's in the '90s and '00s. "The main requirement for being a pro surfer these days is to be able to surf really, really well," says Sam. "You also need to be pretty clued up about the industry, and you've got to get on with the photographers and journalists on trips. Having a stab at the WQS will cost about £20,000 a year. Bearing in mind that few surfers qualify until their fourth year on tour, that's quite an investment."

The first time Cornwall's Robyn Davies made it to the women's final at the British Championships, she faced Linda Sharp, Eden Burberry and Gwynedd Haslock; the four best women surfers from four decades, all surfing in one final. Mentored by Porthleven pro's Jake Boex and Dan 'Mole' Joel, Robyn won the British women's title five times and was Britain's first full-time female pro surfer.

Newquay's Alan Stokes, on the other hand, was honed by Quiksilver training camps. "In our late teens Mark Harris, John Buchorski and me got to go to Europe each year with Quiksilver and surf with Danny Wills, Gary Elkerton, Mick Campbell and all the best European juniors," says Stokesy. "Basically that's what brought us up to the next level and made us capable of winning Open contests. It was a big stepping-stone and an important time in our surfing development."

These surfers have all been outstanding performers in recent years, but none can match the awesome international achievements of Russell Winter. Born in London in 1975, Russ moved to Newquay aged nine. His family intended to buy a hotel — but instead bought a surf shop and burst into British surfing. In the early '90s, Steve, Dean and Russ Winter started dominating national competitions. As Steve puts it, "We all spent every day, all day, from dawn till dusk surfing."

The family began spending winters in Barbados, and while surfing Soup Bowl on the east coast Russ was able to hone his frontside attack and famous hack. His surfing was all about a connection of re-entries, laybacks and gouging power moves. In 1994 Russ won the EPSA European tour. But he set his sights much higher. Aware that he could train all winter in Australia and Barbados, and with reliable British sponsors (like Gul and Animal), Russ set himself a three-year goal to qualify for the ASP WCT. He began the long WQS slog — airports, board charges, hotels, taxis, unfamiliar breaks, snapped boards, sourcing magic boards and heats, hundreds of heats. By December 1997, Europe had its first WCT qualifier. Animal threw a huge party at the Bowgie Inn in Newquay to celebrate.

"Grishka, Randall Davies and Spencer had all won in Europe and led the way," says Russ. "I just followed what they'd done, and then I guess I took it to the next level, qualifying for the WCT. But it's hard coming from a minor league surf country. You have to work harder to prove yourself and get respect. The satisfaction comes from jumping the hurdles and turning situations around."

Between 1998 and 2002 Russ surfed four seasons on the WCT alongside the best surfers in the world at the globe's most intense waves, from Jeffrey's Bay to Teahupoo.

Recently, at Thurso in Scotland, Russ won his second WQS event. It meant qualification for a special luxury boat-based event in Tahiti called the O'Neill Mission, with £18,000 in prizemoney. Tackling Teahupoo would be a big moment for Russ after the reef almost took his life when he was on the WCT (not through a heavywipe out but a tiny reef scratch, which became a serious staph infection that put Russ in intensive care for three weeks). Undeterred, Russ got one of the best barrels of the year in Tahiti. It was an incredible wave, triple overhead and reeling. He was awarded the 'best barrel of The Mission' on a global internet vote and it gained him gallons of respect from surfers all over the world. CARVE magazine's Steve England was on hand to witness the occasion. "I wish I could have bagged that moment and taken it home to show the aspiring pro's, the photo sluts and the groms. He nailed some of the best young pro's in the world at the world's heaviest wave, and all his demons in 10 glorious seconds. It was nothing short of inspirational."

The contemporary icons of British surfing in many ways embody the story of this book. They have been nurtured by the growth of British surf culture. Their success has proved that this small island can produce world-class surfers. Yet for every sponsored rider hacking lips and boosting aerials, there are thousands more just surfing for the fun, far removed from the hustle and bustle of contests, film-shoots and magazines. Free surfing is true surfing for most and for those intent on improving, the real 'contest' is with themselves.

below
Robyn Davies became a successful pro after racking up five British Women's titles in the '90s and '00s.
PHOTO: ALEX WILLIAMS.

Newquay's Russell Winter became the most successful British surfer of the modern era when he qualified for the ASP World Championship tour in 2000. He soon proved his pedigree with ballsy performances at breaks like Teahupoo in Tahiti. PHOTO: PETE FRIEDEN.

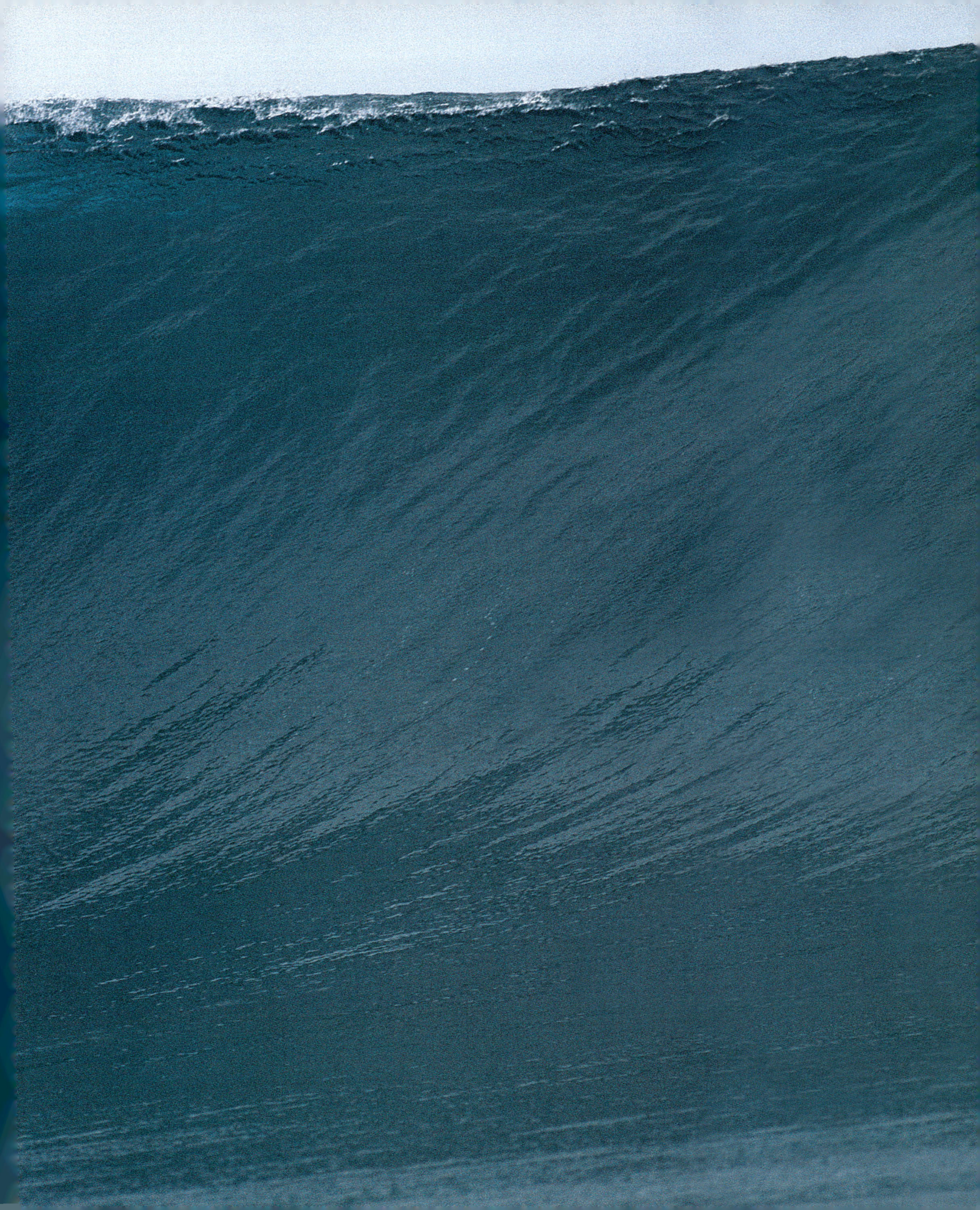

16 | surfing the new wave

GREENING THE GREEN ROOM

If there is one pressing issue for any surfer, it must surely be the environmental crisis. None of us want to surf in polluted waters, and many have now realised just how polluting the surfboard industry itself has been. Surfers are now taking up the challenge of greening the green room.

The green room — inside the tube — has always been the ultimate destination for every surfer. It's a place where time travel seems possible, sliding in surreal slow motion. But despite our quest to surf the perfect wave and find the green room, surfing can hardly claim to be 'environmentally green'. We paddle out in our PVC colour coordinated petrochemical outfit and claim to be clean living! The truth is that nearly everything that makes our surfing life possible comes out of the same oil well — resins, foam, neoprene, urethane leashes, wax, jet plane kerosene.

Despite the dependency on toxic surfboards, it was, however, surfers who first wised up to coastal pollution and began to engage with local politics to keep the sea clean. Spending so much time in the water, it was surfers who noticed how much raw sewage would float past. In the '60s, to add insult to injury, the first crew to tackle the Cribbar had to paddle through the raw sewage outlet at the old Newquay lifeboat slip.

A decade later Bude local Andy James caught hepatitis surfing Summerleaze. The town's sewage was discharged through an outfall pipe straight into the line-up. The illness forced Andy to give up surfing for good. In the early '70s Surf Insight magazine ran an 'environmental issues' full page. By the '80s surfers all over Britain started to object to growing pollution in the sea.

In 1990 a meeting was called in St Agnes, Cornwall, by a group of local surfers who wanted to get active in addressing this very issue on their local beach. The hall was jammed with support. From this gathering, the environmental action group Surfers Against Sewage was born, with Andrew Kingsley-Tubbs, Mike Hendy, Chris Hines, Steve England, Cath Layte, Leslie Pinfold and Roger Mansfield as its founder members and launch committee.

People did not easily believe that the contents of their toilet bowls were being flushed, untreated, into the water just off the beaches. There were "no votes in shit," so the problem had been stoically ignored by politicians for half a century. SAS, with its gas-masked, wetsuited frontline disciples caught the media's attention and slowly turned the arguments against South West Waters' bland assurances under its high-profile media campaign called 'Clean Sweep'. As membership of SAS grew, it transcended from its grass-roots origins and appointed Chris Hines as its full time General Secretary. He was responsible for fund-raising and more effective campaign strategies. The objective was re-defined to clean waters nationally rather than just in Cornwall. SAS was popping up in dirty sea-water all over the country, with its inflatable turd and other eye-catching props. It was also making flamboyant, but legally researched, representations to the Government at Westminster and the European Parliament at Strasbourg.

By the mid '90s the sport of surfing, nationally and internationally, was behind this dynamic surfers' action group. Britain's top performers such as Spencer Hargraves, Carwyn Williams and Chris Griffiths were willing to use their celebrity to push the cause. It took almost 10 years for the tide to turn fully, as private water companies finally ignored shareholders profitable interests and started to invest millions in comprehensive sewage treatment schemes around the nation. SAS had spotlighted Newquay early as 'a suitable case for treatment,' which had caused panic among many

above
Surfers Against Sewage campaigners hold a 'sit down' protest on the beach at Brighton in the early '00s.
PHOTO: MARTIN TAYLOR.

politicians and businesses in the town, fearing a collapse of the tourist trade. The holidaymakers kept coming, and in the end it received a tertiary treatment system managing the whole community's waste. Now the town could justifiably shout its PR mantra, 'The finest surfing beaches in Europe,' and SAS should really take the credit. People power does work if you give it time and energy and today we can be proud of the number of our Blue Flags — a European wide scheme that rewards clean bathing waters.

Despite the green credentials of most British surfers, the majority have stayed loyal to chemical surfboard technology largely pioneered back in the late '50s and '60s by Hobie Alter and Gordon Clark in California. Polyurethane foam and fibreglass gave rise to generations of constantly evolving surfboard designs. But nothing really changed on the materials front because the polyurethane foam was easy to shape, it held detail and its core tolerated thermal ranges. It was also easily and cheaply glassed with polyester resin. The happy marriage of polyurethane foam and clear polyester resin had the perfect cosmetic appeal. But as early as 1987 the World Health Organisation had listed fibreglass as a probable human carcinogenic. Eventually Clark Foam was closed down because their product had become too toxic for American environmental laws. Its demise was a reminder that every piece of equipment a surfer has relied on since the '60s was oil-based.

The reaction to Clark Foam's dominance, then demise, has been a new wave of green-minded surf equipment and attitudes. In boards there has been a shift towards epoxy, which, during construction, uses less polluting VOC's (Volatile Organic Compounds) than '60s style foam and fibreglass. Shapers are embracing a new epoch of surfboard engineering and evolution, and there are many small-scale operations in Britain experimenting with green boards using everything from hemp to balsa and bamboo. The most important of these innovations rests with the Cornishman Tris Cokes at Homeblown. He is making surfboard blanks that are way more environmentally friendly than the carcinogenic and lethal concoction Clark once used. Tris, once an influential shaper on his doorstep, is now becoming a major international voice in the move to green the green room.

HISTORY IS THE FUTURE

In just half a century British surfing has evolved from a misunderstood handful of pioneers riding 'aeroplane wings' with no wetsuits, to a nation where hundreds of thousands ride waves all year long with access to refined equipment even in inland towns. When Jersey was tops, surfers were non-conformists driven by good times. They mirrored the early Hawaiian beach boys, described by American author James Michener as 'perpetual adolescents'. By the '70s surfers were the true 'drop-outs' from mainstream and their close attachment to nature made them some of the first environmentalists. The tide turned dramatically with the professionalism that pervaded the sport by the end of the '80s. Surfers became athletes.

Today in Britain you can track down a handful of pioneering surfers who have surfed for more than four decades and are still riding waves. They are the real role models. Their collective tale is a life devoted to surfing and the ocean. There is a lot to learn from the British trailblazers. If you don't know where you are coming from, how are you going to know where you are heading?

A few of these pioneers still shape surfboards, like Chris Jones, Alan McBride, Steve Harewood and Tim Heyland. Between them there is such a wealth of experience that for every cutting-edge razor-thin shortboard shaped, a complete history of surfing is inscribed in that piece of equipment. And they can readily move from this futuristic stick to build a period board that has the exact feel of 1968. These shapers and many of their friends are walking encyclopaedias. They have been involved in every innovation in British surfing's last 50 years.

In many ways modern Newquay is the result of surfers surfing their way through life and work, through college, through business and into local opportunities. A young surfer who wanted to stick around the coast and keep riding waves had to be opportunistic. Newquay provides an archetypal example of how surfing has pervaded so many aspects of our communal life. Surfers have shifted from being a misunderstood cult group on the edge of town life, to become a prominent and influential social and economic force within the heart of the community. Surfers are now teachers, solicitors, policemen, firemen, and so many other essential workers. In turn surfers provide work on beaches, shops, surf schools, hotels, entertainment venues and media positions.

The downside to surfing's expanding popularity is, of course, the crowds in the lineup. In the summertime, Newquay's population swells from 22,000 to 250,000. Between surf schools, visiting recreational surfers and the local hardcore, there can be over 300 in the ocean at Fistral.

Surfing today is doing something more radical to tourism across coastal Britain than when the railways and roads opened up cheap access to the beaches in the past. In the search for winter waves, surfers are visiting beaches at all times, turning the once fickle tourist economy into a 12-month season. With Newquay Airport poised to receive tens of millions of pounds to help turn it into a fully civilian passenger hub, and Tourist Boards all over the country pushing surfing, crowds will keep rising.

Since the mainstream introduction of the surfing school concept in the early '80s, the opportunity for women to enjoy surfing has increased enormously. According to Barry Hall, the BSA's Head Coach, "More than half our customers are women. Plus, a considerable percentage continue to surf once they've been on a course." This new attitude to women's surfing has been embraced by surf industry giants like Quiksilver with their launch of Roxy, a dedicated female fashion line.

One of the most visually exciting developments along the British coastline in 21st century has been big wave surfing. When South African Chris Bertish was photographed in November 2003 paddling alone into 15-foot waves at Newquay's famous Cribbar reef off the Towan Headland, he opened the door to a renewed interest in this thrilling spectacle. A succession of established names followed his lead to ride breaks such as the Cribbar, and Oyster Falls in Devon, whenever these monsters reared their heads. The peak of publicity for the Cribbar emerged in 2006 when Dan 'Mole' Joel, Llewellyn Whittaker, Duncan Scott and Sam Lamiroy attacked 20-foot waves working in pairs by towing in with jetskis to launch and recover the surfers. This new extreme edge of the sport meant British surfers could access and ride waves previously considered impossible to paddle into.

Within our archipelago the newest and potentially the most dramatic arrival in the lineup of big-wave sites is Aileen's, a reef at the foot of the 230 metre Cliffs of Moher on Ireland's west coast. "It's one of the biggest waves I've ever surfed and seen," says Irish pioneer John McCarthy. "But what makes it unique is the shape — it throws this enormous tube. There are probably only a handful of waves in the world that do something like that. But I don't think there are any with a setting like the Cliffs of Moher."

In September 2006 CARVE Magazine rapidly mobilized a squad of Irish and British surfers as a hurricane swell battered Ireland's shores. Mickey Smith photographed Andrew Cotton, Al Mennie, Dave Blount, Duncan Scott, Russell Winter, Spencer Hargraves, Dan 'Mole' Joel and Sam Lamiroy surfing 25-foot waves. North Atlantic surfers had entered the rising global league of elite big wave tow-in surfing. Ireland now has a cold-water answer to Jaws in Hawaii, where Laird Hamilton pioneered tow-in surfing.

More surf discoveries in Britain are inevitable. The Government's recent edict to allow everyone the 'Right to Roam' guarantees public access to Britain's 7,800 miles of coastline. The opportunity exists for more quality waves to be discovered and enjoyed. Surfing clearly has the potential to continue to grow.

above
In recent years, the use of jetskis has allowed surfers to tackle previously unrideable big-wave spots. Dan 'Mole' Joel has a practice run at Aileen's on the west coast of Ireland.
PHOTO: MICKEY SMITH.

St Ives surfer Tom Lowe pushes the limits at Lauren's, a remote and dangerous reef in West Ireland. PHOTO MICKEY SMITH

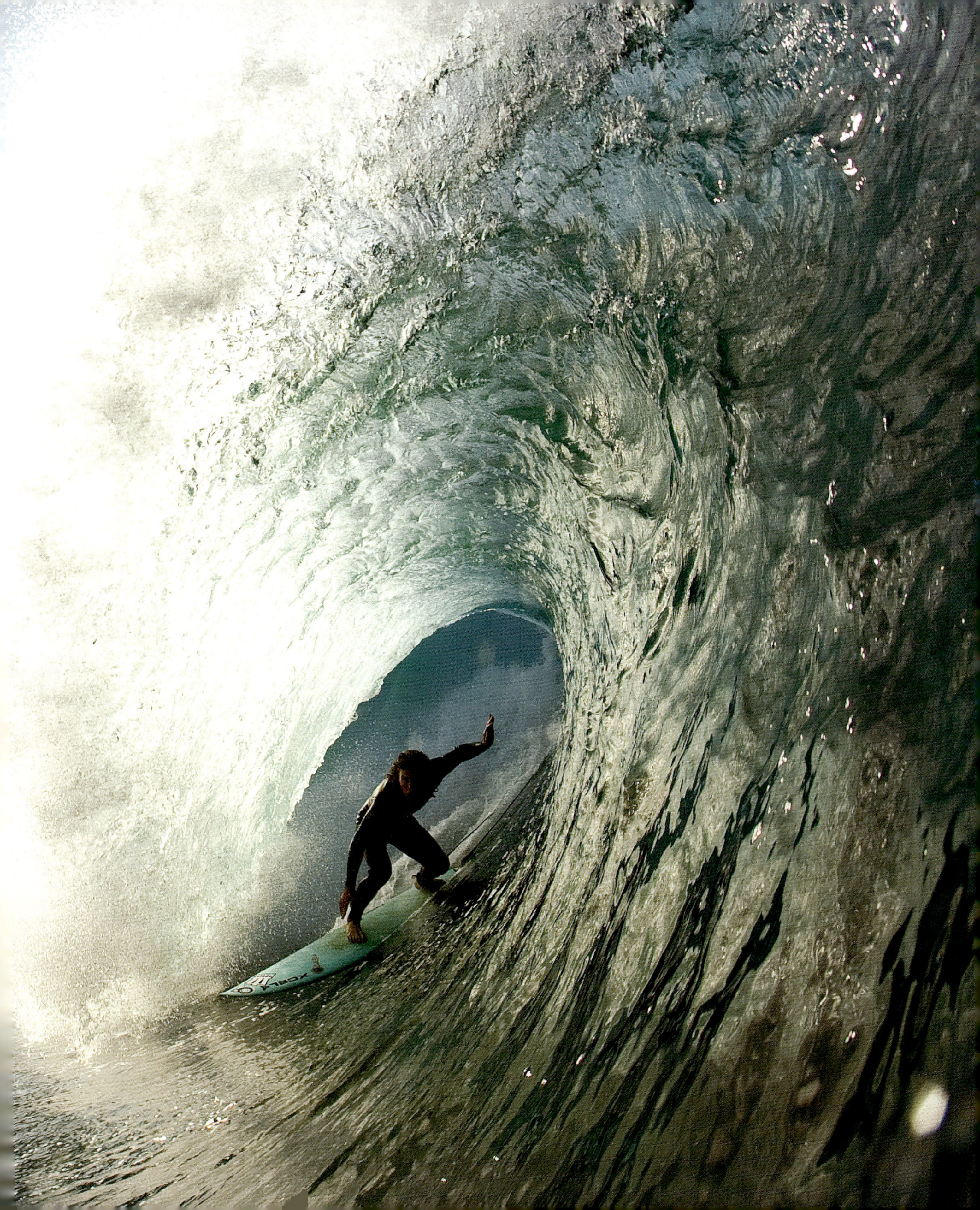

Mole Joel again, on a macker at Aileen's.
PHOTO: MICKEY SMITH

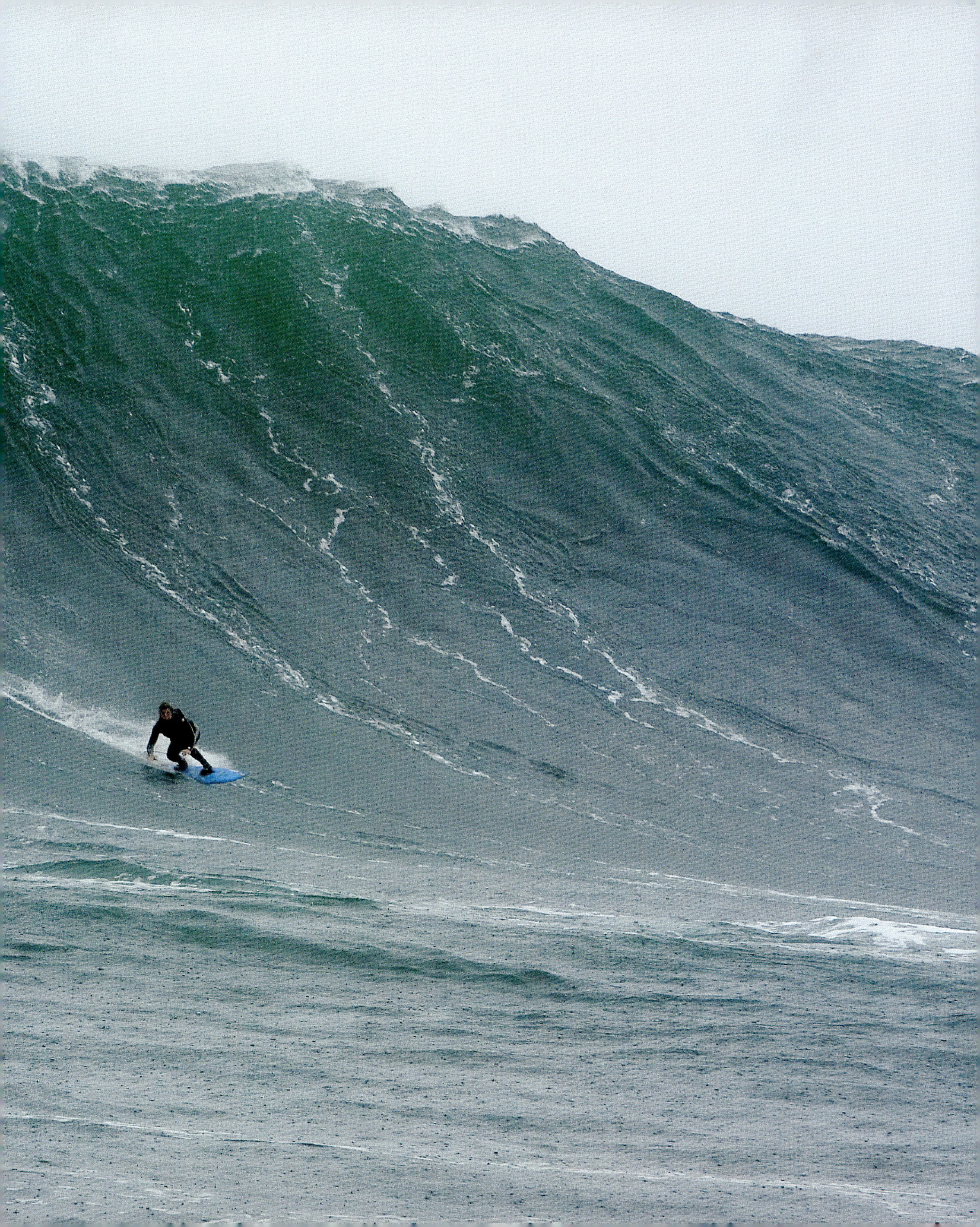

coda

Today surfing means many things to many people. It embraces young and old, hardcore regular, weekend warrior, free-surfing amateur, contest pro and soul surfer.

In essence, surfing has always been about having a relationship with nature – riding energy pulses at the ocean's periphery. Today we are at a cusp in surfing history, as we enter an increasingly ecologically sensitive age. We have shown that surfers are waking up to the fact that they contribute, through their chosen sports equipment, to one of the most polluting industries on the planet, and this must change. The next half century of surfing in Britain – already heralded by innovative green industries, tow surfing, artificial reefs and changes in wetsuit technology – will undoubtedly see some important developments.

"I never in my wildest dreams thought that what I was doing could ever grow and become something so big in Newquay, let alone the whole country," said Pip Staffieri, reflecting on modern British surfing in an interview in 2004. "Surfers now have much more time to enjoy the waves than I did, when work for ordinary people was a much bigger commitment. Plus, now you have wetsuits, which we had no idea about, so you've got much more time in the water, all year. It gives me such pleasure to see all the fantastic things surfers do on waves these days."

Pip, Europe's first legitimate surfer, passed away on 28 June 2005 at 86 years of age. The following words were posted on his obituary: "Thanks for building your board and going surfing Pip. Your passing marks the end of British surfing's humble beginning."

We have shared that beginning in this book, dedicated to British surfers everywhere.

The modern face of British surfing. Offshore perfection at Thurso East on Scotland's north shore. PHOTO: ESTPIX.

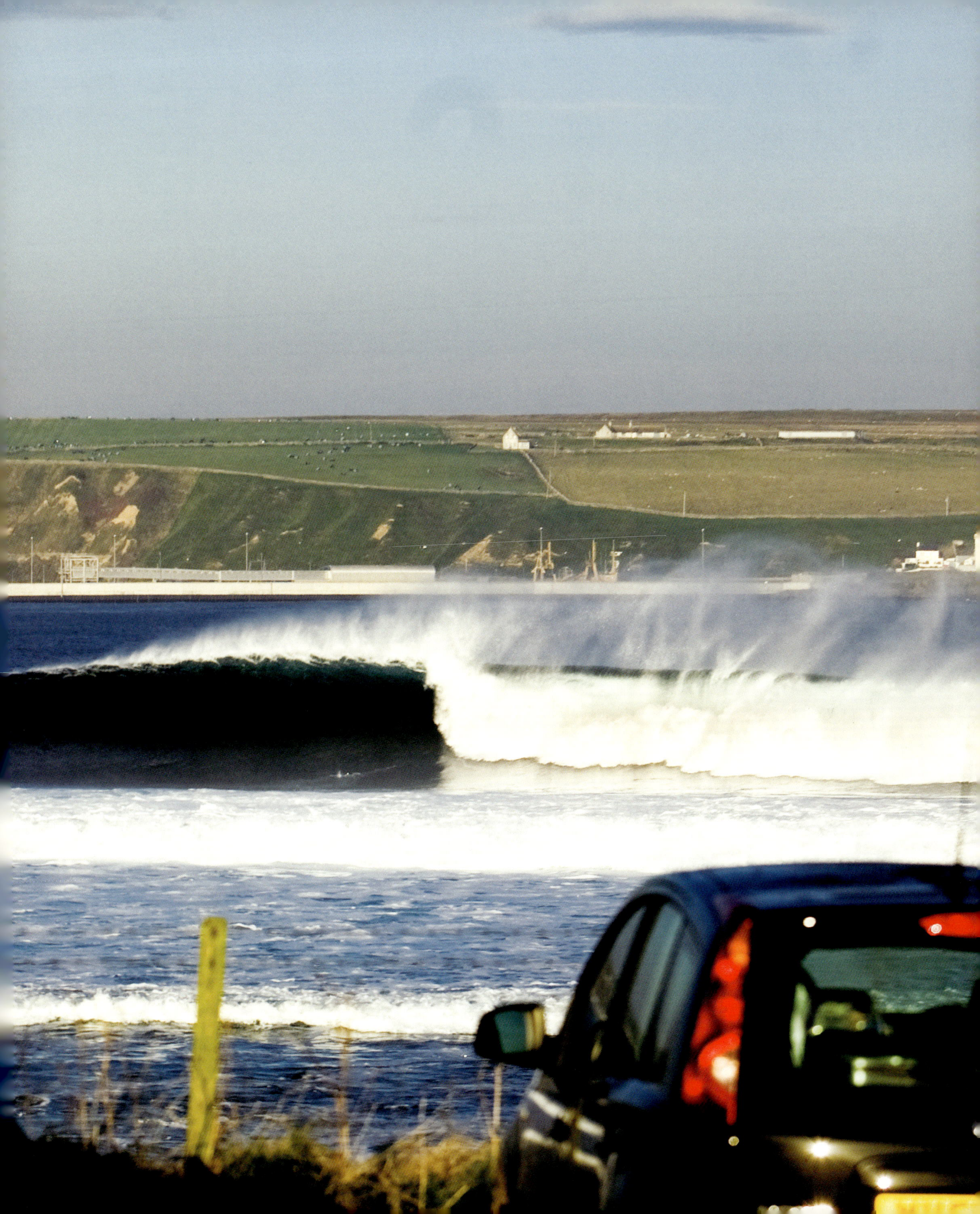

appendix

waves and swells

Waves come in all shapes and sizes but the majority of them are produced in the same way – by winds blowing across the oceans and creating swells. (The exceptions are tsunamis which are caused by submarine earthquakes, and tidal waves such as the Severn Bore, see page 122.)

The best type of swell for surfing is a groundswell, generated many hundreds of miles away by winds revolving around distant low pressure systems. In the North Atlantic, these 'lows' track from west to east, following the course of the jet stream in the upper atmosphere. Classic surfing conditions occur when a solid groundswell combines with offshore winds; lines of swell can be seen stacked up out to sea, and breaking waves will be clean and lined up.

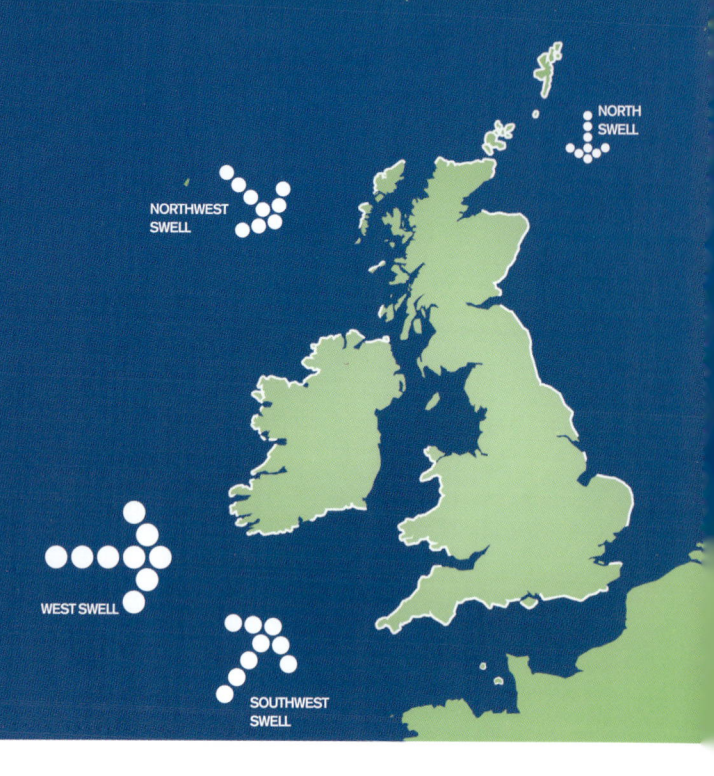

bibliography

Much of the informative content of this book is the recording and compilation of an oral history, recounted directly to the author by the main players in the tale. The author was then charged with authenticating these statements, utilising supportive testimony from others, old surf magazine entries and his own direct life experience in British surfing. It represents original written material.

BOOKS
The History Of Surfing (Nat Young, 1987)
A History Of Surf Culture (Drew Kampion, Bruce Brown, 2003)
Dale Velzy Is Hawk (Paul Holmes, 2006)
You Should Have Been Here Yesterday, The Roots Of British Surfing (Rod Holmes & Doug Wilson, 1994)
The Stormrider Guide, Europe (Ollie Fitzjones, Tim Rainger, 1992)
The Encyclopedia Of Surfing (Matt Warshaw, 2003)
Surfing, A Modern Guide (Reg Prytherch, 1972)

MAGAZINES
Atlantic Surfer, Newquay, Cornwall.
British Surfer, Swansea, West Glamorgan.
CARVE, Newquay, Cornwall.
Surfer, California, USA.
Surf Insight, Newquay, Cornwall.
Surf Scene, Lifton, Devon.
The Surfer's Path, Bude, Cornwall.
Wavelength, Truro, Cornwall.

NEWSLETTERS
BSA Yearbook
Groundswell (BSA newsletter).
Ripple (Lowestoft surf club newsletter, East Anglia).
Shorebreak (Shore surf club newsletter, Sussex).
Surf Chat
SURF
SYM (Sol Y Mar surf club newsletter, North Wales).
Tube News (Wessex surf club newsletter, Dorset).

corrections and clarifications

Have we got a date, a spelling or a fact wrong? Have we missed someone out who you think should be included in this book? Years of research have gone into The Surfing Tribe; facts, dates and spellings have been checked as thoroughly as possible in a quest for accuracy. However, given the nature of the subject matter, it's inevitable that we have inadvertently made a mistake here and there. If we have, please let us know. Please email both the author and the publishing editor (surfing@rogermansfield.com and chris.power@orcasurf.co.uk), or write to: Roger Mansfield, c/o Orca Publications Ltd, Berry Road Studios, Berry Road, Newquay, Cornwall, TR7 1AT.

archive photos

If you have an archive photo that you think should be considered for publication in the next edition of this book, please let us know. Contact the publishing editor (chris.power@orcasurf.co.uk), or write to: Orca Publications Ltd, Berry Road Studios, Berry Road, Newquay, Cornwall, TR7 1AT. Please do NOT send photos or other archive material until requested.

about the author

No one is better qualified to write a history of British surfing than Roger Mansfield. Widely recognised as the leading authority on our surf culture and history, Roger has been central to British surfing for longer than any surfer still styling in home waters.

Roger was born in 1952 in Newquay, Cornwall, where he still lives and surfs. Great Western Beach was his summertime playground, and by age 11 he had become a proficient bellyboarder. The arrival of stand-up surfers in Newquay in the early '60s naturally caught the youngster's attention, and one hot afternoon in the summer of 1963 he got his first taste of real surfing. Lifeguard Bill Bailey lent him a five-foot fibreglass 'paipo' board to try, and Roger eagerly paddled out. "On my third wave, pushed forward by the whitewater, I found the focus to spring to my feet. I stood. Absolutely every sense in my body was trapped in the moment. I felt exhilarated. I had never felt like that before. Straightaway I wanted to do it again."

By the following summer Roger had his own board and he'd become a member of the growing clan of Newquay wave-riders. Many of these individuals became key players on the British scene in later years.

Surf contests became regular events towards the middle of the decade and Roger entered as many as he could. He won the British Junior title three years in a row from 1967-69. The following year, age 18 and just back from the World Championships in Australia, he won the coveted British Open title. Being top dog for the year was the proudest moment of his surfing career and seemingly the fulfilment of his childhood fantasy. But there were no obvious career opportunities in this embryonic sport, except in the surfboard manufacturing industry. So Roger honoured his folks' wishes and headed off to university in South Wales. By 1974 he'd experienced the warmth of the Welsh surfing tribe, won the British Universities Surfing Championships, and graduated with a degree in Psychology. A decade of global surf travel followed, interspersed with occasional working seasons in Newquay.

By the mid '80s he was back as a full-time resident in Newquay – a husband, father and geography schoolteacher. The sport had expanded and his position within it had shifted from original Newquay grommet to experienced older surfer. In a flash of inspiration, Roger threw himself into the waves to earn a living, swapping the classroom for the beach. He set up the Offshore Surfing School, the first surf school in mainland Britain, where novices could learn to surf quickly and safely. The school was highly successful and widely emulated, and Roger taught surfing for ten years before moving onto other things.

Throughout the '80s and '90s he was involved in a variety of surf-related ventures. He wrote for surfing publications; he judged and directed contests; he pioneered the renaissance of longboarding with his Malibu Madness event; and he commentated at the 1986 World Championships at Fistral Beach. This event inspired Roger to resurrect his competitor status, and three years later he won the British Masters title, then the English Longboard title in 1991. In the mid '90s he set up the Newquay Surfboard Company in partnership with Chris Jones, making boards and running a shop in Wesley Yard. Around the same time he also stamped his environmental credentials by becoming a founder member of the pressure group Surfers Against Sewage.

In 2004 Roger was commissioned to organise a museum exhibition about the history of surfing in Britain. Titled *Surf's Up!* the exhibition featured vintage surfboards, archive photos and all kinds of memorabilia. The project was widely praised and the exhibition went on a national tour to several cities.

This book was the logical next step. It represents a lifetime of work and involvement, as the author has not only researched but been part of the history of British surfing. The Surfing Tribe will always be a 'work in progress' but, through decades of research, Roger has laid firm foundations. Finally, the history of British surfing is being turned from anecdote and hearsay into fact.
Sam Bleakley

above
Roger in action at Fistral Beach, Newquay, summer 1971.
PHOTO: DOUG WILSON.

index

A
Adams, John 72, 73, 178, 179
Alder 58, 83, 85, 103, 108, 116, 172, 174, 186
Atlantic Surfboards 49, 50

B
Backhouse, Roger 116
Bailey, Bill 45, 53, 54, 56, 57, 64, 67, 122, 140, 142, 155, 160, 161, 162, 163, 168
Barland-Rott 44
Bartlett, Lee 190, 191
Batten, Bill 130, 131, 133, 134, 135
Baxendale, John 100, 124, 148
Beaugeard, Dave 35, 45
Beddoe, Keith 62, 101, 171
Bennetts, Andy 130, 131, 133, 134, 135
Bickers, Freddy 98, 160
Bilbo 36, 57, 59, 66, 67, 69, 70, 95, 98, 115, 118, 120, 121, 130, 134, 142, 146, 155, 156, 157, 161, 162, 163, 164, 166, 168, 172, 174, 176, 183, 184, 186
Binning, Tanya 154
Blake, Tom 20, 21, 22, 24, 64, 96, 160, 161
Bleakley, Alan 3, 6, 13, 56, 62, 157, 163, 166, 168, 169, 170, 171, 179, 180, 205
Blight, Freddie 48, 54, 56, 57, 67, 82, 162, 169
Bounds, Pete 6, 60, 97, 98, 101, 102, 105, 111, 118, 121, 133, 148, 156, 158
Britton, Barry 13, 147
Brown, Bruce 69, 172, 178
Browning, Richard 44
Bunt, Steve 74, 80, 81
Burberry, Eden 61, 157, 191
Burden, Bobby 30, 33
Burgis, Gordon 33, 34, 35, 36, 37, 40, 41, 43, 45, 70, 139, 142, 145, 169
Butler, Maurice 121

C
Campbell, John 54, 82, 142
Carr, Mike 45, 72, 73
Cavey, Kevin 146, 148
Charlesworth, Barrie 88, 89, 90
Circle One 92, 174
Cokes, Tris 78, 79, 126, 195
Conibear, Paul 100, 102
Conway, John 54, 56, 57, 59, 62, 162, 169, 181, 186, 188
Cooper, Bob 35, 162
Cooper, Roger 116, 117
Cope, Tony 118, 119
Cribbar 58, 59, 60, 194, 196, 197
Cross, Dennis 58, 174
Cunningham, Mike 102, 119

D
Daniel, Steve 62, 76, 84, 92, 93, 108, 118, 128, 133, 168, 179, 184, 186
Davies, Bill 117, 118
Davies, Gabe 124, 126, 127, 128, 190
Davies, Ian 124
Davies, Randall 61, 126, 191
Davies, Robyn 190, 191
Deerhurst, Ted 108, 128, 179, 183, 184
Dix, Jimmy 21, 22, 24, 160
Duke, Alan 147, 148

E
Edwards, John 'Fritz' 96
English Surfing Federation 91, 126
European Professional Surfing Association 'EPSA' 108
European Surfing Championships 36, 41, 145, 148
Everett, Denis 31, 33

F
Farrow, Dave 121
Fielding, Glyn 130
Findlay, Malcolm 130, 131
Fistral 13, 35, 45, 53, 56, 61, 62, 64, 77, 91, 116, 119, 156, 183, 184, 186, 187
Force Nine 58
Fosters Surfmasters 62, 187
Friar, Dave 45, 54, 56, 59, 98, 138, 162, 172

G
Ganz, Viv 96, 103
Gill, Paul 111, 133, 181
Gladders, Tim 124
globes 191
Gould, Peter 33, 37, 40, 142
Gould, Renny 37, 38, 133
Gower Surf Club 97, 102
Griffey, Pete 90
Griffiths, Chris 'Guts' 103, 171
Groves, Bob 45, 91, 116, 117, 118, 160
Guernsey Surf Club 44

H
Halpin, Dai 100, 148
Harewood, Charles 30, 32, 35
Harewood, Ian 33, 142
Harewood, Steve 34, 35, 36, 76, 165, 166, 169, 196
Hargraves, Spencer 61, 62, 126, 133, 181, 188, 190, 194, 197
Haslock, Gwynedd 155, 157, 158, 191
Head, Bob 32, 34, 54, 56, 57, 66, 67, 79, 89, 122, 123, 142, 146, 156, 160, 162, 163, 168
Hendy, Mike 78, 80, 126, 194
Heyland, Tim 89, 90, 94, 95, 98, 148, 165, 169, 196
Highams, Tim 85
Hill, Ian 146
Hole, Tony 45, 50, 72, 73
Holmes, Paul 56, 57, 66, 67, 118, 141, 157, 162, 164, 166, 169, 179, 180, 183
Honeysett, Cliff 30, 33
Hughes, Annette 154

I
Island Surf Club 18, 30, 146

J
Jackman, Mick 58, 59, 66, 162
Jeffs, Tony 100
Jenkins, Barry 33, 35, 36, 41
Jersey Surfboard Club 6, 31, 32, 33, 34, 35, 45
Johns, Frank 78, 81
Jones, Chris 2, 9, 52, 54, 56, 57, 59, 61, 67, 70, 76, 80, 86, 98, 100, 102, 106, 107, 108, 115, 118, 123, 161, 162, 164, 165, 166, 168, 169, 170, 176, 179, 184, 196
Jones, Pete 'PJ' 98, 106

Jury, Paul 'Ju' 85

K

Kahanamoku, Duke 20, 21, 147, 154
Ka'iulani, Princess Victoria 115
Kennedy, Alan 26, 78, 84
Kieran, Pat 133
Kift, Alan 88, 90
Knowles, Paul 120, 121

L

Lamiroy, Sam 124, 126, 127, 190, 191, 197
Lascelles, Pete 'Chops' 80, 170, 184
Lawson, Dave 122, 123

M

Mahoney, Jerry 115, 116
Male, Bobby 36, 37, 150
Maltman, Arlene 37, 156, 157
Manetta, Johnny 80, 126
Mansfield, Roger 3, 6, 10, 36, 54, 56, 59, 61, 67, 86, 145, 154, 166, 170, 176, 194, 204
Martin, Mike 85
Matthews, Stuart 90, 123
McBride, Alan 'Mac' 56, 138
McDonald, Doug 54, 64
Mitchell, Warren 54, 82
Moraiz, Jo 33, 142
Moran, Hugh O'Brien 148
Morcom, Ian 'Porky' 56, 95, 98, 162
Moreno, Gary 175
Moss, Jill 157

N

Newling, Chris 'Tigger' 9, 36, 74, 76, 80, 82, 83, 86, 87, 100, 101, 148, 154, 157, 166, 169, 174, 179
Newling, John 82
Newling, Sarah 154, 157
Newton, Bez 100, 124
Nile, Graham 74, 92, 101, 107, 118, 169, 184

O

Ocean Magic 62, 167, 184, 186
Oxenden, Nigel 18, 30

P

Palmer, Bruce 61, 89, 123
Parkin, John 121, 148
Paterson, Jock 116, 171, 176
Patience, Dave 'Moby' 54, 56
Paull, Keith 35, 59, 98, 162, 164
Porthmeor 45, 46, 48, 49, 50, 51, 73
Potter, Martin 'Pottz' 62, 176, 187, 190
Powers, Bob 88, 89
Prytherch, Reginald 'Reg' 118

R

Raven, Mike 83, 84, 85
Raynes, George 130
Reed, Dave 187
Renvoize, Simonne 123, 155, 157, 164, 178
Roberts, Grishka 61, 62, 108, 181, 188, 190
Roberts, Trevor 54, 56, 57, 156, 162
Robin, Hansen 97, 98
Rochlen, Dave 48, 49, 50, 172
Rogers, Gary 124, 127
Rosnay, Joel de 33, 141
Roughton, John 124
Russell, Paul 83, 108, 126, 184
Russell, Pete 59, 60, 61, 162

S

Schofield, Brian 162, 164, 169
Scottish Surfing Federation 131, 133, 134, 135
Semmens, Nigel 60, 61, 62, 74, 91, 92, 101, 108, 118, 128, 133, 167, 179, 181, 184, 186
Sharp, Linda 102, 118, 156, 157, 158, 191
Skewjack 76, 77
Slocombe, Keith 45, 46, 47, 48, 49, 73, 78, 96
Smith, Dave 89, 95, 98
Smith, Denzil 102
Smith, John 'The Bull' 124
Smith, Mike 116, 170
Sol Y Mar Surf Club 100, 101, 102
Steadman, Roger 146, 147
Stone, Jed 168, 176
Sumpter, Rodney 6, 8, 34, 36, 40, 41, 45, 54, 59, 61, 69, 70, 71, 79, 86, 123, 133, 142, 147, 148, 154, 156, 157, 158, 162, 164, 170, 171, 178, 180, 183
Surfers Against Sewage 81, 194, 195
Surfer's Path (The) 181
Surf Insight 36, 76, 121, 131, 135, 157, 169, 180, 194
Surf Scene 121
Sweet, Dave 'Doc' 85

T

Tait, Willie 130
Thompson, Derek 116
Thompson, Des 100, 148
Tiki 89, 90, 94, 95, 98, 106, 158, 169, 174
Tiley, Ian 27, 54, 82, 142
Treeby, Bob 131, 133
Trewella, Richard 53, 54, 56, 64, 138
Tris 78, 79, 80, 126, 195
Troy, Peter 33
Tucker, Simon 83, 102, 103, 108
Tydeman, Geoff 74, 168, 178
Tyler, Chris 72, 76, 77

V

Vance, Desmond 'Bow' 147
Veitch, Nigel 124, 126, 128, 176

Viertel, Peter 141

W

Ward, Dave 37
Ward, Rob 116, 152, 153
Ward, Vince 115, 163
Watersplash 30, 33, 34
Watson, Neil 120, 121
Welsh Surfing Federation 102, 158
Westlake, Bob 58, 83, 172
Wetteland, Max 48, 54
Williams, Carwyn 83, 102, 108, 133, 176, 188, 194
Williams, Charles 34, 36, 46, 48, 49, 50, 51, 70, 98, 160, 169, 172, 174, 178
Williams, James 46, 72, 76, 78, 79
Williams, Ron 102
Wilson, Colin 73, 76, 77, 123, 179
Wilson, Doug 2, 6, 8, 11, 26, 27, 45, 50, 53, 54, 56, 57, 58, 59, 61, 64, 66, 67, 70, 71, 79, 82, 115, 142, 145, 154, 162, 163, 164, 172, 174, 180, 183
Winter, Russell 13, 157, 169, 187, 188, 191, 192, 197
Wishart, Ian 130, 133, 135
Woodcock, Nigel 62, 121, 171
World Championships 35, 40, 41, 45, 59, 62, 69, 74, 81, 83, 86, 91, 102, 103, 107, 118, 119, 147, 154, 156, 158, 166, 169, 171, 183
Wright, Martin 'Wiggins' 80

X, Y

Z

Zuma Jay surf shop 85

MICKEY SMITH